The Time-Life Gardener's Guide

ANNUALS

A

REDEFINITION

BOOK

The Time-Life Gardener's Guide

ANNUALS

TIME-LIFE BOOKS, ALEXANDRIA, VIRGINIA

CONTENTS

Annuals are among the most cheerful flowers in the garden. They come in a vast array of colors, and because they are here this year and gone the next, they allow the gardener endless opportunities for experimenting and for yielding to whims of the season. This volume will show you how to take full advantage of annuals' flexibility and variety. The first chapter explains how to prepare the soil and various ways of planting annuals—in beds, in window boxes and hanging containers, among flowering perennials and bulbs—and how to cut and dry them for indoor enjoyment. The second tells how to propagate, by sowing seeds and planting stem cuttings, and how to create your own hybrids. The third describes methods of keeping the garden in shape—and what to do at summer's end to give your annuals a head start for the following year. Following is a section with a handy frost-date map that indicates when annuals can be safely planted, depending on where you live, a checklist for maintenance and tips on troubleshooting. Finally, the volume concludes with a dictionary describing the genus and species of more than 150 of the beautiful flowers that grow as annuals.

4
MAKING THE MOST OF NATURE

5
DICTIONARY OF ANNUALS

1
NONSTOP COLOR

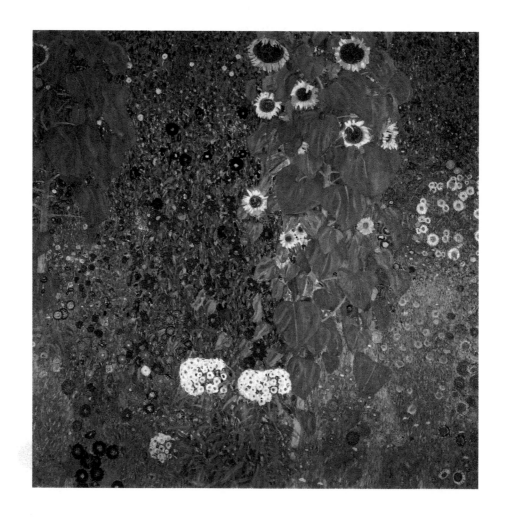

Few of the flowers that grace a garden are more ingratiating and dependable than the annuals—that enormous group of plants that live and die in a single year. Beginning in spring with the brightly colored faces of early-blooming petunias, ending in late fall with the frost-defying foliage of ornamental cabbage, annuals bloom continuously, often under conditions that other, less sturdy plants cannot tolerate. Where would gardeners be without periwinkle, verbena and portulaca, which thrive in midsummer heat and drought? What other plant brightens deep shade as effectively as the artless, confetti-like impatiens? Think of summer evenings without the sweet smell of night-blooming nicotiana, or of summer days without the sight of petunias, nasturtiums, marigolds, zinnias, geraniums and morning glories flowering, and then flowering again with a minimum of human intervention.

Given their continuous display of color, annuals are natural candidates for all sorts of decorative uses. They are ideal subjects for massed plantings in formal, geometrical beds, the modern, modified equivalents of the splendid parterres of Versailles. Tucked among spring bulbs and spring-flowering shrubs, they mask the inevitable decline of these seasonal blooms. Many of them make long-lasting cut flowers and are traditional choices for the cutting garden; others are literally ever-lasting—they can be dried for winter bouquets. Annuals with a trailing habit of growth are favorites for window boxes and hanging baskets, and those that are vines make handsome quick-growing covers for trellises, screens and fences.

A sampling of these many uses for annuals is explored on the following pages, along with instructions for preparing the soil, laying out the beds, choosing and blending flowers for different colors and habits of growth, along with some helpful guidelines for putting together window boxes and hanging baskets that provide the best conditions for growing annuals in confined spaces.

STARTING RIGHT
WITH RICH AND HEALTHY SOIL

Few plants are as easy to grow as flowering annuals. Even in poor soil they will produce some blooms. Nevertheless, most annuals prefer to sink their roots into firm-textured, moist and nourishing earth. Making an ideal bed for them is a comparatively simple task requiring few tools and only a moderate amount of effort.

Before digging the bed *(right)*, test the soil for its pH level—its acid-alkaline balance. Most annuals thrive in slightly acidic soil—soil that measures 5.8 to 6.8 (over 7 is too alkaline). To start the test, scoop up at least four samples of earth from different parts of the bed. With a trowel, blend them together. Send a half-pint of the mixture to the nearest agricultural extension service for analysis. Or test the mixture at home; kits are available at garden supply centers. If the soil is too alkaline, add sulfur or acidic organic substances such as leaf mold or peat moss when turning the bed. For excessively acid soil, add lime; spreading five pounds per 100 square feet will raise the pH one point.

Once you have adjusted the chemistry, improve the soil structure. Few garden plots start with rich, loamy earth. Most tend to have soil that is too thin and sandy, or too compact and clayey. In either case the remedy is the same; generous mixtures of humus —organic matter like peat moss or shredded leaves. Mixed with sandy soil, humus helps retain moisture that would otherwise drain away too swiftly, and adds nutrients. Worked into clay, it breaks up heavy clods, lets in air and gives the roots room to grow.

The best time to turn a bed is in autumn; the amendments will decompose and add their nutrients to the soil over the winter. Whatever the season, do not dig a garden after a heavy rain; wet earth is hard to work with.

Red and yellow snapdragons, coral petunias, tall pink-and-white spider plants and pale yellow marguerites grow side by side with purple veronica and purple salvia in a well-prepared annual border.

1 Remove grass and discard it. Dig a trench to a depth of about 12 inches and loosen the soil at the bottom of the trench; you need turn the soil no deeper than 12 inches because annuals have shallow roots. Place the removed earth in a wheelbarrow for later use.

2 Dig a second trench parallel to the first and turn the soil from the first into the second *(right)*. Then dig a third trench and place its soil in the second. Break up clods as you work.

3 Continue digging trenches until you have turned the entire plot. When you have dug the last trench, fill it with the soil you set aside in the wheelbarrow.

4 When you have finished digging, add soil amendments—lime or sulfur if your soil test indicates the need for either, organic matter for texture and richness, and fertilizer. A layer 3 inches deep is about right. Thoroughly mix the various additions into the soil with your spade, chop up any remaining clods and rake the bed smooth. □

A FLOWER BED TO SHOW OFF ANNUALS

The words "formal garden" seem to imply a Victorian horticultural extravaganza, or perhaps the ornate plantings at Versailles. But what the term means today is merely a flower bed laid out in a geometric design and filled as often as not with old-fashioned, everyday annuals like marigolds and petunias. Because many annuals are densely flowered, they perfectly suit a formal, symmetrical bed, and look their best framed in one. Such a precisely shaped garden cannot be bent to fit in a yard where slopes or rocks make the ground uneven. But in an open, level area, a formal bed with strong, straight lines can be striking. The bold design makes the most of a small lot, and the plot's regular shape makes it easy to plant even for a beginning gardener.

The equipment needed to lay one out is simple: stakes, some string and a length of ordinary board, as shown below and at right. The plank, marked to serve as a spacing guide, helps you plant the annuals in the precise rows the design calls for.

To make the formal pattern, plant in blocks of colors and limit the kinds of plants you use. Two or three varieties are enough; more shapes and colors can spoil the visual effect. Favorite candidates besides petunias and marigolds include dusty miller, wax begonias, periwinkles, China aster and snapdragon. Be sure to pick plants that have similar space requirements so that the rows will be even (see the Dictionary of Annuals, *pages 82-137).* All is not lost, however, should two plants with different spacing needs—one of 12 inches, say, and the other 10— prove irresistible. You can plant them both either 10 or 12 inches apart, whichever seems better suited to the overall spacing of the bed.

Rows of silvery dusty miller enclose several inner bands of purple and white salvia, giving a formal garden a severe but pleasing geometric design.

1 After deciding on the size of your formal garden plot—it should be at least 3 feet by 6—turn and enrich the soil as shown on pages 8-9. Then mark out one straight side by sinking stakes at the corners and connecting them with string.

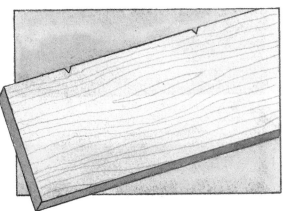

2 To plant annuals in straight rows, buy a plank as wide as the spacing required by the annuals you have chosen. For plants needing 10 inches between them, for example, get a 10-inch-wide board. Starting 5 inches in from the end, cut notches at 10-inch intervals *(inset, above)*. Place the board so that its short end lies against the string defining the plot's long side, and so that at least 5 inches of soil show between the board and the short edge of the bed. Kneel on the board and begin planting your annuals *(right)*.

3 When you have finished one row, lift the board and move it back one full width. Since you have been kneeling on it, the board will have left an impression in the soil, which will help you realign it. Continue planting and moving until the bed is finished. ☐

CHANGING COLORS
FROM SEASON TO SEASON

Annuals are endlessly versatile. They work perfectly well in a new-made bed of their own, but they can also lend wonderful color and variety to an already established landscaping scheme. A landscape's walks and walls are permanent; shrubs usually remain in the same locations for several seasons; even perennials generally stay put. Annuals, however, are uniquely and intriguingly impermanent. They must be planted afresh each year, giving the gardener the chance to alter the look of the landscape and its color scheme from season to season.

Some attention should be paid, of course, to which colors will go best in certain settings—and which will clash. Pink zinnias, for example, would be virtually invisible if planted in front of a red brick wall, and they might be an eyesore located next to a bed of orange marigolds. Where two strong hues are chosen, plants with white or silver blooms can be put between them as a buffer.

Contrasts of shape and size also enliven a landscape. There are tall spiky annuals as well as short round ones. Mixing them can add visual interest. In any case, the best way to work out pleasing combinations is to draw a map of the basic landscape features *(right)* and then make an overlay *(opposite)* on which various plantings can be sketched in. If you want to try various combinations, make an overlay for each one. A well-devised plan can prevent mistaken color pairings and other minor disasters, and will indicate ahead of time approximately how many plants will be needed.

Two bright annuals, yellow snapdragons and pink petunias, occupy a raised bed between a walk and a row of shrubs that includes pink hydrangea.

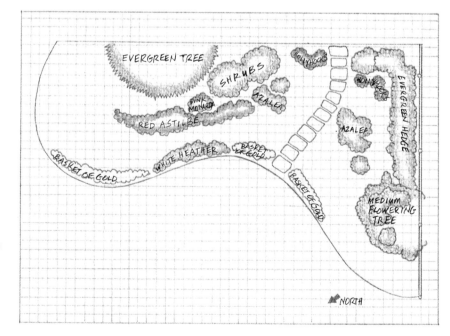

1 After measuring your garden site, transfer the measurements to a sheet of graph paper, letting a square on the paper equal 1 foot. Draw in the main features of your landscape—trees, walks, shrubs and perennial beds. Color-code and label the various areas.

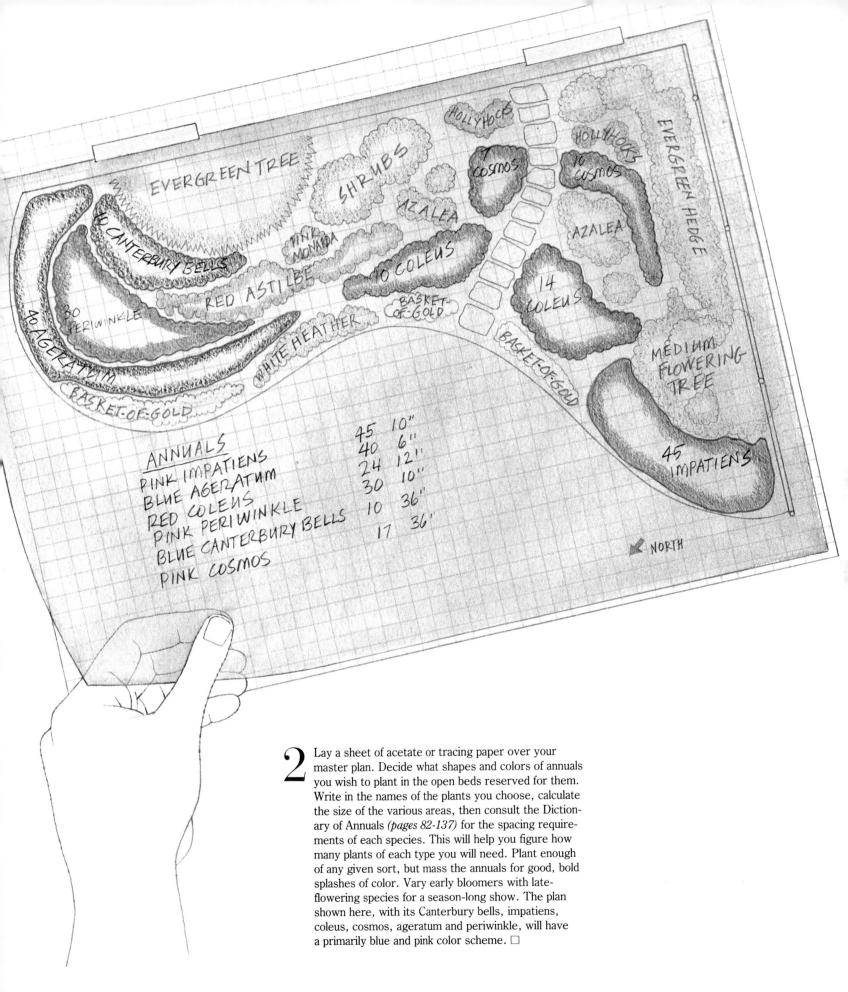

EVERGREEN TREE

SHRUBS

HOLLYHOCKS

HOLLYHOCKS

7 COSMOS

10 COSMOS

EVERGREEN HEDGE

AZALEA

AZALEA

10 CANTERBURY BELLS

PINK MONARDA

RED ASTILBE

10 COLEUS

14 COLEUS

30 PERIWINKLE

40 AGERATUM

BASKET-OF-GOLD

WHITE HEATHER

BASKET-OF-GOLD

BASKET-OF-GOLD

MEDIUM FLOWERING TREE

45 IMPATIENS

ANNUALS

PINK IMPATIENS	45	10"
BLUE AGERATUM	40	6"
RED COLEUS	24	12"
PINK PERIWINKLE	30	10"
BLUE CANTERBURY BELLS	10	36"
PINK COSMOS	17	36"

← NORTH

2 Lay a sheet of acetate or tracing paper over your master plan. Decide what shapes and colors of annuals you wish to plant in the open beds reserved for them. Write in the names of the plants you choose, calculate the size of the various areas, then consult the Dictionary of Annuals *(pages 82-137)* for the spacing requirements of each species. This will help you figure how many plants of each type you will need. Plant enough of any given sort, but mass the annuals for good, bold splashes of color. Vary early bloomers with late-flowering species for a season-long show. The plan shown here, with its Canterbury bells, impatiens, coleus, cosmos, ageratum and periwinkle, will have a primarily blue and pink color scheme. ☐

FLOWERS
AND THEIR LIFE CYCLES

Virtually all garden plants go through four stages of development before they die. They germinate from seed, sprout leaves, flower, and set seed—that is, produce seeds. Depending on how long they take to flower, whether or not (and when) they reflower, and how long they take to complete an entire life cycle, plants are classified as annuals, biennials or perennials. Plants that live and die in the same year are called annuals. To ensure the survival of their kind, annuals must produce a great many seeds every year; for gardeners, this means prolific flower production and long blooming seasons. Biennials spread their life cycle over two years. During the first year they concentrate on developing roots and foliage; only in the second year do they put out flowers. Perennials are plants that have growth cycles extended over many years. Even though the foliage and the flowers die every winter, the roots survive underground

Annuals, biennials and perennials bloom together in lush profusion. By artfully arranging different kinds of plants, a gardener can have kaleidoscopic shifts of shapes, colors and textures with the changing seasons.

and put out new shoots when spring returns. Unlike annuals, perennials do not depend for survival solely on setting seed; they also perpetuate themselves by spreading their roots.

Climate—especially the severity of winters—plays a big role in determining the length of a plant's life cycle. In its native tropics, for example, impatiens is a perennial. But left outside for the winter in most parts of North America it perishes, so gardeners here treat it as an annual. Some plants (like foxglove) are classified as biennials by botanists, but they can be forced to bloom in their first year if started indoors in January and transplanted outside as soon as temperatures moderate.

The most pleasing garden designs are built around judicious combinations of these basic categories. By mixing perennials with annuals and biennials whose blooming seasons complement one another, you can ensure a spring-to-fall display of color that no single category of plants can provide.

ANNUAL

An annual (like the marigold shown to the right) sprouts from a seed in spring, sending some delicate roots belowground and some tender green shoots above. By early summer the plant has grown fuller and begun to blossom. It then blooms with increasing fullness and vigor, reaching its peak in late summer. In fall its roots, stems and flowers have begun to wither; by winter they will have died.

ONE YEAR

A seed sown
in spring

SPRING   EARLY SUMMER

BIENNIAL

A biennial (like the sweet William illustrated here) normally divides its life cycle into two distinct periods. After a seed has sprouted in spring, the plant develops roots and foliage throughout the summer, but no flowers. The roots and foliage cease to grow but survive the winter and then have a spurt of new growth early in the second spring. Flowers appear in late spring. In midsummer the plant sets seed and withers; by fall it will have died.

FIRST YEAR

A seed sown
in spring

SPRING   SUMMER

PERENNIAL

A perennial (shown here is a Shasta daisy) goes through a yearly cycle of growth after a seed sprouts in spring, but one cycle does not end with the plant's death as it does in annuals; instead it repeats itself. In the first summer the plant develops roots and foliage, but no flowers. In fall the foliage withers and the roots go dormant underground and survive the winter. In spring the plant reawakens; over the summer and into the fall, its roots and foliage put out new growth, and flowers appear. From now on the plant will continue to go dormant in winter and to produce new growth and new flowers season after season. □

FIRST YEAR   SECOND YEAR

A seed sown
in spring

SUMMER   SPRING

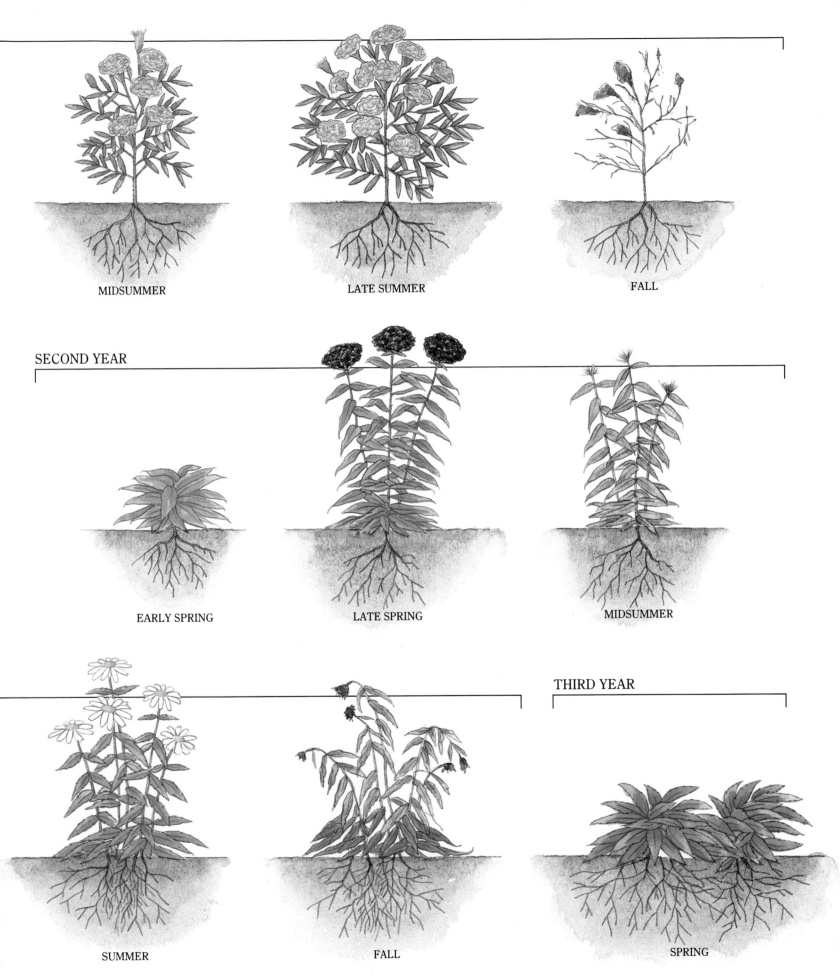

MIDSUMMER

LATE SUMMER

FALL

SECOND YEAR

EARLY SPRING

LATE SPRING

MIDSUMMER

SUMMER

FALL

THIRD YEAR

SPRING

17

SPOTS OF COLOR
TO ENLIVEN A GARDEN

Nestled in front of a row of perennial lilies and iris that retain only their green foliage after their blooming season has ended, annuals in the form of deep purple and rose pink petunias and light purple ageratum add midsummer color.

Not the least of the appealing features of annuals is that they can be used to fill out flower beds that are devoted mainly to other sorts of plants—to perennials, or perennials mixed with bulbs. Most perennials bloom for only a few weeks, if that long. Bulbs generally flower in the early spring and then rest until the next year. A bed or a border containing just these types of plants can go through dull periods when nothing much blooms.

The remedy, of course, is to interplant with annuals, which provide color when all the other plants seem to be on vacation. Many annuals are known for their bright season-long blooms. Some others—pansies and violets, for example—enjoy cool weather and bloom in the spring. Marigolds and zinnias, on the other hand, are warm-weather plants and bloom on through the fall. A judicious mixture of early bloomers with later-flowering species will give a garden bold splashes of color throughout the growing season. Annuals cover the spectrum—which means color combinations are virtually unlimited and can be fresh and different from one year to the next.

Annuals are usually added to the beds of more permanent plants in the spring, as quick follow-ups when the early bulbs have faded. Planting is easy, as the drawings at right demonstrate. Simply select fairly open spots between clumps of perennials or clusters of bulbs—and dig carefully so as not to injure the roots of the established inhabitants.

1 When adding to an established bed, plant
annuals one at a time in the bare spots.
First, clear away any mulch from the area
and loosen the soil with a trowel. Add a tea-
spoonful of all-purpose fertilizer and a handful
of compost or other fine organic matter. Mix
the additions thoroughly into the soil.

2 Dig a hole in the loosened, amended soil
with the trowel. Loosen the roots and the
soil of a new annual and place it in the hole.
Be sure the plant sits at the same depth as
it did in its container. Firm the soil around
the plant and respread the mulch. Water
generously to help the roots recover quickly
from the stress of transplanting. □

A WINDOW BOX:
COLOR ON A SMALL SCALE

Standing tall above a mix of purple heliotrope and nierembergia, deep pink geraniums highlight this overflowing window box. Trailing lamiastrum and lacy white artemisia provide a cool contrast.

Window boxes of annuals in bloom can do more than beautify windowsills. They can also brighten porch railings or add decorative accents to outdoor staircases. In addition they offer an opportunity to create beauty on a small scale, with control of the environment. You can determine the location, the exposure and the growth medium.

In planting window boxes, avoid oversized containers; they will be much heavier when filled with soil and difficult to mount. Make sure when you mount one that you affix it securely; it may have to be bolted in place.

Since plants in window boxes are more exposed to the drying effects of sun and wind than plants in the ground, they need more water. During July and August you may have to give them several good soakings every day. All that water will quickly wash away nutrients, so enrich the soil once a week with diluted fertilizer. For sunny locations, use only boxes made of wood or clay; soil in metal or thin plastic containers can overheat in direct sunlight and "bake" roots to death.

When combining different annuals in one window box, include only plants that have similar requirements for sun and shade. Place the taller, more upright varieties in the back of the box, and those of intermediate height in front of them. For a cascading effect, fill the front of the box with trailing plants like alyssum or lobelia.

1 If you make your own wooden window box or buy one without drainage holes, use an electric drill to perforate the bottom *(right)*. Turn the box upside down so that the sides rest on a secure foundation. With a ruler and a pencil, mark the bottom of the box at intervals of 3 to 4 inches. Drill, using a bit that makes holes at least ¼ of an inch wide.

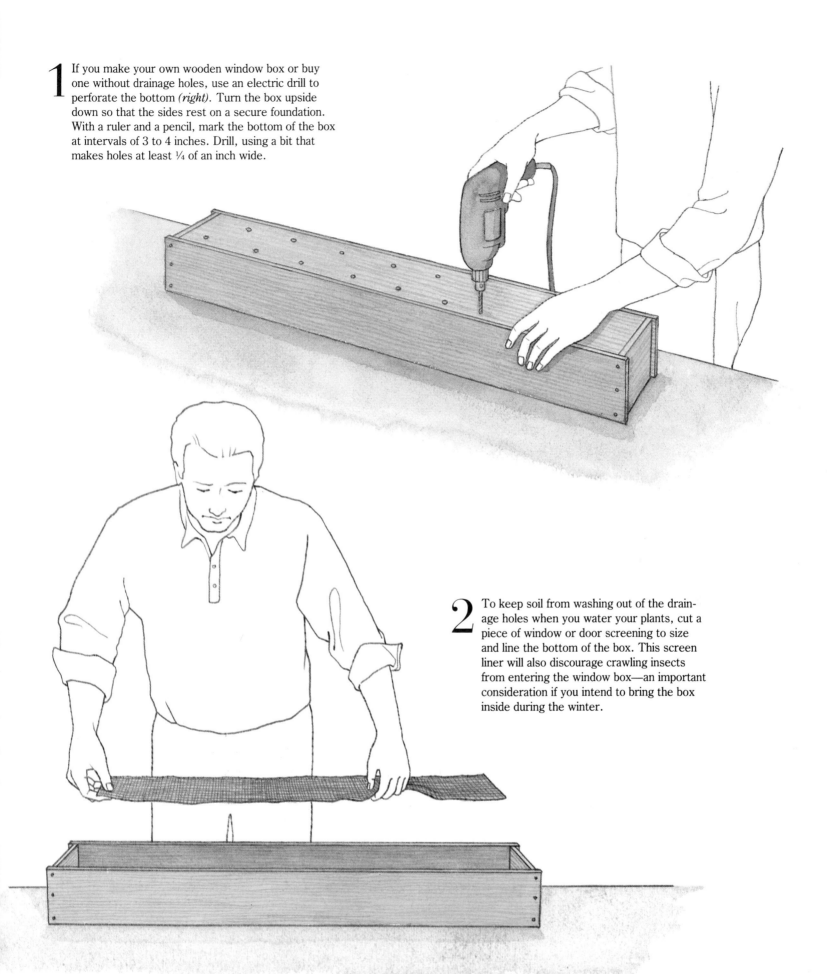

2 To keep soil from washing out of the drainage holes when you water your plants, cut a piece of window or door screening to size and line the bottom of the box. This screen liner will also discourage crawling insects from entering the window box—an important consideration if you intend to bring the box inside during the winter.

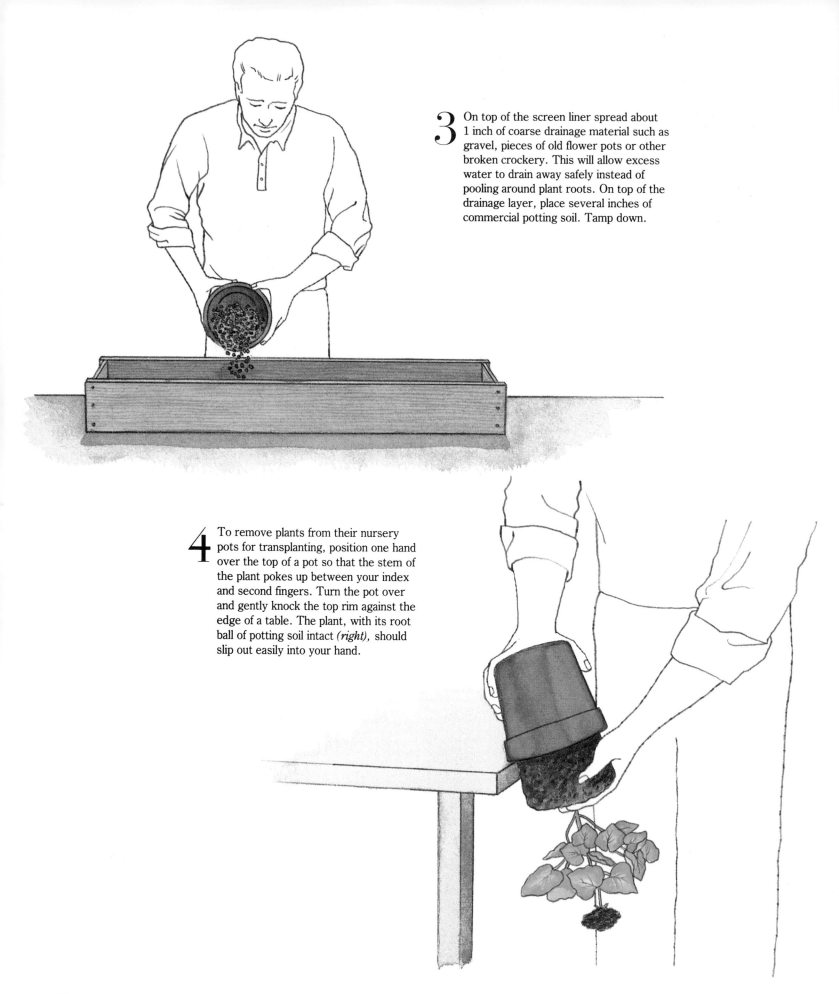

3 On top of the screen liner spread about 1 inch of coarse drainage material such as gravel, pieces of old flower pots or other broken crockery. This will allow excess water to drain away safely instead of pooling around plant roots. On top of the drainage layer, place several inches of commercial potting soil. Tamp down.

4 To remove plants from their nursery pots for transplanting, position one hand over the top of a pot so that the stem of the plant pokes up between your index and second fingers. Turn the pot over and gently knock the top rim against the edge of a table. The plant, with its root ball of potting soil intact *(right)*, should slip out easily into your hand.

5 Take each plant out of its nursery pot. To fit the plants into the window box you may have to pare some soil from the root balls with your fingers *(left)*. Take care not to disturb the roots too much.

6 Arrange all the plants in the window box. Fill in around each plant with potting soil; make sure that each plant is sitting at the same depth in the window box as it did in its nursery pot, and that the soil line is about 1 inch below the rim of the box. Water thoroughly (until water begins running out of the drainage holes). □

CASCADES OF BLOSSOMS FROM A HANGING BASKET

Nothing does more to brighten a patio, dress up a porch or give a warm welcome to visitors at an entryway than a hanging planter filled with flowering annuals. Any container light enough to be suspended from a ceiling or a beam can serve as a midair planter. You can purchase ready-to-fill plastic pots or convert old wooden or ceramic bowls. But a moss-lined wire basket that shows its lush greenery and freshly opened blossoms from all sides *(right and following pages)* offers a uniquely appealing blend of nature and artifice.

All annuals with trailing or spreading growth habits are good candidates for hanging baskets. These include impatiens, begonia, alyssum, lobelia, ivy geranium, petunia and verbena. Purchase healthy starter plants in plastic cell packs and take care to combine plants that thrive in the same soil conditions and mix of sunlight and shade. Wire basket frames (complete with hangers) and bags of sphagnum moss can be purchased at garden supply centers.

Water your hanging basket frequently—as often as three times a day during the height of summer. Hanging plants dry out much more quickly than ordinary plants, since they are exposed to air on all sides. For a thorough soaking, take down the basket and water it with a hose that has a breaker attachment—one that disperses water in a fine spray. Be sure to hang your basket where dripping water is not a problem. And remember that a freshly watered basket is heavy to lift. For ease of handling, limit your basket to 10 inches in width.

Its moss-lined wire framework concealed beneath dense foliage, this hanging planter becomes a living bouquet of geraniums, petunias, marigolds, lobelias and African daisies.

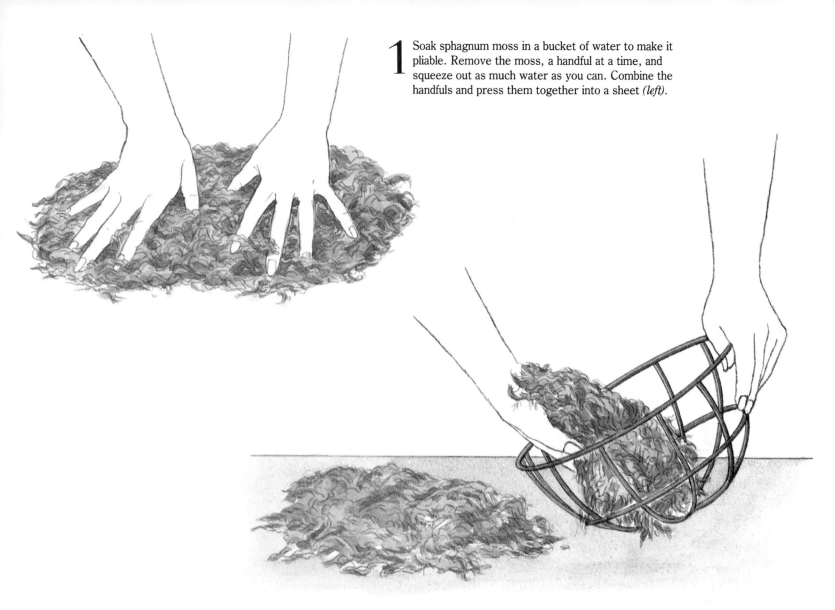

1 Soak sphagnum moss in a bucket of water to make it pliable. Remove the moss, a handful at a time, and squeeze out as much water as you can. Combine the handfuls and press them together into a sheet *(left)*.

2 Remove the wire hanger from the basket frame. Arrange the moss in a sheet against the inside of the basket *(above)* and press down. Line the entire frame with a layer of moss about 1 inch thick.

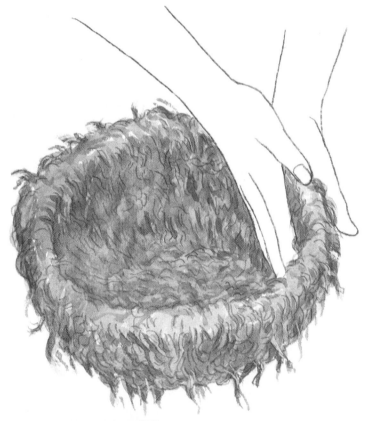

3 With your fingers and palms, feel around the lining for thick and thin spots *(left)*. Even out the width by removing pieces of moss from the thicker spots and pressing them into the thinner spots. Cover up any wire showing on the outside of the frame in the same way. Use more moss as needed.

4 Attach the wire hanger and hang up the basket. Use scissors or garden shears to trim any long dangling strands of moss from the outside of the frame *(right)*. The moss-lined basket should look "natural" but neat.

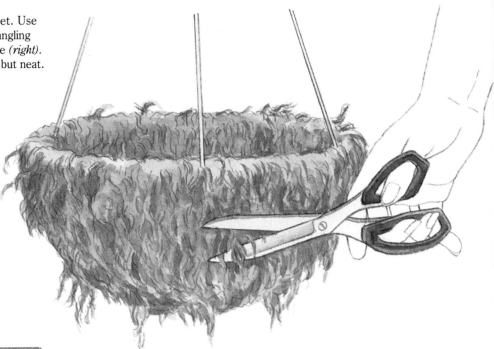

5 Pour into a clean bucket enough commercial potting mix to fill the hanging basket. Mix in 1 tablespoon of slow-release fertilizer and a few handfuls of moisture-retaining peat moss. Cover the sphagnum moss on the bottom of the basket with this enriched mixture. Using your finger, a pencil or a dibble, make an opening in the moss lining near the bottom of the basket.

6 Remove a starter plant from its cell pack. With one hand grasping the plant and the other hand inside the basket, ease the root ball through the opening in the moss lining; if necessary, scrape some soil from the root ball for easier insertion. When the root ball is entirely inside the basket, firm the moss around the crown of the plant on the outside of the basket.

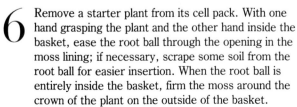

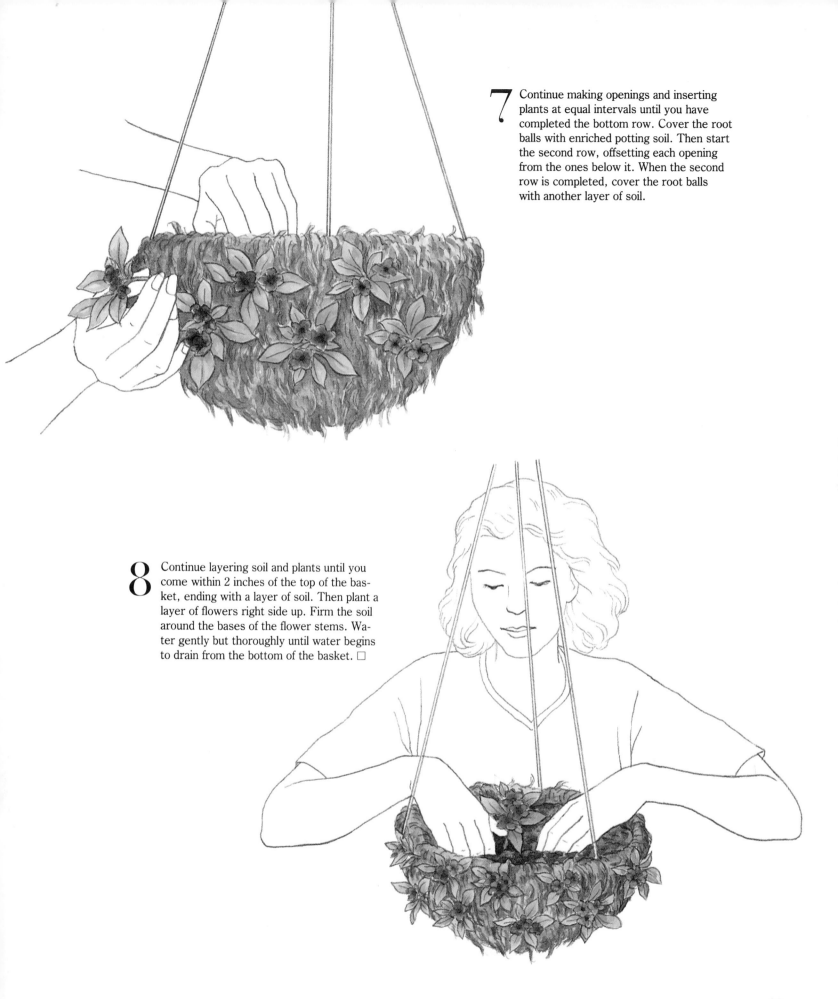

7 Continue making openings and inserting plants at equal intervals until you have completed the bottom row. Cover the root balls with enriched potting soil. Then start the second row, offsetting each opening from the ones below it. When the second row is completed, cover the root balls with another layer of soil.

8 Continue layering soil and plants until you come within 2 inches of the top of the basket, ending with a layer of soil. Then plant a layer of flowers right side up. Firm the soil around the bases of the flower stems. Water gently but thoroughly until water begins to drain from the bottom of the basket. □

FLOWERING VINES ON FENCE AND TRELLIS

A number of bright-blooming annuals are essentially vines that can be trained up trellises, fences or similar frameworks with wonderful effect. A trellis interlaced with flowers and lush foliage can provide a vertical garden of head-high color at the edge of a terrace or in front of a porch, and can also serve as a sunshade, a windbreak or a screen to afford extra privacy. And annual vines are ideal climbers, growing swiftly in the spring, then conveniently dying back in the autumn to let pass the precious rays of the winter sun.

Climbing annuals include several much-loved standbys: nasturtiums, sweet peas and morning glories. Nasturtiums are that rarity in horticulture, plants that positively thrive on neglect. They need little if any fertilizer, and not much water either, to produce flowers in abundance. Once nasturtiums are sown as seeds in early spring, they will grow and flower all summer long.

Sweet peas, with their sweet-scented and many-colored flowers, require a little more attention. Growing well in cool weather —and disliking heat—they should be planted early, right after the last hard frost. During the hot months, they should be protected by a 2- to 4-inch-thick carpet of mulch laid around their stems, which will keep down the soil temperature.

The all-time favorites are morning glories, seen at right and on the opposite page. Their blooms are large and festive, and the plants produce thick foliage with astonishing rapidity. They do not begin to grow, however, until the spring sun has warmed the earth to about 50° F. In temperate zones, therefore, they should (unlike sweet peas) be planted late, in mid-May at the earliest.

Lavender-and-white morning glories climb and trail and drip luxuriantly as they cling to an open, trellis-like garden fence. A freestanding trellis is easy to tack together from similar slats of painted wood; fiberglass ones can be purchased at garden supply centers.

1 Having prepared the soil as described on pages 8-9, firmly anchor your trellis in the ground. Then dig a shallow trench 4 or 5 inches in front of it and plant your seeds. Cover the seeds with soil and water them. When the seedlings have come up, you will need to thin them; keep the healthiest ones.

2 Once your vines have grown high enough to reach the trellis, you can begin helping the stems wrap themselves about the framework. Some plants naturally twist clockwise, some the reverse. Note the direction your vines naturally incline to and help them twine that way. If at first they do not take hold, you can secure them with bits of string.

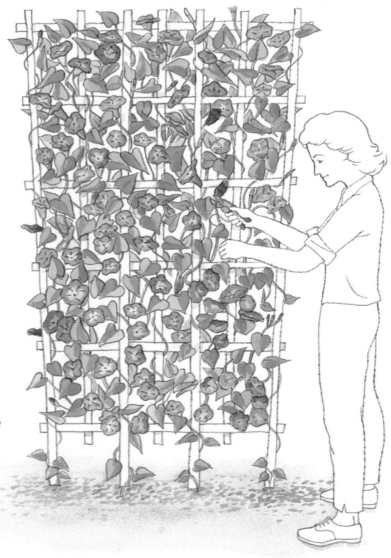

3 When the vines have climbed about a third of the way up the trellis, start pinching back the stem tips to encourage branching. As the plant grows taller and produces flowers *(right)*, remove dead blooms regularly to maintain the trellis's appearance and promote continued flowering. □

A SPECIAL GARDEN
FOR FRESH-CUT FLOWERS

Having a steady supply of fresh-cut flowers to bring indoors is one of the great pleasures of growing annuals. But you may hesitate to cut from your flower beds for fear of ruining the display if you take too many. The answer is to plant an old-fashioned cutting garden, a garden where you select and plant flowers especially for use indoors.

If you can place it where it will be hidden from view, you are free to mix colors and flower shapes in the cutting garden without worrying about design. Even in a relatively small space you can have a wide variety of flowers. But to ensure a good selection at cutting time, include at least four to six plants of each kind you choose.

Select a site for your garden that receives full sun. Be careful to place taller plants where they won't block the sun away from their shorter neighbors. Arrange the garden so that there is enough room between rows to walk through when you go to cut.

The best times for cutting flowers are early in the morning, late in the evening or any time on a cloudy day. These are the times the blossoms will have the most moisture inside. Select partially opened flowers rather than fully mature ones.

Take a sharp knife or a shears into the garden along with a bucket of warm water; stems will take up warm water faster than cold. Later, when you arrange the flowers in a vase, add a floral preservative to the water. The preservative will help the flowers last longer by providing nutrients and reducing the growth of stem-clogging bacteria.

In a well-planned cutting garden an abundance of annuals—yellow marigolds, scarlet sage and verbena, and tall salpiglossis in yellow and reds —stand ready to be cut for arrangements.

1 Select a stem that will be tall enough for your arrangement but still have enough leaves remaining on the plant to support its future growth. With a knife or a shears, cut the stem just above a node (the point of attachment to a leaf or a pair of leaves) and plunge it into a bucket of warm water.

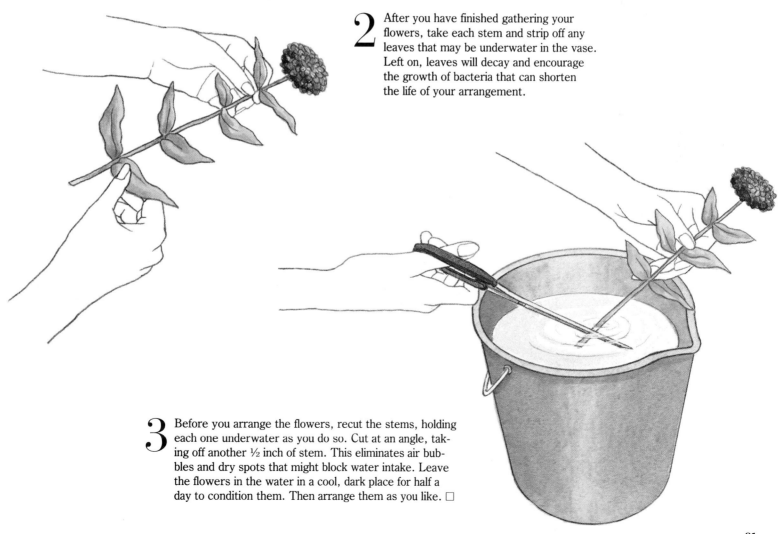

2 After you have finished gathering your flowers, take each stem and strip off any leaves that may be underwater in the vase. Left on, leaves will decay and encourage the growth of bacteria that can shorten the life of your arrangement.

3 Before you arrange the flowers, recut the stems, holding each one underwater as you do so. Cut at an angle, taking off another ½ inch of stem. This eliminates air bubbles and dry spots that might block water intake. Leave the flowers in the water in a cool, dark place for half a day to condition them. Then arrange them as you like. □

DRYING SUMMER'S BLOOMS FOR WINTER BOUQUETS

One intriguing and satisfying way to capture some of summertime's color, and brighten the house with it through the dark days of winter, is to preserve flowers by drying them. A number of annuals are ideal for the purpose. Once dried, the blooms last almost indefinitely, and can be made into handsome arrangements. An added advantage is economy. Dried bouquets made at home require only a few inexpensive supplies. Similar arrangements bought at a florist's shop can be quite costly—and so can a winter's worth of cut fresh flowers.

Some aficionados of flower drying make it a complex craft, employing special flower presses and drying compounds. But novices can get excellent results with the simple air drying techniques explained at right and on the following pages. The only supplies necessary are thin florist's wire, preservative sealer and green florist's tape. All are available at craft shops.

The time to begin picking annuals for drying is in midsummer or, at the latest, in early fall. The damp weather of late autumn will spoil most blooms. And because the purpose is to dry the flowers, they should be picked on a warm sunny day after the morning's dew has evaporated.

Select blossoms that are healthy and undamaged by insects; no amount of drying will make a faulty flower look any better. And look for blooms that have not fully opened, since they will continue to mature after picking. Unless they are gathered while still young, blossoms may open too far and shatter when handled.

In all cases, foliage should be stripped from the stems; it rarely dries attractively. Practically all annuals that can be dried do best when their stems are fastened in bunches with rubber bands and the bunches are hung upside down from strings or wires in a dark, dry, airy place *(page 35)*. Strawflowers *(opposite)* are a special case; the stems are so weak that they need to be removed and replaced with wire.

A pale gray vase holds a dried winter arrangement of large, champagne-colored strawflowers and statice that varies in color from reddish purple to pale lavender.

1 When picking strawflowers, one of the most popular and satisfactory candidates for drying, cut off the flower heads with shears or a knife, leaving only about ¼ inch of stem attached.

2 Once you have snipped off all the strawflower heads you will need, lay them in a single layer on a tray, a shallow pan or the top of a wooden box. Then put them in a warm, dry place—an attic, a basement, a garage or a shed should prove suitable—and let them dry for two or three weeks.

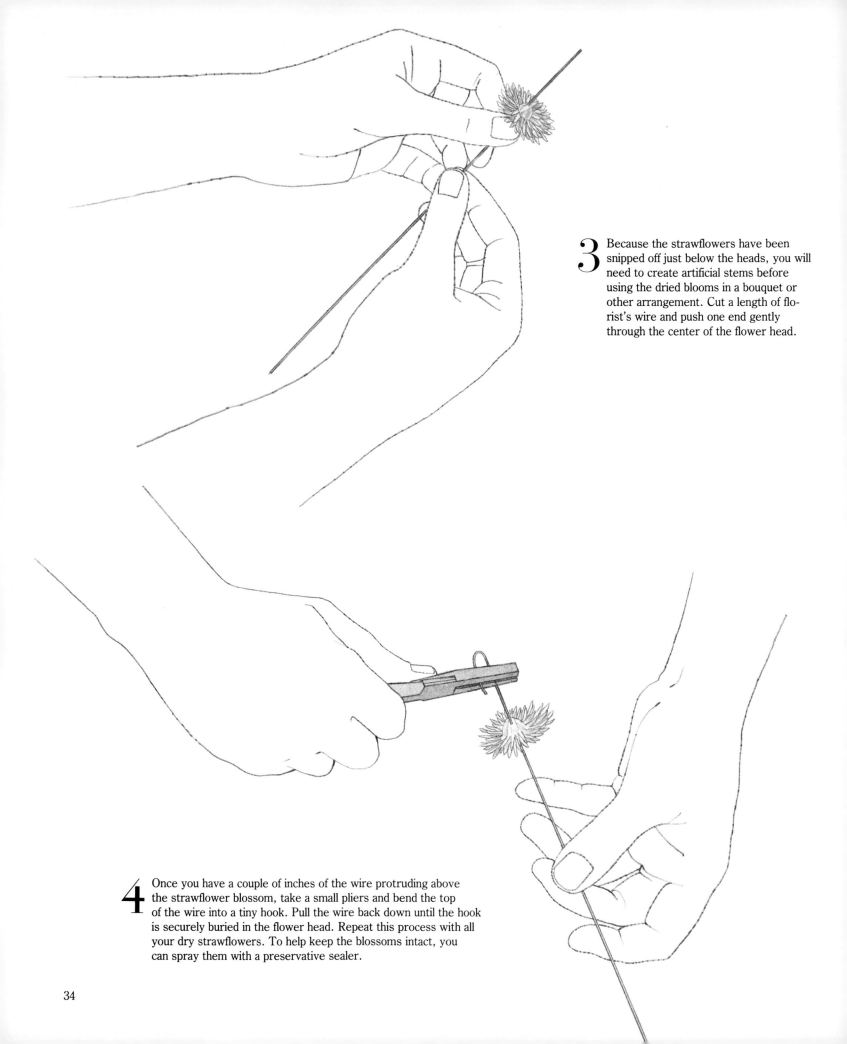

3 Because the strawflowers have been snipped off just below the heads, you will need to create artificial stems before using the dried blooms in a bouquet or other arrangement. Cut a length of florist's wire and push one end gently through the center of the flower head.

4 Once you have a couple of inches of the wire protruding above the strawflower blossom, take a small pliers and bend the top of the wire into a tiny hook. Pull the wire back down until the hook is securely buried in the flower head. Repeat this process with all your dry strawflowers. To help keep the blossoms intact, you can spray them with a preservative sealer.

5 Finish the artificial stems with green florist's tape. To do so, hold the tape in one hand and the wire stem in the other; rotate the stem so that the tape winds itself around it. This done, your strawflowers are ready for arranging in any manner you want—standing in an upright vase, lying in a shallow basket or tied in a bouquet. □

HANGING ANNUALS TO DRY

Three annuals that rival strawflowers as favorites for drying are shown here. Left to right they are: globe amaranth, statice and celosia. All have papery blossoms that dry easily, and all but celosia are members of a plant group known as everlasting. Other annuals that dry well are honesty, starflower and bells-of-Ireland. They dry best hung upside down, as shown here. The drying place should be dark as well as airy; too much light can fade the blossoms while they dry. It should also be moderately warm—50° to 60° F—but not hot. Drying can take as little as one week and should not take more than three. You can test by gently touching the bunches with your hand.

2
SEEDS
AND CUTTINGS

S tarting plants from seed may not be the quickest way to get a garden but it is the most magical. Nothing in the prosaic covering of a zinnia or petunia seed hints at the blossom that will eventually erupt from within it. Very likely, it is this magic that has led gardeners for years to experiment with seeds and the process of growing them. The following pages describe some methods for growing plants from seed. Included is the common practice of starting seeds indoors, well in advance of the date they would normally be sown outdoors. This, of course, is what nurseries do, but when done at home it permits the gardener to explore far more plant varieties than the local nursery can possibly offer. For proof, one has only to look at the pages devoted, for example, to petunias and marigolds in a seed catalog. Less common is the practice of collecting seeds from flowers particularly admired, which not only extends the pleasure they give into a second summer but is an economical way to increase that pleasure. Finally, there is the practice of pollinating flowers by hand, which, of course, is what hybridizers do. Pollination requires careful attention to the flower while it is in bloom, but its result can be the most magical of all—the creation of a brand-new plant type.

Then, bypassing seeds entirely, there are instructions for creating new plants from favorite annuals, such as coleus, by taking stem cuttings, and for prolonging the life of geraniums—which, overwintered indoors, can be made to bloom again next season.

SOWING SEEDS
IN THE GARDEN

There are many good reasons for sowing seeds directly in the garden. Some annuals grow so fast that nothing is gained by starting them indoors. Some—such as poppy, larkspur and others that have long taproots—do not flourish when moved, so you are likely to have a higher survival rate with sown seeds than with transplanted seedlings. And some, like certain daisies, sweet peas and forget-me-nots, do better when started in cool soil; they can even withstand frost.

No matter what seeds you are sowing, and whether or not the last frost date in your area has passed, the soil must be in condition for planting. Take a handful and squeeze it; if it sticks together, it is still too wet to work. Wait a few more days and test it again. When the soil is moist but crumbles in your hand, it is ready for planting.

There are two methods of sowing. One is to broadcast seeds—toss them into the soil at random. A light watering, and the job is done. This method is useful for such fine seeds as portulaca and petunia, which are too fine to measure.

A second method is to sow seeds in furrows *(opposite)*. It requires more work in the planting, but it enables you to control the arrangement of the flowers. That may be important if you are planting a formal bed *(pages 10-11)* and want precise geometric lines.

A crowd of gloriosa daisies—some with solid yellow petals, others splashed with orange—nod in the midsummer sun. As hardy annuals, they do well when sown directly in the soil, early in the season.

1 Mark the boundaries of the bed with stakes and string. Use the edge of a mattock or a hoe to loosen the surface soil and make a furrow about 1 inch deep—or as deep as the seed packet instructions indicate. Follow the seed packet instructions, too, for spacing between furrows.

2 Sprinkle the seeds out of the packet evenly into the furrows. To ensure sufficient germination, sow about four seeds for every plant you expect to retain. Look at the seed packet to see whether or not the seeds need covering with a thin layer of soil.

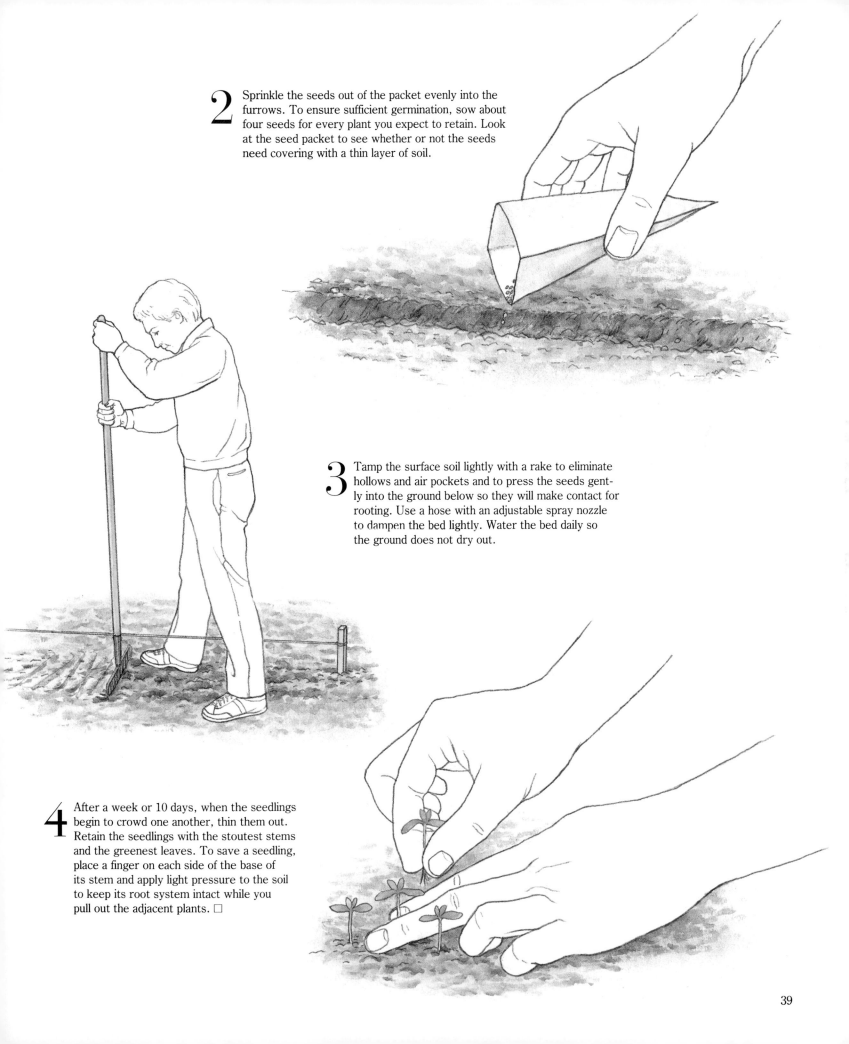

3 Tamp the surface soil lightly with a rake to eliminate hollows and air pockets and to press the seeds gently into the ground below so they will make contact for rooting. Use a hose with an adjustable spray nozzle to dampen the bed lightly. Water the bed daily so the ground does not dry out.

4 After a week or 10 days, when the seedlings begin to crowd one another, thin them out. Retain the seedlings with the stoutest stems and the greenest leaves. To save a seedling, place a finger on each side of the base of its stem and apply light pressure to the soil to keep its root system intact while you pull out the adjacent plants. □

INDOOR SOWING
FOR EARLY BLOOMS

Red and pink wax begonias form a mass of blooms in a garden bed edged in stone. Begonias do best if started in a tray indoors and then transplanted, because their seeds are so small that, sown outdoors, they can easily be dispersed by the wind or washed away by rain.

Some annuals have tiny seeds that may be lost if sown outdoors. Others need a long time to grow before they flower. If you want to get a jump on the season and have such flowers as marigold, zinnia, geranium and verbena blooming in your garden in early summer, they must be sown four to 12 weeks (depending on species) before the last frost date in your area *(pages 70-71)*. That means they must be sown indoors. When you start seeds indoors *(opposite),* an aluminum foil loaf pan makes a convenient planter. Use a soilless mix, or use potting soil combined with peat moss and perlite or vermiculite. Do not use garden soil; it may harbor pests and diseases. While germinating, most seeds need light, but a few, such as sweet peas and morning glories, germinate in the dark. All need some water, but too much can cause damping-off, a disease that kills seedlings. Water your seedlings with a misty spray or set the planting container in a tray of water.

After the seedlings have germinated, transfer the best of them to individual peat pots. When the last frost date has passed, plant them in the garden, peat pot and all. Inside the peat pot, their roots remain intact and suffer no disturbance; and because peat pots are made of organic matter, plant roots can grow right through them. The pot gradually decomposes in the soil.

1 In the bottom of a disposable aluminum foil loaf pan, make drainage holes with the point of a pencil or other instrument. Fill the pan to within ½ inch of the top with moist potting soil mixed with peat moss and perlite or vermiculite.

2 Lay a pencil on its side and mark two shallow furrows in the soil. Sprinkle seeds evenly in the grooves and press them in place with your fingers. Cover them with a light layer of vermiculite to hold them in place and help hold in moisture.

3 Set the pan in a tray of warm water for about half an hour, or until the moisture rises to the top of the soil mixture. Then set the pan in a warm, bright spot, such as near a sunny window or under an artificial light. If nights turn cold, move the pan away from the windowsill; most seeds germinate best when the soil temperature is about 70° F.

4 In a week or two, the seedlings will start sprouting with two leaves and a fragile stem. The seedlings should stand as far apart as they are tall. If they are crowded, thin them by pulling out the least healthy ones with your fingers or by snipping them off at the soil line with a scissors.

5 When the seedlings have produced a second set of leaves, they can be transplanted into individual peat pots. Lift out a small clump of seedlings from the pan with your fingers.

6 Put the clump on a flat surface and gently separate the seedlings from one another with your fingers. Separate them at their roots and be careful not to break the delicate stems.

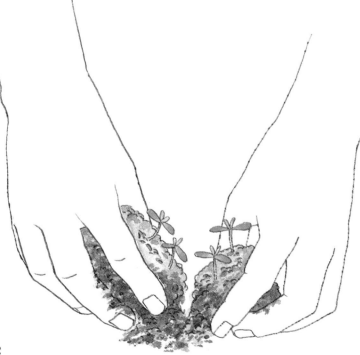

7 Fill each peat pot with a moist, sterile potting soil or with a mixture of potting soil, peat moss, and perlite or vermiculite. Stick a pencil in the center of the soil and gently rotate it to make a hole about as deep as the roots.

8 Hold a seedling by its leaf (the plant can grow another leaf, but the stem is tender and may be easily injured by handling) and put it into the hole at the same depth that it grew in the pan. Make sure you do not bend the roots.

9 Gently tamp down the soil. Place the peat pot in a tray of water and let it soak until the soil is saturated. Put the pan in a warm, bright spot. Fertilize with a weak solution of liquid fertilizer once a week until after the last frost date has passed and it is safe to plant outdoors. Before transplanting your seedlings into the garden soil, acclimate them to outdoor conditions by putting them outside a few hours a day, gradually lengthening the exposure time. □

SAVING AND SORTING SEEDS FROM YOUR GARDEN

Most home gardens are sown from commercial seed, because the seeds cast by many of the flowers in your garden are likely to be hybrids, and hybrids will not breed true; what comes up often bears little resemblance to the plants that produced the seed. But if you are willing to experiment and don't mind surprises, planting seeds that you have stored yourself can be a satisfying and inexpensive way to enlarge and enjoy your garden.

Plants vary greatly in their seed-bearing mechanisms. Some produce a few large seeds, with each encased in its own protective shell; the seedpods of other plants harbor a multitude of tiny seeds. Obviously, collection procedures vary from plant to plant. But by following a few general rules, you can improve your chances of raising new plants from seeds you have collected and stored.

Only ripe seeds will germinate. Wait until your flowers mature and turn brown before you try to collect seeds from them. Always collect on a dry day so that the flower heads contain as little moisture as possible; moisture encourages the growth of mold, which can spoil stored seeds. Store fully dried seeds in closed, labeled containers in a cool, dry place; for optimum conditions, look no farther than your kitchen refrigerator.

Zinnias are among the easiest flowers to collect seeds from. When these rose pink blossoms turn brown, their seeds can be stripped by hand—and laid away until the advent of a new planting season.

1 With a scissors or a shears, cut off old flower heads. Group them by variety, place them in paper bags, fold over the tops of the bags and bring them indoors to dry. Store them in a dry place for four or five days.

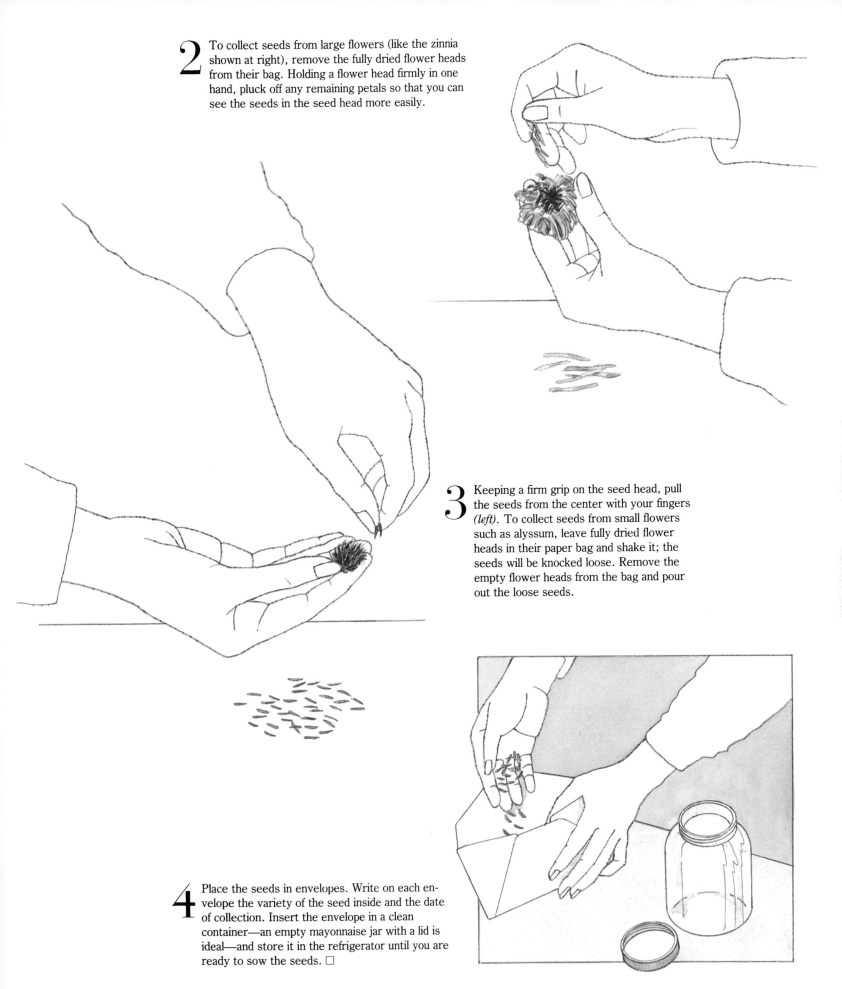

2 To collect seeds from large flowers (like the zinnia shown at right), remove the fully dried flower heads from their bag. Holding a flower head firmly in one hand, pluck off any remaining petals so that you can see the seeds in the seed head more easily.

3 Keeping a firm grip on the seed head, pull the seeds from the center with your fingers *(left)*. To collect seeds from small flowers such as alyssum, leave fully dried flower heads in their paper bag and shake it; the seeds will be knocked loose. Remove the empty flower heads from the bag and pour out the loose seeds.

4 Place the seeds in envelopes. Write on each envelope the variety of the seed inside and the date of collection. Insert the envelope in a clean container—an empty mayonnaise jar with a lid is ideal—and store it in the refrigerator until you are ready to sow the seeds. □

HOMEGROWN HYBRIDS: EXPERIMENTS WITH POLLINATION

Professional plant breeders are constantly introducing new hybrids that are distinguished by never-before-seen colors, greater vigor, more desirable growth habits and better resistance to disease. Improving specific traits through hybridization is a time-consuming task best left to professionals. But using a simplified version of the method that commercial growers use, you can experiment with making your own hybrids—just for the fun of seeing what comes up.

The flowers of most annuals contain both a male sex organ (the pollen-producing stamen) and a female sex organ (the egg-producing pistil). While many flowers are capable of self-pollination, their eggs can also be fertilized by pollen carried from other plants on the wind or on the bodies of insects like honeybees. Each offspring of such cross-pollination between different "parents" is a hybrid.

To create hybrids in your garden, you mimic this natural process—transferring pollen from the stamen of one plant to the pistil of another. For best results, choose parents that are members of the same species, and take care to guard against accidental pollination. You will be working outdoors, so you will need to work fast and cover your plants to protect them from being fertilized by wind-borne pollen.

A reasonable goal for your first hybrid is the creation of a new petal color: for example, crossing a yellow-flowered portulaca with a red-flowered portulaca to make an orange-colored hybrid. But be prepared for surprises; even experts have trouble predicting the outcome of a particular cross.

Hybrid portulacas growing in a rock garden show some of the rich colors and double blooms that have been created by crossing carefully selected parents.

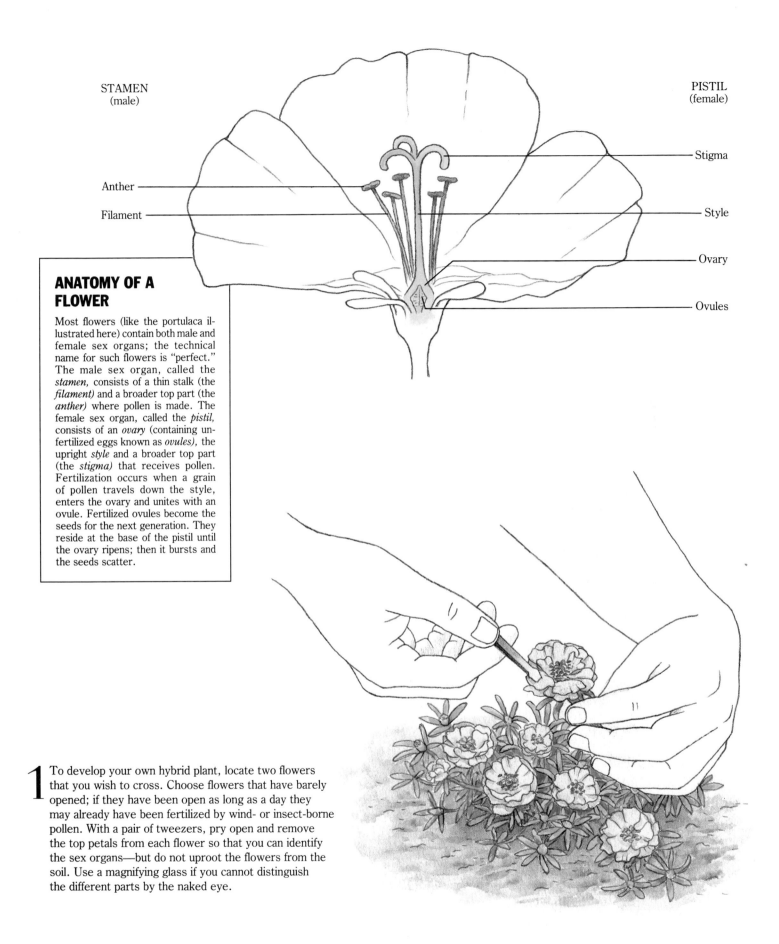

STAMEN
(male)

PISTIL
(female)

Anther —

Filament —

— Stigma

— Style

— Ovary

— Ovules

ANATOMY OF A FLOWER

Most flowers (like the portulaca illustrated here) contain both male and female sex organs; the technical name for such flowers is "perfect." The male sex organ, called the *stamen,* consists of a thin stalk (the *filament)* and a broader top part (the *anther)* where pollen is made. The female sex organ, called the *pistil,* consists of an *ovary* (containing unfertilized eggs known as *ovules),* the upright *style* and a broader top part (the *stigma)* that receives pollen. Fertilization occurs when a grain of pollen travels down the style, enters the ovary and unites with an ovule. Fertilized ovules become the seeds for the next generation. They reside at the base of the pistil until the ovary ripens; then it bursts and the seeds scatter.

1 To develop your own hybrid plant, locate two flowers that you wish to cross. Choose flowers that have barely opened; if they have been open as long as a day they may already have been fertilized by wind- or insect-borne pollen. With a pair of tweezers, pry open and remove the top petals from each flower so that you can identify the sex organs—but do not uproot the flowers from the soil. Use a magnifying glass if you cannot distinguish the different parts by the naked eye.

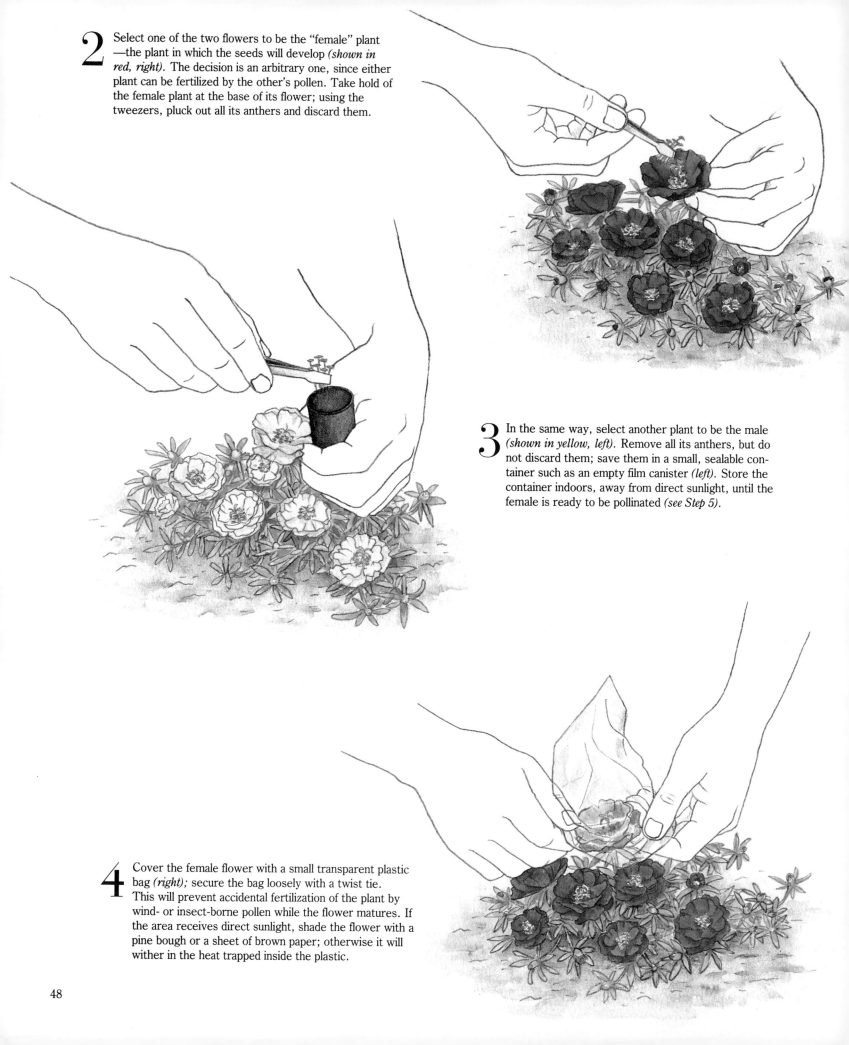

2 Select one of the two flowers to be the "female" plant —the plant in which the seeds will develop *(shown in red, right)*. The decision is an arbitrary one, since either plant can be fertilized by the other's pollen. Take hold of the female plant at the base of its flower; using the tweezers, pluck out all its anthers and discard them.

3 In the same way, select another plant to be the male *(shown in yellow, left)*. Remove all its anthers, but do not discard them; save them in a small, sealable container such as an empty film canister *(left)*. Store the container indoors, away from direct sunlight, until the female is ready to be pollinated *(see Step 5)*.

4 Cover the female flower with a small transparent plastic bag *(right)*; secure the bag loosely with a twist tie. This will prevent accidental fertilization of the plant by wind- or insect-borne pollen while the flower matures. If the area receives direct sunlight, shade the flower with a pine bough or a sheet of brown paper; otherwise it will wither in the heat trapped inside the plastic.

5 Check the flower daily (for five or six days) to see if the pistil is ready to receive pollen. Look for a tiny drop of sticky substance—like a dewdrop—on the stigma. When this appears, dip a clean, fine-tipped paintbrush into the canister of anthers to bring out some pollen. With the brush-tip, "paint" the pollen onto the stigma.

6 Cover the newly pollinated flower with a clean plastic bag; discard the old bag, as it may contain pollen from other plants that could interfere with your cross. Secure the new plastic loosely with a twist tie (right) and shade it from the sun again. Attach a tag to identify the cross for future reference.

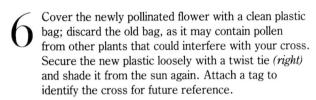

7 Within a few days the petals of the pollinated flower will wither and fall off. Remove the plastic. Look for a swelling of the ovary (left); this indicates the development of seeds within. To keep the swollen seedpod from bursting and scattering its seeds, wrap the pod in a piece of cheesecloth until you are ready to collect and store the seeds (pages 44-45). □

PROPAGATING
FROM STEM CUTTINGS

Because every seed carries within it its entire genetic history, you never know which traits will turn up in the progeny of a given plant's seeds next season. If you want an exact reproduction of a plant you are particularly fond of, the best way to get it is often by stem cuttings—in other words, by cloning. That way you can be sure of duplicating the color, size and form that you start with. In the case of some annuals—particularly coleus, impatiens and geranium—you will also get sturdier plants faster than you can with seeds.

Propagation by stem cutting works best with healthy young plants that have no blooms; if your plant does have flowers, cut them off because flowers sap energy that the plant will need to direct to the forming of roots. The cut should be from 4 to 6 inches long and should be young growth; it can be a side stem or a length taken from the top of a single-stemmed plant. Either of these cuts permits the donor plant to replace the removed portions.

To root the cutting, prepare a small pot by filling it with a light, loose medium. Perlite, vermiculite and coarse sand are all effective mediums for this purpose.

Before the cutting is set in the medium, the entire pot should be placed in a tray filled with warm water and allowed to soak up as much moisture as possible. For quick results—especially if you are using an old plant with stems that have become woody—you may want to coat the tip of the cutting with a powdered or liquid root hormone. This product, which stimulates root growth, is available in various strengths and formulations at garden supply stores. Be sure to check labels to determine which hormone is suitable for your plant.

When kept moistened and in a well-lighted location—but not in direct sunlight—the cutting will root and be ready for transplanting in one to three weeks.

This lavender-flowered coleus is an annual that is easily propagated from stem cuttings; it has firm and succulent stems that root readily.

1 Using a sharp knife, make a clean cut about 4 to 6 inches from the top of the stem (exclusive of flowers) and about ¼ inch below one of the nodes where the plant's leaves emerge *(inset)*. In holding the stem, be careful not to crush it.

2 Carefully strip the leaves from the bottom 1 to 2 inches of the stem, but retain the leaves at the top. Pinch off any flowers or buds from the top of the stem portion.

3 Moisten the rooting medium and with your fingers or a pencil make a 1-inch hole in it. If you are using a rooting hormone, place a small amount on a sheet of paper and roll the cut end of the stem in it. Place the stem in the hole and gently tamp the medium around the stem to hold it upright.

4 Cover the pot with a plastic bag, making sure the cutting is not cramped. Secure the plastic to the bottom of the pot with a rubber band and place the pot where it will receive indirect sunlight. In two weeks, remove the plastic and check root growth by tugging gently on the stem. Resistance indicates that roots have formed and the cutting can be transplanted. □

51

HOLDING GERANIUMS OVER THE WINTER

The geranium is an annual like no other. Actually, in its native environment, South Africa, it is a perennial, which means that in soil and climate that are warm enough, it will bloom again and again, season after season. In northern climates it is generally treated as an annual because it cannot survive cold winters. But it does not have to be thrown out with the trash in autumn. After summer has waned, the geranium can be dug up, potted and brought indoors, and kept alive through the winter in a dormant state *(opposite)*.

Any plant that is to be brought indoors should of course be disease-free and insect-free. If it is, it may be dug up a few weeks before the onset of cold weather, stripped of much of its top growth and then transplanted to a pot. After being given a week in cool, shady space outdoors, it may be gradually introduced into a warmer location indoors.

Once indoors, the plant should be kept in a cool, well-ventilated spot out of direct sunlight. During the early winter months it should be watered lightly—just enough to keep the soil from becoming bone-dry; too much watering may stimulate early growth. By March or April it should have more water and be moved to a spot where it will have light for a few hours each day. Soon new growth will start to appear. After all danger of frost is past, the plant can be acclimated to the outdoors and returned to the ground to bloom for another season.

Planted once again in a garden after successfully spending a winter indoors, vigorous geraniums having brilliant red blossoms and scalloped leaves share a decorative border with some silvery dusty miller and pale purple ageratum.

1 Moisten the soil at the base of a geranium and, with a spade, dig up the plant carefully. Take care to leave the major roots intact and to keep as much soil as possible around them.

2 Choose a pot that will house the root ball without much room to spare. Partially fill it with soil, place the plant on the surface and then add more soil so the plant will sit at the same level as it did when growing in the garden.

3 Using clippers, remove dead leaves and flowers and cut back about a third of the plant. Moisten the soil and put the potted plant in a shady spot for a week to allow the plant to adjust itself to the pot. Then bring it indoors and set it in a cool place out of direct sunlight. Mist the soil when it feels dry. At the end of winter, expose the plant gradually to direct sunlight and, after the last frost, to the out-of-doors. □

3
CARE
AND FEEDING

Annuals are known for being undemanding in their needs; many of them seem to spring from the earth unbidden. But even the sturdiest of them benefits from a little tender care. If they are watered at regular intervals, fed at least once with a fertilizer designed to encourage flowers and kept free of weeds, the plants will be better looking—bushier, fuller, with larger and more abundant flowers. Other small attentions that improve their performance are stakes or some other form of support to protect the plants from the high winds and pelting rains of summer thunderstorms. These stakes, or their substitutes, are especially needed for such tender-stemmed plants as cosmos, and for such tall-growing favorites as sunflowers, zinnias and larkspur. They should be, of course, as inconspicuous as possible, lest the bed of annuals begin to resemble the vegetable patch.

Perhaps the most important garden chore connected with growing annuals is a religiously practiced program of pinching and "deadheading," that is, removing spent flowers. Pinching back the tips of such fast-growing plants as petunias helps keep them from becoming leggy and scraggly as summer wears on, and deadheading not only removes unsightly flowers but encourages the plant to bloom over and over again, often well past the cutoff date nature intended.

There are many ways to handle these routine gardening tasks, some of them especially useful for annuals. You can water with a watering can, for instance, or with a subsoil soaker hose; you can pull weeds by hand as they appear, or discourage their appearance with a mulch. These and other measures for caring for annuals are discussed on the pages that follow.

WATERING
DOWN TO THE ROOTS

Thick, moisture-conserving mulch lies between the plants in this handsome, curving annual border that mixes red geraniums with the massed white blooms of densely growing impatiens.

Most annuals need a steady supply of moisture to grow and flourish. About 1 inch of water each week, from rainfall or from a hose, is normally enough. But it should be a regular 1 inch, and most of it should filter down to the plants' roots, where it will do the most good.

It takes quite a bit of rainfall to add up to an inch. The best way to be certain enough has accumulated is to set out a rain gauge. Simple and inexpensive ones are available at most hardware stores.

So that moisture will be retained, be sure to spread a 1- to 2-inch layer of good mulch, which helps slow evaporation and retards the growth of weeds that can leach water the annuals need. Shredded leaves make an effective mulch; so do tree bark, straw and pine needles. Some gardeners in farming areas swear by buckwheat hulls and ground-up corncobs.

When watering with a hose, it is better to do it generously twice a week than to sprinkle lightly every day. A good soaking gets the moisture down to a depth of 6 inches or more. This is essential if annuals are to be strong and healthy. Deep watering helps their roots grow down into the soil, where they can absorb not only extra moisture, but also larger supplies of soil nutrients.

For these twice-weekly waterings, a sprinkler that rotates or oscillates is satisfactory. More effective, however, are soaker hoses such as the one shown at right. The more durable ones, made of rubber, are porous and flexible, and drip moisture directly into the ground where it is needed with a minimum of evaporation and waste.

1 Having bought a soaker hose, place the cap provided on one end, then loop the hose between rows of plants—leaving enough free to extend back to the garden faucet. The loops can be up to 4 feet apart; the water will spread as it drips out. If the hose is new and resists lying flat, weight it down with bricks or stones while you work.

2 When you have determined the best route for your hose, clear any mulch from its path, then cut a shallow trench in the soil with a trowel or a small mattock. Place the hose in the trench.

3 Cover the hose with the dug-up earth (right) and add a layer of mulch. The covering sends most of the water straight into the earth, cuts down on evaporation and also shields the hose from the sun's rays. With this sort of drip irrigation, you can water the entire garden efficiently with a turn of the garden faucet. The system can be made automatic with the addition of a clock timer. □

FERTILIZING
FOR A MIDSUMMER BOOST

Gently curving rows of yellow rudbeckia, dainty pink and pale yellow snapdragons and bicolored petunias bloom in a well-tended garden. A midsummer boost of fertilizer rich in phosphorus enhances their beauty and extends their growing season.

Many annuals will bloom splendidly all summer long without benefit of fertilizer. But a number of them, such as petunias, begonias, geraniums and sweet peas, grow better when fertilizer is mixed into the soil at planting time, and perk up visibly when they receive a second application in midsummer.

Commercial fertilizers are available in a wide assortment of solids and liquids. Some gardeners like to use natural, or organic, fertilizers made from such substances as fish emulsion, manure, cottonseed meal, blood meal, bone meal and activated sludge. But most gardeners find chemical fertilizers easier to use; they are less expensive and they break down faster in the soil.

These fertilizers, usually packaged in granular form, contain three essential chemical elements: nitrogen for foliage and stem growth, phosphorus for flowering and root growth, and potassium for general vigor. The ratios of these elements vary to meet the needs of different plants. Annuals require relatively low quantities of nitrogen and relatively high quantities of phosphorus, in a ratio of one part nitrogen to two parts phosphorus and two parts potassium. That ratio usually appears on fertilizer packages as 5-10-10, indicating that the package contains 5 percent nitrogen, 10 percent phosphorus and 10 percent potassium. The remaining 75 percent is filler material and tiny amounts of other chemicals.

The most effective way to use chemical fertilizer in a flower garden is to mix it into the soil at the time of planting, following directions on the package to determine the proper amount. A second application in midsummer can provide additional nourishment, replacing fertilizer absorbed by the plants or washed away by heavy rainfall.

1 Prepare for a midsummer feeding by clearing away mulch. Use a trowel, a hoe or a mattock to cut a 1-inch-deep groove on either side of a plant row and close to the drip lines (the edges of the foliage). For a plant that stands alone, cut a circular groove around the plant.

2 Sprinkle a small amount of fertilizer into the groove by gently shaking it from a trowel. Then use the trowel to distribute the fertilizer evenly in the soil.

3 Cover the groove with soil and replace or add mulch to hold moisture. Water the area well to activate the fertilizer. In regions where the growing season is long and summer is hot, an additional feeding six weeks later provides a late-summer boost. □

LENDING SUPPORT WITH STAKES AND STRING

Towering above a bed of cosmos, salvia and other plants, sunflowers nod in a breeze. Their tall stems need staking about halfway up.

Some of the most decorative annuals grow so tall, top-heavy or thin-stemmed that a stiff breeze may topple them. Especially vulnerable are those with large flower heads, such as dahlias, sunflowers and zinnias. Also endangered are slender plants such as cosmos, and tall, spiky annuals such as hollyhocks and foxgloves. The best way to prevent broken stems and bedraggled blooms is to provide the plants with stakes—before the plants produce full-blown flowers and need support. One method is to stake them in groups *(right)*. This works best with species that tend to sprawl sideways or grow upward—zinnias and marigolds, for example—and with slender plants like cosmos that are normally planted in clumps. Single staking—using one stake per plant *(following pages)*—is essential for the annuals that grow very tall or have heavy blooms or both.

The stakes can be inconspicuous. Ideal are lengths of green-stained bamboo, which are thin but strong and blend into the surrounding foliage. They should be long enough to support the height of the mature plants and leave an extra 8 inches to push into the ground.

PERIPHERAL STAKING

1 To begin staking a bed of slender-stemmed annuals, drive several stakes into the ground at the corners. The stakes should be close enough to help the plants stay upright, but without crowding. Then loop a length of soft twine around the stakes about 1 foot above the ground and tie the ends. This first string will help support the lower foliage as the plant grows taller. A long bed of vulnerable annuals may require additional stakes, say three on each side or more. If you live in a windy area, you can give the plants extra support by running additional strings in a crisscross pattern through the flower bed.

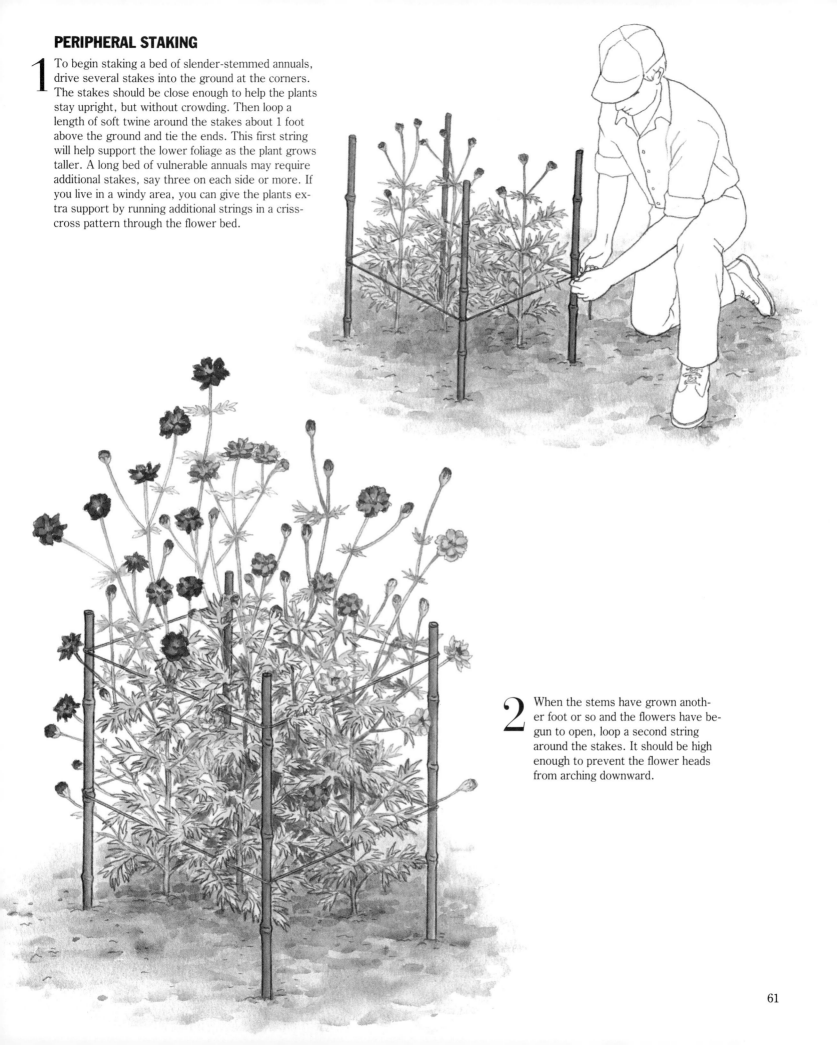

2 When the stems have grown another foot or so and the flowers have begun to open, loop a second string around the stakes. It should be high enough to prevent the flower heads from arching downward.

61

SINGLE STAKING

1 Shoring up individual plants with their own stakes requires only a little more time than the peripheral staking shown on the previous page. First, drive a stake of bamboo or other hard wood into the ground about 3 inches from the plant. Loop a piece of twine (or a long plastic tie) around the stake and around the stem, as illustrated in the box at right. Be sure the loop enclosing the stem is loose; otherwise you may injure the plant.

2 As the plants continue to grow, add more ties as needed to keep up. Annuals that produce large blossoms should have a tie near the base of the flower head *(right)*. A plant that has a particularly tall flower head may need still another piece of twine added among the upper blossoms *(far right)* to keep the flower head from snapping off in a strong wind. □

KEEPING FLOWERS AT THEIR PEAK ALL SUMMER LONG

A massed planting of golden yellow marigolds and pink petunias makes a dazzling midsummer show. Both these annuals are free-flowering plants that, with a little maintenance in spring and summer, will make a fine display all season long.

Annuals are such prolific bloomers that even if you just put them in the ground and leave them alone, they will produce great quantities of flowers all by themselves. But if you give them a little attention, they will reward you by blooming even more abundantly. Regular maintenance is particularly useful in warm-weather areas, where growing seasons are long.

Three methods used both to control and to take advantage of the naturally fast growth of annuals are pinching, deadheading and shearing. What you are actually doing when you perform these tasks is redirecting the growth of the plant so that its energy goes into making as many flowers as possible.

You begin in the springtime with pinching —nipping stem tips in the bud. This encourages branching and results in larger and bushier growth for the plant.

As the season progresses, start deadheading—removing spent blossoms; this gives you not only a more attractive garden immediately but more flowers in the long run.

Sometimes you may have to shear your plants—cut them all the way back to within a few inches of the ground. Though this may seem drastic, in fact it will rejuvenate the plants and allow them to get a fresh start and begin growing again.

Even in a large garden, these activities don't have to consume great amounts of time. To keep them from becoming chores, make grooming your plants a part of a daily stroll among the flowers. At the end of your walk, you'll be able to turn around and see a much more beautiful yard.

PINCHING FOR FULLNESS

To pinch back a stem, grasp the growing tip—the point of the stem above the top pair of mature leaves—between your thumb and forefinger and remove it. This growing tip contains a plant hormone that inhibits the growth of buds farther down on the stem. By removing the tip, you allow the dormant buds to begin to grow. Seedlings can be first pinched when they have three or four sets of leaves. Transplants bought from a nursery can be pinched back as you plant them in the ground. Pinch the new growth on your plants after about three weeks to encourage them to become even bushier.

SHEARING FOR FRESH GROWTH

Annuals such as impatiens, lobelia, portulaca, alyssum and others that flower on many small stems may need shearing because deadheading flower by flower is impractical. After a period of early rapid growth, these plants may slow down in midseason and begin producing fewer flowers. At this point shearing the plants back will allow them to begin fresh growth and they will soon be blooming again.

DEADHEADING FADED FLOWERS

To deadhead, you can use shears for large plants; pluck off smaller flowers with your fingers. Deadheading will not only make the plants more attractive, it will also prevent them from producing seeds. Except for certain newly developed annuals that do not produce viable seeds, plants will usually stop blooming after they have gone to seed, so deadheading is doubly effective in keeping the garden looking attractive. If the stems are long and would be left as unsightly stubs when the flowers have been removed, you may want to take a pair of shears and cut the stems down among the leaves. □

FALL CHORES
FOR A SPRING PAYOFF

With the first frost of fall, it's time to say good-by to most of your annuals. But fall is by no means the end of the gardener's year. By taking proper precautions before the onset of winter, you can ensure an early and successful rebirth of your garden in the spring.

Since frost-killed plants may harbor insect pests and disease-causing organisms, remove all dead foliage as soon as possible. If the entire bed is devoted to annuals, simply pull up the plants and throw them on the compost heap, or discard them as trash.

If the bed also contains bulbs, perennials or biennials that will survive the winter, cut the annuals off at the ground with a pair of shears so that you can remove them without injuring the plants that remain. Leave the roots of the cut annuals in the ground to die.

A bed emptied of annuals can be brightened by filling in the bare spots with hardy annuals like ornamental cabbage or biennials like pansies. In many climates, these plants will bring color to your garden until the end of December. Buy them at a garden center or start your own from seed in midsummer and transplant them outdoors in the fall.

All newly transplanted biennials and any plants with evergreen foliage need the protection of a winter mulch. The mulch helps maintain a stable ground temperature; without it, alternate freezing and thawing can cause roots to heave above the surface, where the cold dry air will quickly kill them.

Some commonly used winter mulches are straw, shredded leaves and pine needles. Choose whatever is cheap and available in your region. For best results, mulch to a depth of 2 to 3 inches; too thick a layer can harm plants by blocking the passage of air, sunlight and water.

In a late-autumn bed where frost-killed annuals have been removed, foxgloves and newly transplanted pansies poke above a winter mulch of pine needles.

1 Where pulling would disturb the roots of neighboring biennials, remove dead annuals by cutting them to the ground *(right)*. Gather them in bundles and throw them on a compost heap or discard them with the trash. The roots of the cut annuals will die in the ground.

2 To protect the roots of a biennial during the winter months, mulch with 2 to 3 inches of straw, shredded leaves, pine needles or other readily available insulating material. Work the mulch under the foliage, taking care not to bury it *(left)*.

3 If you live in a region where winter temperatures drop below 20° F, lay an extra cover of very thin mulch on top of the plants *(right)*. If you have high winds, shelter the plants with small boughs cut from evergreens. In either case, make sure the protective cover is thin enough to permit air, sunlight and water to pass through. □

4
MAKING THE MOST OF NATURE

Annuals may be among the least troublesome of all garden plants to grow; they are by nature rugged and tenacious. Even so, they are more likely to stay healthy and thus look their best if the gardener pays attention to such fundamental matters as timing, grooming and troubleshooting. On the following pages you will find some handy guides to all those considerations.

As much as anything else, success with annuals depends on good timing. Some annuals are hardy enough to withstand —even to need—cool soil, and thus should be planted early in spring or late in fall; others are tender and must not be put in the ground till after all danger of frost is past. But spring comes earlier in California and South Carolina than it does in Michigan and Maine. For a general guide to timely planting in your area, see the map on pages 70-71; it indicates the average date of the last frost in nine regions across the United States and Canada. Then, for a checklist of chores to do and when to do them, see the chart on pages 72-75; if you live in western Nebraska (Region 3) you'll only just be turning the soil in May and June, whereas fellow gardeners in Georgia will already be cutting flowers.

Even in the best of gardens, trouble arises from time to time, and a given plant or group of plants may look sickly or distressed. Pages 76-79 provide a collection of common garden ailments. The text and illustrations are designed to help you identify such garden pests as beetles and scale, for instance—or how to distinguish the damage done by particular pests if, like leaf miners, they are too small to see with the naked eye. The text also gives information on how to correct the conditions that such pests bring on. Finally, this section concludes with suggestions for enhancing the beauty and well-being of your garden in the form of handy tips that require more common sense and forethought than hard labor.

THE ZONE MAP AND PLANTING

Annuals get off to the best start when soil conditions, day length and air temperatures are just right. To some extent, those conditions depend on the calendar, to some on locality and to some on the annuals themselves. Annuals are classified as hardy, half-hardy and tender. The hardy ones can withstand light frost and cool soil; they can be planted in early spring, as soon as the soil can be worked, usually four to six weeks before the last frost. Half-hardy annuals are best planted after the last frost, but if an unexpected late frost should occur, the plants will survive. Tender annuals need warm weather and soil. They cannot be planted outdoors until all danger of frost has passed.

The map at right is a guide for linking frost dates with regions. It is based on average last spring frost dates collected from weather stations over a 30-year period and compiled by the United States Department of Commerce. It divides North America into nine regions. Region 1, which includes the northern part of the continent, has the coldest temperatures, the longest winters and the latest spring frost. Region 9, which lies in the warmest areas of California, Florida and Texas, has the earliest spring frost-free date. Some parts of Region 9 may never experience frost at all.

The regions on the map, like the frost dates, are to be used only as general guidelines. Within regions, frost-free dates can vary with altitude, and they can vary from year to year when temperatures are higher or lower than normal. For information specific to your area and the year, consult a local agricultural extension service.

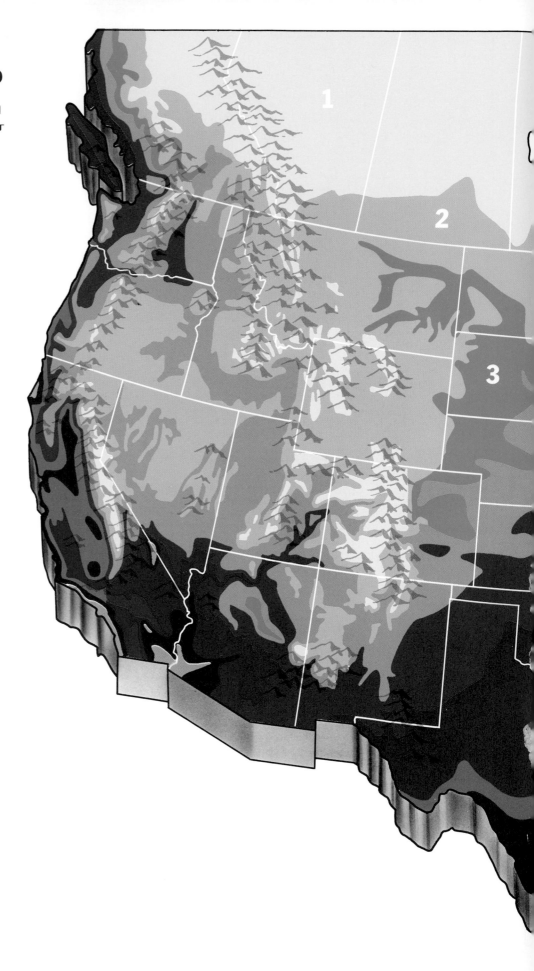

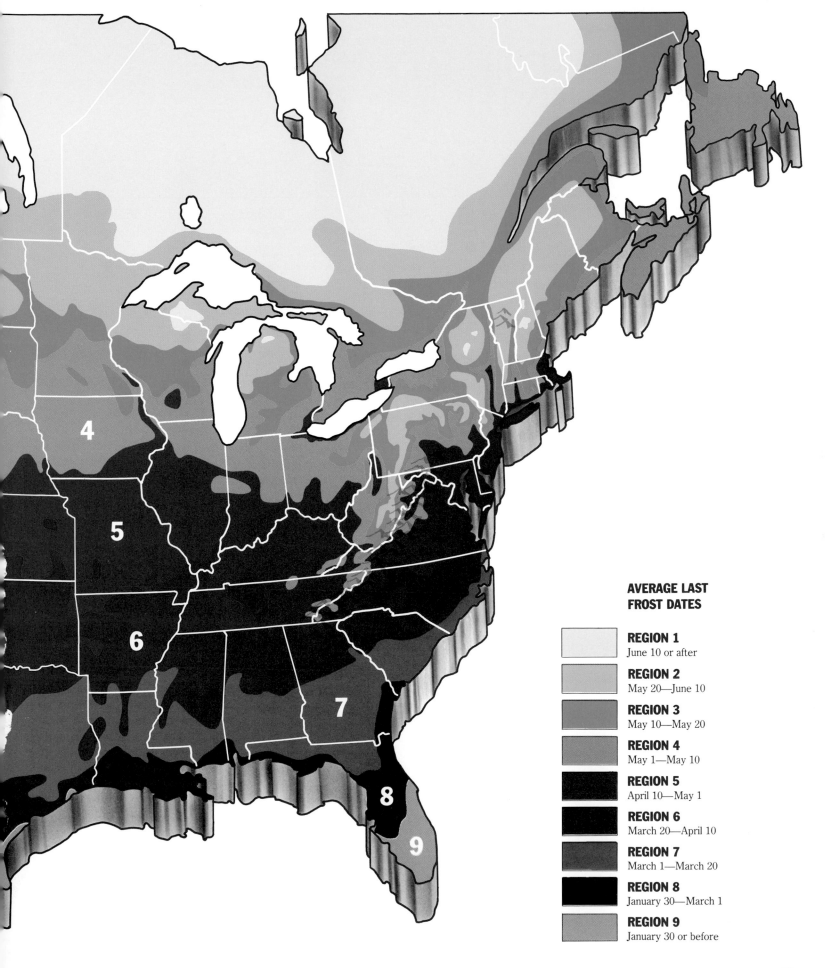

AVERAGE LAST FROST DATES

REGION 1
June 10 or after

REGION 2
May 20—June 10

REGION 3
May 10—May 20

REGION 4
May 1—May 10

REGION 5
April 10—May 1

REGION 6
March 20—April 10

REGION 7
March 1—March 20

REGION 8
January 30—March 1

REGION 9
January 30 or before

A CHECKLIST FOR MAINTENANCE MONTH BY MONTH

	REGION 1	REGION 2	REGION 3	REGION 4	REGION 5
JANUARY/FEBRUARY	• Study seed catalogs and order seeds • Clean, sharpen and repair tools • Plan and design flower beds	• Study seed catalogs and order seeds • Clean, sharpen and repair tools • Plan and design flower beds	• Study seed catalogs and order seeds • Clean, sharpen and repair tools • Plan and design flower beds	• Study seed catalogs and order seeds • Clean, sharpen and repair tools • Plan and design flower beds • Start tender annual seeds indoors if they require 12 weeks or more to develop • Start hardy annual seeds indoors for planting outdoors as soon as the soil can be worked	• Study seed catalogs and order seeds • Clean, sharpen and repair tools • Plan and design flower beds • Start tender annual seeds indoors if they require 10 weeks to develop • Start hardy annual seeds indoors for planting outdoors as soon as the soil can be worked
MARCH/APRIL	• Start any seeds indoors • Start dahlias indoors	• Start any seeds indoors • Start dahlias indoors	• Start any seeds indoors • Start dahlias indoors	• Start tender annual seeds indoors if they require 12 weeks or more to develop • Start dahlias indoors • Prepare planting beds as soon as the ground can be worked • Plant hardy annuals • Sow hardy annual seeds outdoors	• Start tender annual seeds indoors • Start dahlias indoors • Prepare planting beds as soon as the ground can be worked • Plant hardy annuals outdoors • Sow annual seeds outdoors • Weed flower beds
MAY/JUNE	• Prepare planting beds as soon as the ground can be worked • Plant any annuals outdoors • Water as necessary • Weed flower beds • Apply insecticides and fungicides as needed • Mulch flower beds	• Prepare planting beds as soon as the ground can be worked • Plant any annuals outdoors • Water as necessary • Weed flower beds • Apply insecticides and fungicides as needed • Mulch flower beds	• Prepare planting beds as soon as the ground can be worked • Plant any annuals outdoors • Water as necessary • Weed flower beds • Apply insecticides and fungicides as needed • Mulch flower beds	• Plant tender annuals outdoors • Sow tender annual seeds outdoors • Water as necessary • Weed flower beds • Thin seedlings • Place slug and snail bait • Apply insecticides and fungicides as needed • Train vines • Mulch flower beds	• Plant tender annuals outdoors • Sow tender annual seeds outdoors • Water as necessary • Weed flower beds • Thin seedlings • Place slug and snail bait • Apply insecticides and fungicides as needed • Train vines • Mulch flower beds

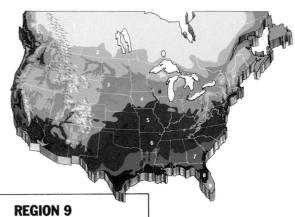

	REGION 6	REGION 7	REGION 8	REGION 9	
JANUARY/FEBRUARY	• Study seed catalogs and order seeds • Clean, sharpen and repair tools • Plan and design flower beds • Start any seeds indoors	• Study seed catalogs and order seeds • Clean, sharpen and repair tools • Plan and design flower beds • Start any seeds indoors • Prepare planting beds as soon as the ground can be worked	• Study seed catalogs and order seeds • Clean, sharpen and repair tools • Plan and design flower beds • Start any seeds indoors • Prepare planting beds • Plant hardy annual seedlings • Sow hardy annual seeds outdoors • Water as necessary • Weed flower beds	• Study seed catalogs and order seeds • Clean, sharpen and repair tools • Plan and design flower beds • Start seeds indoors • Prepare planting beds • Plant hardy annuals • Sow hardy annual seeds outdoors • Water as necessary • Weed flower beds • Thin seedlings • Place snail and slug bait • Apply insecticides and fungicides as needed	
MARCH/APRIL	• Start dahlias indoors • Prepare planting beds as soon as the ground can be worked • Plant hardy and tender annuals outdoors • Sow any annual seeds outdoors • Water as necessary • Weed flower beds	• Start dahlias indoors • Prepare planting beds • Plant hardy and tender annuals • Sow any annual seeds outdoors • Water as necessary • Weed flower beds • Thin seedlings • Place slug and snail bait • Apply insecticides and fungicides as needed • Train vines	• Plant any annuals outdoors • Sow any annual seeds outdoors • Water as necessary • Weed flower beds • Thin seedlings • Place slug and snail bait • Apply insecticides and fungicides as needed • Train vines • Mulch flower beds • Remove faded flowers • Pinch back tall-growing plants as necessary • Shear low-growing plants as necessary • Fertilize plants as necessary • Cut flowers for indoor displays	• Plant any annuals outdoors • Sow any annual seeds outdoors • Water as necessary • Weed flower beds • Thin seedlings • Place slug and snail bait • Apply insecticides and fungicides as needed • Train vines • Mulch flower beds • Remove faded flowers • Pinch back tall-growing plants as necessary • Shear low-growing plants as necessary • Fertilize plants as necessary • Cut flowers for indoor displays	
MAY/JUNE	• Plant tender annuals outdoors • Sow tender annual seeds outdoors • Water as necessary • Weed flower beds • Thin seedlings • Place slug and snail bait • Apply insecticides and fungicides as needed • Train vines • Mulch flower beds • Remove faded flowers • Pinch back tall-growing plants as necessary • Shear low-growing plants as necessary • Fertilize plants as necessary	• Plant tender annuals outdoors • Water as necessary • Weed flower beds • Place slug and snail bait • Apply insecticides and fungicides as needed • Train vines • Mulch flower beds • Remove faded flowers • Pinch back tall-growing plants as necessary • Shear low-growing plants as necessary • Fertilize plants as necessary • Cut flowers for indoor displays • Cut flowers for drying	• Plant tender annuals outdoors • Water as necessary • Weed flower beds • Place slug and snail bait • Apply insecticides and fungicides as needed • Train vines • Remove faded flowers • Pinch back tall-growing plants as necessary • Shear low-growing plants as necessary • Fertilize plants as necessary • Cut flowers for indoor displays • Cut flowers for drying • Remove spent hardy annuals	• Plant tender annuals outdoors • Water as necessary • Weed flower beds • Place slug and snail bait • Apply insecticides and fungicides as needed • Train vines • Remove faded flowers • Pinch back tall-growing plants as necessary • Shear low-growing plants as necessary • Fertilize plants as necessary • Cut flowers for indoor displays • Cut flowers for drying • Remove spent hardy annuals	

	REGION 1	REGION 2	REGION 3	REGION 4	REGION 5
JULY/AUGUST	• Water as necessary • Weed flower beds • Apply insecticides and fungicides as needed • Train vines • Remove faded flowers • Pinch back tall-growing plants as necessary • Shear low-growing plants as necessary • Fertilize plants as necessary • Cut flowers for indoor displays • Cut flowers for drying • Take cuttings to root indoors	• Water as necessary • Weed flower beds • Apply insecticides and fungicides as needed • Train vines • Remove faded flowers • Pinch back tall-growing plants as necessary • Shear low-growing plants as necessary • Fertilize plants as necessary • Cut flowers for indoor displays • Cut flowers for drying • Take cuttings to root indoors	• Water as necessary • Weed flower beds • Apply insecticides and fungicides as needed • Train vines • Remove faded flowers • Pinch back tall-growing plants as necessary • Shear low-growing plants as necessary • Fertilize plants as necessary • Cut flowers for indoor displays • Cut flowers for drying • Take cuttings to root indoors • Sow biennial seeds indoors or outdoors • Plant biennials outdoors	• Water as necessary • Weed flower beds • Apply insecticides and fungicides as needed • Train vines • Remove faded flowers • Pinch back tall-growing plants as necessary • Shear low-growing plants as necessary • Fertilize plants as necessary • Cut flowers for indoor displays • Cut flowers for drying • Take cuttings to root indoors • Sow biennial seeds indoors or outdoors	• Water as necessary • Weed flower beds • Apply insecticides and fungicides as needed • Train vines • Remove faded flowers • Pinch back tall-growing plants as necessary • Shear low-growing plants as necessary • Fertilize plants as necessary • Cut flowers for indoor displays • Cut flowers for drying • Sow hardy annual seeds indoors or outdoors • Sow biennial seeds indoors or outdoors
SEPTEMBER/OCTOBER	• Remove annuals killed by frost • Check and repair trellises and raised beds • Dig up dahlias and store them	• Water as necessary • Cut flowers for indoor displays • Cut flowers for drying • Remove annuals killed by frost • Check and repair trellises and raised beds • Dig up dahlias and store them	• Water as necessary • Weed flower beds • Cut flowers for indoor displays • Cut flowers for drying • Remove annuals killed by frost • Check and repair trellises and raised beds • Dig up dahlias and store them • Mulch biennials	• Water as necessary • Weed flower beds • Cut flowers for indoor displays • Cut flowers for drying • Remove faded flowers • Remove annuals killed by frost • Check and repair trellises and raised beds • Dig up dahlias and store them • Plant and mulch hardy biennials • Plant ornamental kale and cabbage	• Water as necessary • Weed flower beds • Cut flowers for indoor displays • Cut flowers for drying • Remove faded flowers • Take cuttings to root indoors • Plant hardy annuals outdoors • Plant biennials outdoors
NOVEMBER/DECEMBER					• Remove annuals killed by frost • Check and repair trellises and raised beds • Dig up dahlias and store them • Plant ornamental kale and cabbage • Mulch hardy annuals • Mulch biennials

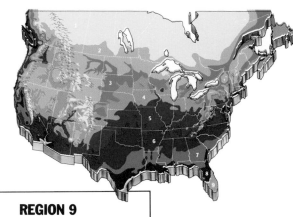

REGION 6	REGION 7	REGION 8	REGION 9	
<ul><li>Water as necessary</li><li>Weed flower beds</li><li>Apply insecticides and fungicides as needed</li><li>Train vines</li><li>Remove faded flowers</li><li>Pinch back tall-growing plants as necessary</li><li>Shear low-growing plants as necessary</li><li>Fertilize plants as necessary</li><li>Cut flowers for indoor displays</li><li>Cut flowers for drying</li><li>Sow hardy annual seeds indoors or outdoors</li><li>Sow biennial seeds indoors or outdoors</li></ul>	<ul><li>Water as necessary</li><li>Weed flower beds</li><li>Apply insecticides and fungicides as needed</li><li>Train vines</li><li>Remove faded flowers</li><li>Pinch back tall-growing plants as necessary</li><li>Shear low-growing plants as necessary</li><li>Fertilize plants as necessary</li><li>Cut flowers for indoor displays</li><li>Cut flowers for drying</li><li>Sow hardy annual seeds indoors or outdoors</li><li>Sow biennial seeds indoors or outdoors</li><li>Remove spent annuals</li></ul>	<ul><li>Water as necessary</li><li>Weed flower beds</li><li>Apply insecticides and fungicides as needed</li><li>Train vines</li><li>Remove faded flowers</li><li>Pinch back tall-growing plants as necessary</li><li>Shear low-growing plants as necessary</li><li>Fertilize plants as necessary</li><li>Cut flowers for indoor displays</li><li>Cut flowers for drying</li><li>Sow hardy annual seeds indoors or outdoors</li><li>Sow biennial seeds indoors or outdoors</li><li>Remove spent annuals</li></ul>	<ul><li>Water as necessary</li><li>Weed flower beds</li><li>Apply insecticides and fungicides as needed</li><li>Train vines</li><li>Remove faded flowers</li><li>Pinch back tall-growing plants as necessary</li><li>Shear low-growing plants as necessary</li><li>Fertilize plants as necessary</li><li>Cut flowers for indoor displays</li><li>Cut flowers for drying</li><li>Sow hardy annual seeds indoors or outdoors</li><li>Sow biennial seeds indoors or outdoors</li><li>Remove spent annuals</li></ul>	**JULY/AUGUST**
<ul><li>Water as necessary</li><li>Weed flower beds</li><li>Apply insecticides and fungicides as needed</li><li>Cut flowers for indoor displays</li><li>Cut flowers for drying</li><li>Remove faded flowers</li><li>Take cuttings to root indoors</li><li>Plant hardy annuals outdoors</li><li>Plant biennials outdoors</li></ul>	<ul><li>Water as necessary</li><li>Weed flower beds</li><li>Place slug and snail bait</li><li>Apply insecticides and fungicides as needed</li><li>Remove faded flowers</li><li>Pinch back tall-growing plants as necessary</li><li>Shear low-growing plants as necessary</li><li>Fertilize plants as necessary</li><li>Cut flowers for indoor displays</li><li>Cut flowers for drying</li><li>Remove spent annuals</li><li>Take cuttings to root indoors</li><li>Plant hardy annuals outdoors</li><li>Plant biennials outdoors</li></ul>	<ul><li>Water as necessary</li><li>Weed flower beds</li><li>Place slug and snail bait</li><li>Apply insecticides and fungicides as needed</li><li>Remove faded flowers</li><li>Pinch back tall-growing plants as necessary</li><li>Shear low-growing plants as necessary</li><li>Fertilize plants as necessary</li><li>Cut flowers for indoor displays</li><li>Cut flowers for drying</li><li>Remove spent annuals</li><li>Take cuttings to root indoors</li><li>Plant hardy annuals outdoors</li><li>Plant biennials outdoors</li></ul>	<ul><li>Water as necessary</li><li>Weed flower beds</li><li>Place slug and snail bait</li><li>Apply insecticides and fungicides as needed</li><li>Remove faded flowers</li><li>Pinch back tall-growing plants as necessary</li><li>Shear low-growing plants as necessary</li><li>Fertilize plants as necessary</li><li>Cut flowers for indoor displays</li><li>Cut flowers for drying</li><li>Remove spent annuals</li><li>Take cuttings to root indoors</li><li>Plant hardy annuals outdoors</li><li>Plant biennials outdoors</li></ul>	**SEPTEMBER/OCTOBER**
<ul><li>Remove annuals killed by frost</li><li>Check and repair trellises and raised beds</li><li>Dig up dahlias and store them</li><li>Plant ornamental kale and cabbage</li><li>Mulch hardy annuals</li><li>Mulch biennials</li></ul>	<ul><li>Take cuttings to root indoors</li><li>Remove annuals killed by frost</li><li>Check and repair trellises and raised beds</li><li>Dig up dahlias and store them</li><li>Plant ornamental kale and cabbage</li><li>Mulch hardy annuals</li><li>Mulch biennials</li><li>Study seed catalogs and order seeds</li></ul>	<ul><li>Take cuttings to root indoors</li><li>Remove annuals killed by frost</li><li>Check and repair trellises and raised beds</li><li>Dig up dahlias and store them</li><li>Plant ornamental kale and cabbage</li><li>Mulch hardy annuals</li><li>Mulch biennials</li><li>Study seed catalogs and order seeds</li><li>Start any seeds indoors</li></ul>	<ul><li>Water as necessary</li><li>Weed flower beds</li><li>Place slug and snail bait</li><li>Apply insecticides and fungicides as needed</li><li>Fertilize plants as necessary</li><li>Remove spent annuals</li><li>Check and repair trellises and raised beds</li><li>Dig up dahlias and store them</li><li>Take cuttings to root indoors</li><li>Mulch hardy annuals</li><li>Mulch biennials</li><li>Study seed catalogs and order seeds</li><li>Start any seeds indoors</li><li>Prepare planting beds for spring</li></ul>	**NOVEMBER/DECEMBER**

WHAT TO DO
WHEN THINGS GO WRONG

PROBLEM	CAUSE	SOLUTION
Dark brown blotches appear on the leaves of calendula, celosia, chrysanthemum, geranium, heliotrope, lobelia, monkey flower and zinnia. Foliage eventually yellows, dies and falls off the plant.	Leaf spot disease, which is caused by various fungi. The fungi, which thrive in cool, moist conditions, are spread by wind and water.	Remove and destroy all infected leaves. Thin plants to increase air circulation. Water plants in the morning; damp soil and cool night air foster the spread of the disease. Several fungicides will prevent leaf spot, but they will not cure infected plants. Sulfur can help control the disease.
Seedlings suddenly topple over and die. Any annual is susceptible, but annual phlox and sweet alyssum are especially prone.	Damping-off, a disease caused by fungi that live in the soil and attack roots and stems.	Before sowing seeds indoors, drench the flats with an approved fungicide. Use a sterile, soilless planting medium. Do not overwater seedlings. Plant only in garden soil that has good drainage.
Orange or brown powdery spots develop primarily on the undersides of leaves. Leaves may wilt; plant growth may be stunted. Susceptible annuals include amaranthus, baby's breath, China aster, chrysanthemum, cornflower, hollyhock, lobelia, morning glory and snapdragon.	Rust, a disease caused by a fungus that thrives when days are hot and humid and nights are cool.	Remove and destroy infected plants. Water only in the morning to prevent disease spread. Sulfur and a number of approved fungicides will help control the disease. Rust-resistant varieties of snapdragon are available.
Color fades from African daisy, forget-me-not, geranium, ice plant, Livingstone daisy, nemesia, pansy, sweet pea and other annuals. Plants may be stunted and may wilt. Roots are damp, soft and discolored.	Root rot, caused by one of several fungi that thrive in heavy wet soil.	Plant only in well-drained soil. Remove and discard infected plants, and flush the soil with an approved fungicide.
Leaves, stems and flower buds are coated with a fine, white powder. Plants and flowers may be distorted in shape. Annual phlox, bellflower, fuchsia, monkey flower, spider flower, sweet pea, verbena and zinnia are particularly susceptible.	Powdery mildew, a disease caused by a fungus. The fungus is spread by wind and water, and it thrives in both hot, dry weather and periods of high humidity.	Plants should not be crowded; good air circulation reduces the spread of the disease. Remove and destroy infected plant parts. Sulfur-based fungicides can both prevent the disease and eliminate it on infected plants. Mildew-resistant varieties of zinnia are available.

PROBLEM	CAUSE	SOLUTION
Tips, leaves and the centers of forget-me-not, fuchsia, geranium, heliotrope, lobelia, petunia, snapdragon, stock and strawflower turn black or brown, often accompanied by a fuzzy, gray growth. The problem occurs most often in cool, damp conditions.	Botrytis blight, also called gray mold, a disease caused by the fungus *Botrytis cinerea*.	Avoid overhead watering and provide good air circulation. Cut away any infected areas of plants and destroy them. A number of approved fungicides can control the disease.
Foliage turns yellow, plants may be stunted and new growth is distorted. Flower buds may not open or may be deformed. Primarily aster, but also cosmos, kochia, globe amaranth, marigold, salpiglossis and pincushion flower can be affected.	Aster yellows, a disease caused by mycoplasmas, organisms similar to bacteria. The mycoplasmas are spread by leafhoppers.	To control aster yellows, leafhoppers must be controlled *(page 78)*. Remove and destroy infected plants. Keep the garden weeded. Some varieties of aster are resistant.
Yellow or brown streaks and spots develop on the foliage of bellflower, calendula, California poppy, celosia, chrysanthemum, coleus, cosmos, dahlia, forget-me-not, geranium, marigold or pincushion flower. Plants may be stunted.	A virus infection. There are several different virus infections, including the common mosaic virus. Infections can be unsightly, but they usually cause little damage to plants and may subside by themselves.	Remove damaged plant parts. There are no chemical controls for viruses, but they can be spread by aphids, which should be controlled *(page 78)*.
Wilting occurs in Cape marigold, China aster, chrysanthemum, coleus, cosmos, dahlia, impatiens, lobelia, marigold, nasturtium and pansy; plants stop growing and eventually die. A cross section of a stem will show dark brown spots or streaks.	Wilt, a disease caused by soil-dwelling fungi or bacteria that penetrate plants through the roots or the base of the stem and clog plant tissue.	In replanting, choose wilt-resistant varieties. There are no chemical preventatives or controls for wilt. Remove infected plants and destroy them. If the soil is heavily infested and the problem recurs, the soil may need professional fumigation.
Irregular dark brown spots appear on the leaves and stems of foxglove, lavatera, linaria, pansy, poor man's orchid and snapdragon. Spots may have purplish borders and black centers.	Anthracnose, a disease caused by a fungus that thrives in warm, wet weather.	Remove and discard any infected plant parts. Spray remaining plants with a recommended fungicide or lime sulfur when the temperature is below 85° F.
Upper surfaces of leaves have yellowish flecks or streaks of a bleached, whitish color. Leaf edges may curl.	Air pollution and smog.	There are no controls for pollution. In high heat and humidity, provide shade for plants; these conditions, combined with intense sunlight, cause leaf pores to open, making them more susceptible to pollutants. If you live in a smoggy area, plant varieties that are resistant to smog and pollution.

PROBLEM	CAUSE	SOLUTION
Leaves curl, wither and may turn yellow. Flowers may be distorted in shape. A shiny substance appears along stems and leaves. Many annuals are susceptible.	Aphids, also called plant lice, ⅛-inch-long, semitransparent insects found in colonies along buds and stems. They secrete a sticky, shiny substance that attracts ants.	Aphids can be knocked off plants with a strong stream of water. If infestation is severe, apply an approved chemical insecticide or insecticidal soap.
Foliage turns yellow on African daisy, browallia, lobelia, marigold, salvia, and strawflower. Plants may be stunted.	Leafhoppers, gray or green, wedge-shaped, winged insects up to ⅕ inch long.	Leafhoppers spread disease and should be controlled with an organic spray or an approved insecticide. Heavy sprays of water will knock them off plants but may not kill them.
Oblong or irregular-shaped holes appear in leaves and flowers. Eventually, plants may be stripped of all foliage. Many annuals, including balsam, China aster, nicotiana, phlox and zinnia are susceptible.	Any of several beetles, including Colorado potato, cucumber and Japanese, which are ¼- to ½-inch insects with hard shells.	Beetles can be hand-picked and destroyed. The easiest way to control beetles is to destroy their larvae with milky spore, a bacterium fatal to beetles but harmless to plants and other animals. Plants may be sprayed with an approved insecticide.
Leaf surfaces have colorless areas with light green or brown tunnels. Castor bean, chrysanthemum, dahlia, morning glory, nasturtium, verbena and winged everlasting can be affected.	Leaf miners, flies that lay their eggs on the leaves; when the eggs hatch, the larvae tunnel into the leaves.	Cut off and destroy infested leaves. Keep the garden well weeded; flies lay eggs in weedy areas. If the problem persists, use an approved insecticide.
Plants suddenly lose their color and wilt. Roots are damaged or deformed and have knots and swellings. African daisy, bellflower, California poppy, chrysanthemum, cornflower, statice and sweet pea can be affected.	Nematodes, microscopic worms that live in the soil and attack plant roots. Since they cannot be seen, only a soil test can confirm their presence.	Remove and destroy affected plants. Large plantings of marigolds will kill nematodes. Do not plant susceptible annuals in an area that has been infested within the past three years. If the problem persists, professional soil treatment may be needed.
Leaves of many annuals turn yellow or reddish and their surface becomes dull. Foliage may curl and wither. Tiny black specks are visible on the undersides of foliage. Eventually, webs will appear on plants.	Spider mites, tiny pests that suck the juice from leaves.	Keep plants well watered; mites thrive in hot, dry conditions. A heavy spray of water can knock mites off plants. They can be controlled with an approved miticide or an insecticidal soap. Ladybugs are natural predators.

78

PROBLEM	CAUSE	SOLUTION
Leaves of bellflower, chrysanthemum, gaillardia, gerbera, mignonette, monkey flower and pansy develop small patches of white, yellow or brown around the edges, curl up, then wither and die. Flower buds are discolored and may not open; if they do open, the petals will have brown edges.	Thrips, slender winged insects just visible to the eye.	Remove infected flower buds and plant tips; remove severely infested plants altogether. Spray remaining plants with an approved chemical insecticide or an insecticidal soap.
Entire plants, especially calendula and coleus, become discolored. When a plant is shaken, a cloud of white specks appears.	Whitefly, a white, 1/16-inch insect that collects in colonies on the undersides of leaves.	Check for signs of whitefly before buying bedding plants. Whitefly may be controlled with insecticidal soap, an organic spray or an approved chemical insecticide. Whitefly is attracted to yellow; yellow flypaper is available.
Large holes are eaten in the foliage of forget-me-not, geranium, hibiscus, marigold, nicotiana, pansy and petunia. Entire young seedlings may be eaten. Shiny silver streaks appear on plants and garden paths.	Slugs (shell-less snails) and snails, night-feeding pests up to 3 inches long.	Bait can be purchased and applied at dusk; it will need to be reapplied after rain or watering. Shallow saucers of beer or inverted grapefruit halves will trap slugs and snails.
The upper leaf surfaces of balsam, calendula, China aster, dahlia, gaillardia, marigold, snapdragon and zinnia become spotted. Foliage may lose color, wilt and fall from the plant. Flower buds may be deformed.	Plant bugs, also called true bugs, orange, green or black insects 1/4 inch long that suck plant juices.	Use an organic spray or an approved chemical insecticide.
Light green oval spots and white patches resembling cotton appear on leaves and stems of alternanthera, gerbera, hibiscus, ice plant and impatiens. Plants become discolored and may wilt.	Scale, a 1/8- to 1/4-inch insect with an oval shell. The white patches are egg sacs.	Scale can be controlled with insecticidal soap or an approved chemical insecticide.
Leaves are eaten and entire plants may be stripped, primarily in late spring. Castor bean, heliotrope, hollyhock, mignonette and verbena are the most susceptible annuals.	Any of a number of caterpillars.	*Bacillus thuringiensis,* called Bt, a bacterium that kills caterpillars but does not harm plants or other animals. If caterpillars return to your garden every spring, Bt can be sprayed in anticipation of the problem.
A white, foamy substance appears between leaves and stems.	Spittlebugs. When their eggs hatch, the young insects produce the foam for protection while they feed on leaves and stems.	Wash bugs off plants with a heavy spray of water. If infestation is severe, spray with an approved insecticide.

79

TIPS AND TECHNIQUES

ACCENT ON FOLIAGE

Most gardeners plant annuals for their colorful flowers, but the main features of some varieties are the rich textures and patterns of their foliage.

Coleus leaves have splashes and streaks of color ranging from pale green to red. Dusty miller foliage has a glimmering, silver tone and a soft, feltlike texture. Both of these annuals are low-growing and can be used for edging and borders *(right)*.

To fill garden beds, there are foliage annuals that grow to 5 feet in height, such as bloodleaf, which has deeply veined, bright red curled leaves, and kochia, which resembles a small evergreen shrub with narrow, light green leaves until the fall, when the foliage turns a bright pinkish red. Castor bean is a sprawling plant with large, deeply lobed green leaves to 2 feet across.

COLOR IN THE SHADE

When you want to enliven a shady garden, you can plant annuals that add color to the yard without the benefit of direct sunlight. The most common of these are begonias and impatiens because they bloom continuously from midsummer to fall and tolerate a wide range of climates.

Where summers are hot, good choices for shady garden beds are the tall spikes of foxglove and salvia. Large areas can be filled with mass plantings of flowering tobacco. For edgings and borders, lobelia and sweet alyssum may be used. In cool-summer climates, monkey flower and wishbone flower are compact plants good in shady borders. Salpiglossis can be used in large beds.

For the best results with annuals under trees, thin the lowest branches to create high, open shade. Since the annuals will compete with tree roots for nutrients, add extra organic matter to the soil before planting.

TESTING SEEDS

Many gardeners collect or buy seeds and save them from one year to the next. But not all seeds keep for long periods. Before you expend time and energy sowing stored seeds, it's a good idea to test them to see if they will germinate at the normal rate.

To test the percentage of germination, place 10 seeds in a moistened paper towel. Fold the towel and put it in a plastic bag. If the annual needs cool temperatures to germinate, place the bag in a dark, cool spot; if the annual needs warmth to germinate, keep the bag in a warm place out of direct sunlight.

Most annuals sprout in 10 to 14 days. A few take up to 28 days to germinate. Check the days required for the annual you are testing in the Dictionary of Annuals, and after the appropriate time, count the number of seeds that have sprouted. If it's eight or more, the seeds are as good as new. If five to eight have sprouted, the seeds are usable, but you will need to sow more than usual. If fewer than five have sprouted, the seeds will produce few flowers, and sowing is not recommended.

FRAGRANT ANNUALS

In addition to bringing lively color to the garden, many annuals will also fill the air with fragrance. These flowers should be planted where their scents will be most often enjoyed—along the pathway to the front door, under windows that are frequently open and near favorite outdoor relaxation spots.

Sweet alyssum and sweet William *(left)* can be used in containers and along garden borders. Four-o'clock, heliotrope, mignonette or stock can be used to fill large areas with scented flowers. Other bedding plants that are lighter in fragrance but still add a sweet scent to the air are flowering tobacco, nasturtium, pincushion flower, snapdragon, sweet sultan and wallflower.

When you want an aromatic vine to bring added appeal to a fence or a trellis, you can use moonflower and sweet pea, which produce fragrant, colorful blossoms.

EDIBLE ANNUALS

Most annuals are not considered to be edible, but there are several that can add color and flavor to various recipes.

Nasturtium leaves and flowers *(right)* add a peppery flavor to garden salads; dianthus flower petals add a taste of clove. Impatiens, pansies and violas are bland in flavor but can be used as a colorful garnish in salads or floating atop cold, creamy soups. Chrysanthemum petals, with their tangy, slightly bitter taste, can be sprinkled over salads, soups and cooked vegetables. Similar in taste to chrysanthemum are the golden petals of calendula and marigold.

Sunflower seeds are well known to be edible. Less well known is that the buds of sunflowers can also be cooked and used for flavor accents similar to those of capers.

If you spray edible flowers to control pests, use only those pesticides recommended for vegetables.

THE CONTAINED GARDEN

Even in the limited space of a tiny yard, balcony or patio, you can enjoy the beauty of brilliant flowers all summer long. Many annuals are compact plants that will thrive in containers, which can also be interesting design elements.

Besides the traditional barrels, window boxes, planters and pots, there are several inexpensive and attractive alternatives. Clay drainage pipes set on end can be filled with cascading petunias *(left)*. A child's red wagon, an old wheelbarrow or even an unused birdcage can be filled with flowers.

In addition to a container, all you need is a potting mix and a nearby source of water.

5
DICTIONARY OF ANNUALS

Annuals come in so many hundreds of thousands of varieties that, given their short life span of a single season, it would be possible for a legion of gardeners to grow annuals all the summers of their lifetimes and never repeat the same garden twice. Uncounted genera exist in nature; some of those have thousands of species, and seed breeders experiment so prodigiously that hundreds of new cultivars are developed every year.

Out of such a plethora of flowering forms, it would be impossible to catalog them all. The dictionary that follows describes approximately 150 of them. Most are annuals in the strictest sense, in that they germinate, bloom, produce seeds and die in one year only. But also included among the entries are some biennials, which have a life cycle similar to that of annuals *(pages 14-17)* but extend it over two years instead of one, and some species that may be perennials in warm climates and annuals only in cold ones, for the simple reason that their roots cannot survive Northern winters.

All entries are listed by their botanical names, because that is how horticulturists designate them, and because some plants having different characteristics share the same common name. The name dusty miller, for instance, is applied to plants of three separate genera—*Centaurea, Chrysanthemum* and *Senecio.* But so that you can find a plant whether or not you know its botanical name, the common names appear in alphabetical order, with cross-references to the botanical names.

Each entry contains a broad description of the genus, a more detailed description of one or more selected species and varieties, and information about growing conditions—whether the plant does best in sun or shade, and what kind of soil it requires. Every entry is accompanied by a photograph of at least one species; sometimes, where species vary greatly in color, size or form, there may be two or more photographs.

ABELMOSCHUS MANIHOT

ABUTILON HYBRIDUM

AGERATUM HOUSTONIANUM

Abelmoschus
(ah-bel-MOE-shuss)

A plant native to Asia; has lobed or divided leaves and single funnel-shaped flowers.

Selected species and varieties. *A. manihot* (formerly known as *Hibiscus manihot*), sunset hibiscus: a perennial grown as an annual in temperate regions. It grows 5 to 6 feet tall and in late summer bears 6-inch yellow flowers with brown or maroon centers. Excellent for an accent or the back of a border. 'Grandiflora' is a large-flowered cultivar.

Growing Conditions. Sow seeds outdoors where the plants are to grow, after danger of frost has passed. Or sow indoors six to eight weeks before the last frost date; transplant to the garden when danger of frost is past. Sowing seeds in individual peat pots will improve chances of transplanting success. Space plants 2 to 3 feet apart in full sun or light shade and a rich, moist, well-drained soil. Fertilize with 5-10-5 at planting time only. Water well during the growing season and to help plants tolerate high temperatures.

Abutilon (ah-BOO-tih-lon)
Flowering maple

Approximately 150 species of tropical plants, having leaves resembling those of the maple tree and showy, often trumpet-shaped flowers. A tender perennial that is usually grown as a house plant, flowering maple can be grown outdoors as an annual. Use it for the middle of a border, in containers, as a hedge, or as a specimen plant.

Selected species and varieties. *A. hybridum,* flowering maple, Chinese lantern: hairy foliage, either solid green or variegated. Plants grow in a mounded shape to 3 feet tall and are bathed in drooping bell-shaped 3-inch flowers that are orange, red, pink, yellow or white and have the texture of crepe paper. 'Eclipse' is a cultivar with pink flowers; leaves are variegated with yellow. 'Insigne' bears white flowers with red and purple veins. 'Splendens' bears deep red blooms.

Growing conditions. Flowering maple may be grown from seeds started indoors and will germinate in 14 to 21 days. However, since plants need at least 20 weeks after sowing to produce flowers, you may prefer to buy plants for the garden. This plant is also easily propagated from stem cuttings, taken in fall before the first frost or in early spring from plants overwintered indoors. Space plants 18 inches apart in full sun or light shade in a rich, moist soil. In areas where day temperatures are above 90° F, plants will benefit from afternoon shade. Keep them well watered; fertilize lightly. Pinch back stem tips to keep plants bushy.

African daisy see *Arctotis; Lonas*

Ageratum (ah-jer-AY-tum)
Ageratum, floss flower

A group of 30 species, most with oval-shaped leaves and scalloped edges, and tiny, compact flowers. One species is among the most popular of all edging plants.

Selected species and varieties. *A. houstonianum:* bears fluffy, powder-puff-like flower heads, primarily purplish blue but sometimes pink or white; plants are mounded, short and compact with heart-shaped leaves. 'Blue Blazer' bears radiant deep-blue flowers, but the plants often vary between 4 and 7 inches in height and may not be suitable where a neat, even edging is wanted. 'Blue Danube', also called 'Blue Puffs', is acclaimed by many gardeners as the best ageratum for evenness of size and flowering. Flowers are purplish blue; plants uniformly reach 7 inches in height. 'Pink Powderpuffs' bears rose pink flowers that don't turn brown as they mature; plants grow to 5 inches. 'Summer Snow' is a 5-inch plant with pure white flowers.

Growing conditions. For best results, grow ageratums by setting plants into the garden, using either purchased bedding plants or seedlings you have grown indoors. Start seeds six to eight weeks before the outdoor planting date and do not cover them; they need light during their five- to 10-day germination. Space plants 6 to 8 inches apart in a warm location, in full sun or light shade. Where summers are long and hot, ageratums grow best in light shade. They dislike excessive heat and humidity; in the South and in hot areas of the West they make better plants for spring and fall than for summer. Ageratums are not fussy about soil, but will perform best if soil is rich, moist and well drained. Water when the ground starts to become dry. Fertilize with 5-10-5 at planting time and again monthly. Ageratums are low-maintenance plants; their flowers fall cleanly as they fade. If plants become leggy, shear them back.

—

Alcea (al-SEE-ah)
Hollyhock

Bears stiff spikes of paper-like flowers, on stems clothed with maple-like leaves. Most hollyhocks are stately plants growing 4 to 6 feet tall, but there are dwarf cultivars that grow to only 2 feet. Although hollyhocks are all biennials or short-lived perennials, many of the newer cultivars can also be grown as annuals. All hollyhocks may be used as accent plants; the taller types do well at the back of a border.

Selected species and varieties. *A. rosea*, the garden hollyhock: flowers may be single or double in a wide range of colors (except blue). 'Majorette' is a bushy 2-foot dwarf with large double lacy flowers of white, pink, yellow, red, rose and salmon. 'Powder Puffs' grows 6 to 8 feet tall and bears fully double blooms. 'Summer Carnival' grows 4 to 6 feet tall, with double flowers appearing early in summer.

Growing conditions. To grow hollyhocks as annuals, start seeds indoors six to eight weeks before the last frost. Barely cover the seeds; they need light during the 10- to 14-day germination. To grow hollyhocks as biennials, sow seeds outdoors after danger of frost is past; plants will probably not bloom until the following summer. Set hollyhocks 18 to 24 inches apart, in full sun or very light shade. Soil should be rich and well drained. Fertilize with 5-10-5 at planting time and monthly during the growing season. Water heavily. Taller cultivars of hollyhocks may require staking.

Hollyhocks that are grown as annuals or biennials look their best during the first summer of bloom; their later growth and flowering will be less vigorous. For the showiest displays, start new seeds each year. Hollyhocks will self-sow very easily, but cultivars do not reproduce true from seed, so if self-sowing occurs, inferior plants will soon take over. It is best to cut the flowers off before the seeds drop.

Hollyhocks are susceptible to rust, a fungus disease that produces orange-brown spots on the leaves. To prevent its occurrence, dust or spray weekly with a fungicide.

Alonsoa (al-on-ZO-a)
Mask flower

Mask flower is grown for its open-faced blooms of red to amber with prominent stamens. The flowers appear in loose clusters atop thin stems. This annual from tropical America can be used in the middle of a border and as a cut flower.

Selected species and varieties. *A.* × *meridionalis* 'Amber Glow' has amber-colored 1-inch flowers on a 24- to 36-inch plant. *A. warscewiczii* has flowers in shades of red and orange. 'Compacta' bears scarlet flowers ⅝ to ¾ inch wide on 18- to 24-inch plants.

Growing conditions. Start seeds indoors six to eight weeks before the last frost. Germination will take 10 to 14 days. Set plants 8 to 12 inches apart in full sun and average, well-drained soil. Keep plants well watered and lightly fertilized. Mask flowers do best in cool northern gardens and along the California coast. However, unlike many annuals that prefer cool conditions, they will not tolerate frost.

Alternanthera
(al-ter-nan-THEE-rah)
Alternanthera, copperleaf, Joseph's-coat

A tender perennial grown as an annual for its ornamental foliage. An excellent choice where an intricate, formal design or a neatly edged bed is called for in the landscape.

Selected species and varieties. *A. ficoidea:* plants range from 4 to 8 inches in height; foliage may be green, red with orange, yellow, yellow with red, rose, purple and copper, or blood red; flowers are inconspicuous.

Growing conditions. Alternanthera is propagated by cuttings or division, because plants do not come true from seed. Purchase plants from a local nursery or get cuttings from a fellow gardener. Move plants to the garden in spring after danger of frost has passed, spacing them 8 to 10 inches apart in a warm, sunny location with average garden soil. Keep plants clipped to maintain a uniform size. Cuttings rooted in the late summer can overwinter indoors or in a greenhouse or hotbed. To achieve uniform height and to keep the inconspicuous flowers from blooming, shear the plants periodically during the summer.

ALCEA ROSEA

ALONSOA WARSCEWICZII

ALTERNANTHERA FICOIDEA

AMARANTHUS CAUDATUS

AMARANTHUS TRICOLOR SALICIFOLIUS

AMMOBIUM ALATUM 'GRANDIFLORA'

ANAGALLIS MONELLI LINIFOLIA

Amaranthus (am-ah-RAN-thus)

Grown for their flashy multicolored foliage or for their showy, tassel-like flower spikes, amaranthus make colorful additions to beds, borders, hedges and pots, and they are good accent plants. Leaves can be red, maroon, chocolate, green or yellow; many are variegated, splashed with one or more contrasting colors. The drooping flower spikes are either green or dark red.

Selected species and varieties. *A. caudatus,* love-lies-bleeding, tassel flower: an upright plant that grows 3 to 5 feet tall. It is topped with trailing, ropelike flowers of bright red that can grow to 2 feet long. *A. hybridus erythrostachys,* prince's-feather: leaves and flower spikes are red. *A. tricolor,* tampala: brightly colored forms of this species are known as Joseph's-coat. Their 2½- to 4-inch lance-shaped leaves are deep green, chocolate or yellow at the bottom of the plant, while the upper leaves are bright crimson and gold. Plants grow 24 inches tall. *A. tricolor salicifolius,* fountain plant: has 7-inch-long, ⅜-inch-wide leaves that are gracefully pendant. Many of the cultivars of fountain plant, having dark foliage at the bottom and red leaves at the top, are commonly and collectively called summer poinsettia. 'Early Splendor' grows to 3 feet, with maroon, red or purple pendant leaves at the bottom and bright cerise foliage at the top. 'Flaming Fountain' grows to 24 inches, with willow-like leaves of flaming scarlet on a bushy plant. 'Illumination' is 48 inches tall, has dark green and chocolate leaves and is topped with leaves of crimson touched with gold.

Growing conditions. Amaranthus can be grown from seeds sown outdoors where plants are to grow, when all danger of frost has passed; however, for best results, set plants into the garden at that time. Start with purchased bedding plants or sow seeds indoors three to four weeks before the outdoor planting date. Germination takes 10 to 15 days and seeds require warm (75° F) soil to sprout. Plant amaranthus 18 to 24 inches apart in average soil in a warm, sunny location. Fertilize at planting time with 5-10-5 and do not feed the plants again, because too much fertilizer will make the leaves lose much of their color. Amaranthus will tolerate dry soil and heat, but it should be watered in very dry weather. Take care not to disturb the roots when weeding.

Ammobium (am-MOH-bee-um)

A tender perennial grown as an annual that makes excellent flowers for cutting and for drying. It is native to Australia.

Selected species and varieties. *A. alatum,* winged everlasting: bears 1- to 2-inch flower heads with glistening silvery white bracts and yellow centers. They are borne on thick, branching, 36-inch-long stems that have raised edges resembling wings. 'Grandiflora' has larger heads and will self-sow in sandy soil.

Growing conditions. Sow seeds outdoors where plants are to grow six weeks before the last frost, or start them indoors six to eight weeks before the outdoor planting date. Germination takes five to seven days. In the Sun Belt, seeds may be sown outdoors until two months before the first fall frost and will overwinter in the garden. A light mulching will help protect against frost damage. Set plants 15 inches apart in full sun and sandy, rich, well-drained soil. Keep well watered. Fertilize with 5-10-5 before planting and feed again every other week.

———

Anagallis (an-ah-GAL-is)
Pimpernel

Pimpernels are mostly spreading, somewhat weedy, plants, growing 6 to 9 inches high and up to 18 inches across, bearing bell-shaped, five-lobed flowers. Use them as annual ground covers and in rock gardens.

Selected species and varieties. *A. arvensis,* scarlet pimpernel, poor-man's-weatherglass: has ¼-inch red flowers that close at night and on cloudy days. *A. arvensis caerulea:* similar, but with blue flowers. *A. monelli linifolia,* flaxleaf pimpernel: a tender perennial grown as an annual. Bears ¾-inch blue flowers; leaves are more lance-shaped than those of other pimpernels.

Growing conditions. For best results start seeds indoors eight to 10 weeks before you want to set the seedlings outside. Germination will take 21 to 30 days. Scarlet pimpernels are hardy annuals that prefer cool conditions; transplant them outside two to three weeks before the last frost date. Flaxleaf pimpernel is a tender perennial that prefers warm temperatures; move it to the garden after danger of frost is past. In the North, seeds sown outdoors where the plants are to grow may produce foliage but no flowers before frost. Plant all pimpernels 12 to 18 inches apart in full sunlight and an average soil. Water and fertilize sparingly.

Anchusa (an-KU-sah)
Bugloss

Plants with somewhat hairy foliage and trumpet-shaped flowers borne in clusters.

Selected species and varieties. *A. capensis,* summer forget-me-not: a biennial usually grown as an annual and used for borders, edgings or ground cover. Showy, spreading plants 9 to 18 inches tall bear clusters of tiny ultramarine flowers. Foliage is coarse and lance-shaped. 'Blue Angel' grows 9 inches tall and bears medium-blue flowers. 'Blue Bird' grows to 18 inches and produces darker, indigo flowers.

Growing conditions. Sow seeds indoors six to eight weeks before the last frost date. In the South, seeds can be sown directly into the ground after all danger of frost is past. In the North, seeds sown directly may produce foliage but no flowers before frost. Plant summer forget-me-nots in full sun, 10 to 12 inches apart, in average, light, well-drained soil. Fertilize little, if at all, and do not overwater. To encourage a second bloom, cut back after flowering.

Angel's trumpet see *Datura*

Antirrhinum (an-ti-RY-num)
Snapdragon

A perennial often grown as an annual, valued for its showy flowers in shades of red, bronze, pink, white, rose, yellow, scarlet, primrose, apricot, orange, crimson, magenta, or lilac. Snapdragons do best in borders, beds and rock gardens, and make exquisite and long-lasting cut flowers.

Selected species and varieties. *A. majus:* blooms have a light, spicy fragrance and appear on showy, erect spikes over dark, straplike foliage. When snapdragon was so named, its pouch-shaped, two-lipped flowers resembled the jaws of a dragon ready to snap. Today, however, the traditional snapdragons have been joined by cultivars with open-faced trumpet-like ruffle-edged blooms as well as some with fully double

flowers. 'Bright Butterflies' is a heat-tolerant cultivar bearing up to 10 spikes of open-faced flowers on a 24-to 30-inch plant. 'Coronet' has extra-large, closely spaced florets that bloom uniformly on a 20-inch plant; very weather-tolerant and rust-resistant. 'Floral Carpet' is a mound-shaped dwarf cultivar, 6 to 8 inches tall, that bears traditional snapdragon flowers and will repeat-bloom without shearing. 'Madame Butterfly' is a double-flowered version of 'Bright Butterflies' with tight clusters of very large flowers. 'Rocket' was the first cultivar bred for heat resistance. It bears large florets closely set on vigorous 30- to 36-inch plants.

Growing conditions. In mid-spring, when the soil has begun warming up, snapdragon seeds may be sown where plants are to bloom. However, for best results, sow indoors six to eight weeks before the outside planting date. Do not cover seeds, as they need light for germination, which takes 10 to 14 days. Snapdragon seedlings and bedding plants tolerate light frosts, so they can be set into the garden about four weeks before the last expected frost. Plant them in full sun or light shade, spacing them 6 to 15 inches apart, depending on their ultimate height. Avoid overcrowding, which invites disease. Soil should be light, rich in organic matter and well drained. Fertilize with 5-10-5 before planting and repeat monthly; water when the ground starts to dry out. Pinch young plants to induce branching and more abundant flowers. To encourage re-blooming, cut off faded flower spikes.

Arctotis (ark-TOE-tis)
African daisy

A daisy-family member native to South Africa; has toothed or deeply cut basal leaves and bears flower heads on long, leafless stalks. Used in beds and borders.

Selected species and varieties. *A. stoechadifolia,* blue-eyed African daisy: a perennial grown as an annual. Valued for its daisy-shaped 3-inch flower heads, whose violet centers are surrounded by creamy yellow ray florets with reddish undersides. Grows up to 30 inches tall, with whitish woolly 4-inch leaves mounded at its base. *A. stoechadifolia grandis:* similar, with larger leaves and longer stem. *A. hybrids:* yellow, white, pink, bronze, red, purple, brown and orange flowers on plants 10 to 12 inches tall.

ANCHUSA CAPENSIS 'BLUE ANGEL'

ANTIRRHINUM MAJUS

ARCTOTIS HYBRID

ARGEMONE MEXICANA 'ALBA'

ASARINA ERUBESCENS

BEGONIA × SEMPERFLORENS-CULTORUM

Growing conditions. Seeds can be sown outdoors in early spring as soon as the soil can be worked, but for best results, sow them indoors six to eight weeks before the last frost and set seedlings outside just after last frost. Germination takes 21 to 35 days. Space plants 12 inches apart in full sun. African daisies do best in poor, dry, sandy soil, so avoid overwatering and fertilize little, if at all. They also prefer cool nights. In hot areas, therefore, grow them in spring or fall; in coastal areas and at high elevations, grow them in summer. To prolong flowering and improve appearance, keep faded blooms removed.

Argemone (ar-JEM-oh-ne)
Prickly poppy, argemony

Prickly poppy is named for its large single poppy-like flowers and its prickly seed capsules. The foliage of some prickly poppies is also covered with fine spines. Plants are rather tall and do best in the back of a border.

Selected species and varieties. *A. albaflora texana* (sometimes listed as *A. polyanthemos*): grows 3 to 4 feet tall and bears 4-inch white flowers. *A. grandiflora:* produces 4-inch silky white flowers on 24-inch plants; its prickly foliage is green with white veins. *A. mexicana,* Mexican poppy: bears 2½-inch yellow flowers and grows 36 inches tall. The spiny leaves have silver-blue markings over the veins. The cultivar 'Alba' has white flowers; 'Sanguinea' has red flowers. *A. munita* grows to 5 feet and bears 5-inch white flowers.

Growing conditions. Sow seeds outdoors after all danger of frost has passed, or start them indoors in peat pots four to six weeks before planting outside. Their long taproots make prickly poppies hard to transplant. Germination takes 10 to 15 days. Space plants 2 to 3 feet apart in full sun and a poor, sandy, well-drained, slightly alkaline soil. Water only when dry and do not fertilize.

Asarina (ass-ah-REE-nah)

A genus of vine that can quickly grow to 10 feet. Generally has soft, hairy, triangular leaves and trumpet-shaped flowers resembling those of snapdragons. May be grown on trellises, in hanging baskets or other containers, or as annual ground covers.

Selected species and varieties. *A. barclaiana:* bears pink 1¼-inch flowers that fade to purple as they age. *A. erubescens,* creeping gloxinia: produces 3-inch rose to pink flowers. *A. procumbens:* pale pink 1½-inch flowers. *A. scandens:* 2-inch lavender blooms.

Growing conditions. Seeds may be started indoors 10 to 12 weeks before planting outdoors; germination takes 10 to 15 days. Stem cuttings may be taken at the end of the summer and overwintered in a cold frame or a greenhouse. Plant seedlings or rooted cuttings in the garden several weeks before the last frost. Grow in full sun and a rich, well-drained soil. Fertilize with 5-10-5 at planting time and again during the growing season; keep well watered.

Baby-blue-eyes see *Nemophila*
Baby's breath see *Gypsophilia*
Bachelor's button
see *Centaurea*
Balsam see *Impatiens*
Basket flower see *Centaurea*
Beard tongue see *Penstemon*
Beefsteak plant see *Perilla*

Begonia (be-GON-ee-ah)

More than 1,000 species of plants that have single or double flowers of white, pink, rose or red. Many are spectacular in beds, in edgings, in containers and can be grown indoors as well.

Selected species and varieties. *B. × semperflorens-cultorum,* wax begonia: flowers appear continuously over waxy green, bronze, brown or variegated foliage. Plants grow 6 to 12 inches high and 4 to 8 inches wide, and many varieties are heat- and sun-tolerant. Avalanche series cultivars are specifically bred for hanging baskets and for use as ground covers; they are sun- and heat-tolerant. Cocktail series cultivars, 6 to 8 inches tall, have bronze leaves, large blooms and good heat tolerance. Double Ruffles series cultivars produce fluffy ball-like red, pink or white flowers on 12-inch plants with green foliage. These cultivars are heat-resistant. Party series cultivars have large, 2-inch flowers with good weather tolerance. Pizzazz series cultivars have medium-sized red, white or pink flowers and green leaves on 10-inch plants. These heat-resistant cultivars can be grown in sun or shade. Prelude series cultivars, green-leaved and early-blooming, are uniform 6-inch plants with small flowers of white, pink, rose and scarlet. These cultivars are very rain-tolerant.

Growing conditions. Wax begonias can be propagated from seeds started indoors 12 to 16 weeks before they are planted outside after the last frost. Bedding plants are also readily available in spring. Space plants 6 to 8 inches apart. Begonias prefer partial shade, but can be set in full sun if temperature does not exceed 90° F. In hot areas, select bronze-leaved wax begonias over the green-leaved forms for their greater heat resistance. Soil should be very rich and well drained; wax begonias will tolerate a somewhat dry soil. Fertilize with 5-10-5 before planting and again monthly.

—

Bellflower see *Campanula*

—

Bellis (BELL-iss)
Daisy

A plant having leaves tufted at the base and solitary flowers atop bare stalks.

Selected species and varieties. *B. perennis,* English daisy: a perennial or biennial that is often grown as an annual. Has single or double 2-inch flower heads with white, pink or red ray florets surrounding bright yellow centers. Use in beds, borders or rock gardens.

Growing conditions. When growing English daisies as annuals, start seeds indoors eight to 10 weeks before planting outdoors. Seedlings that have been hardened off (acclimated to the outdoors) and purchased bedding plants can be moved into the garden several weeks before the last expected frost. Germination will take 10 to 15 days.

When growing English daisies as biennials, start seeds indoors or outdoors in late summer. Plants can be mulched for protection and overwintered in the ground or in a cold frame, and will bloom the following spring. English daisies grown as biennials can also be propagated by division. Set plants 6 inches apart in full sun or light shade. Soil should be light and rich in organic matter. Keep the plants well watered and fertilize monthly during the blooming period. English daisies grow best in cool climates; where summers are hot they should be grown in spring. These

plants can easily become weedy if allowed to reseed, so remove all flowers as they fade.

—

Bells-of-Ireland see *Moluccella*
Black-eyed Susan vine see *Thunbergia*
Blanket flower see *Gaillardia*
Blazing star see *Mentzelia*
Bloodleaf see *Iresine*
Blue bird see *Nolana*
Bluebonnet see *Lupinus*
Blue daisy see *Felicia*
Blue daze see *Evolvulus*
Blue lace flower see *Trachymene*
Bluelips see *Collinsia*
Blueweed see *Echium*

—

Brachycome (brah-kih-COE-me)

A large genus of daisy-like plants native to Australia.

Selected species and varieties. *B. iberidifolia,* Swan River daisy: masses of fragrant 1½-inch flower heads of blue, red, rose, white or violet ray florets surrounding centers that may be lime green, yellow or dark brown. Blooms grow profusely on mounded 12- to 18-inch plants in summer. Under the flowers, the feather-like foliage is almost invisible. Well suited for use in rock gardens, pots, window boxes, baskets and borders. Bring it indoors for a long-lasting cut flower.

Growing conditions. Sow seeds indoors four to six weeks before the last frost; germination will take 10 to 18 days. Or start with bedding plants; set them in the garden after all frost danger has passed. Space plants 6 inches apart in full sun and a warm soil that is rich in organic matter. Swan River daisy is not a long-blooming plant, so make successive sowings or plantings three weeks apart to ensure continual bloom. Keep plants well watered and mulched, as they prefer cool temperatures and cool, moist soil. Fertilize monthly.

—

Brassica (BRASS-ih-kah)

A genus that includes the vegetables cabbage, kale, broccoli, mustard greens and cauliflower.

Selected species and varieties. *B. oleracea* (Acephala Group), orna-

BELLIS PERENNIS

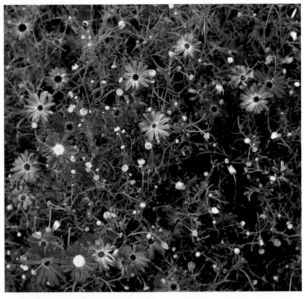
BRACHYCOME IBERIDIFOLIA

BRASSICA OLERACEA (ACEPHALA GROUP)

BROWALLIA SPECIOSA 'BLUE BELLS'

CALANDRINIA UMBELLATA

CALCEOLARIA CRENATIFLORA

mental cabbage, ornamental kale: open rosettes of green leaves with centers of white, pink or purple. Plants measure 12 to 15 inches across and 10 to 12 inches high. They are most unusual and decorative bedding plants, used primarily for their foliage in the fall and winter. 'Nagoya' is a kale with red and white foliage. 'Osaka' is a cabbage in white, red or pink. 'Peacock' is a kale with very finely cut, feathery leaves.

Growing conditions. Ornamental cabbage and kale are most often used in the garden in fall and winter, because they need cool temperatures to grow. Sow seeds indoors in late summer, six to eight weeks before the first expected fall frost. The seeds of ornamental cabbage must be chilled for three days in the refrigerator before sowing and then left uncovered, as they need light to germinate. Ornamental kale needs neither light nor chilling. Seeds germinate in 10 to 14 days. Set the seedlings into the ground about one month before the first expected fall frost, spacing them 12 to 15 inches apart in full sun, in a soil rich in organic matter. Fertilize with 5-10-5 before planting and once a month after that, and keep the soil moist. The foliage begins to turn color when temperatures reach 50° F, and color is intensified by frost. In areas where temperatures do not drop below 20° F, plants will last all winter.

Some say that ornamental kale is edible, but it tastes very bitter.

—

Browallia (bro-WAL-ee-ah)
Browallia, bush violet

Browallias are grown for their abundant 2-inch flowers—starlike, bell-shaped blossoms that are velvety in texture and come in purple, blue or white. Stems grow from 8 to 18 inches long. Browallia is a good choice as a bedding plant in a shaded area, but it is spectacular as a container plant on a patio or a deck; it fills out its container and cascades over the sides.

Selected species and varieties. *B. speciosa* 'Major', sapphire flower: the most common garden browallia. From this cultivar the Bells series cultivars were produced, with stems that trail 10 to 12 inches from the center of the plant. The mix of all available cultivars is called 'Jingle Bells'; individual members of the series are 'Blue Bells' (amethyst), 'Heavenly Bells' (light Cambridge blue), 'Sky Bells' (powder blue), 'Silver Bells' (white) and 'Marine Bells' (indigo).

The Troll series cultivars, available in blue and white, are slow-growing, compact 8- to 10-inch plants, perfect for containers. *B. viscosa* is a similar species but tends to flower more abundantly. 'Alba' has white flowers; 'Compacta' has blue flowers and a more compact habit than the species.

Growing conditions. Sow seeds indoors six to eight weeks before frost danger has passed. Seeds should not be covered as they need light for their 14- to 21-day germination period. Transplant seedlings or purchased bedding plants into the garden when night temperatures will not drop below 65° F. Space plants 6 to 10 inches apart in part shade in a rich, well-drained soil. Fertilize with 5-10-5 before planting. Mulch to keep soil moist and cool.

—

Bugloss see *Anchusa; Echium*
Burning bush see *Kochia*
Bush violet see *Browallia*
Butterfly flower see *Schizanthus*

—

Calandrinia
(kah-lan-DRIN-ee-ah)

A genus of plants having elongated fleshy leaves and short-lived flowers in various shades of red.

Selected species and varieties. *C. umbellata*, Peruvian rock purslane: a spreading, 6-inch plant with single ¾-inch flowers of crimson or magenta. Although a perennial, it is usually grown as an annual. It is a good choice for a rock garden or for an annual ground cover.

Growing conditions. Peruvian rock purslane grows best in the cool North, on the California coast and at high altitudes. Sow seeds outdoors in early spring where plants are to grow, or start them indoors four to six weeks before planting outside. The seeds need a maximum temperature of 60° F during the 14- to 18-day germination period. Set plants into the garden in midspring, spacing them 8 to 10 inches apart in a dry location with full sun. Do not overwater; fertilize little if at all.

—

Calceolaria
(cal-see-oh-LARE-ee-ah)
Pocketbook plant, slipper flower

Masses of flowers unique for the lower lip or petal, which forms a small pocket or slipper-like pouch. The flowers are red, yellow, orange or brown and can be spotted or a solid color. Usually used as houseplants, but can be grown as bedding or container plants in cool areas, especially the Pacific Northwest.

Selected species and varieties. *C. crenatiflora:* Flowers are 1 inch long and come in solid colors and spotted. Most plants reach 10 to 15 inches in height. The Anytime series cultivars are valued for coming into bloom faster than most, and for their compact habit; they grow only 9 inches high. *C. integrifolia* grows 12 inches tall and has yellow to red ½-inch blooms. 'Midas' bears yellow flowers; in frost-free areas, it will grow into a shrub 6 feet tall. *C. mexicana* grows 9 to 12 inches tall, with divided leaves and ½-inch soft-yellow flowers.

Growing conditions. Pocketbook plant can be propagated from seeds and will germinate in 14 to 21 days. However, since the seedlings require temperatures of 50° F to 60° F and can take four to six months to reach transplanting size, it is easier to use purchased plants. The only exception to this rule is the Anytime series, which can be transplanted in three to four months. *C. integrifolia* can also be propagated from cuttings. Set plants outdoors in full sun or light shade, 6 to 8 inches apart in a rich, moist, well-drained soil. Fertilize prior to planting and repeat monthly. Mulch to keep the soil cool. When hot temperatures arrive, the plants will fade and should be replaced by more heat-resistant annuals.

—

Calendula (kah-LEN-du-lah)

A genus from the Mediterranean having large flower heads with rays of yellow, orange or cream.

Selected species and varieties. *C. officinalis,* pot marigold: grown for its bright orange or yellow blooms, which make a conspicuous display in pots and in massed plantings; sometimes used as an ingredient of teas and a colorful garnish on food. The crisp, 3- to 4-inch flower heads, borne atop fuzzy stems, are single or double and daisy-like or chrysanthemum-like. Bon Bon series has large, 2½- to 3-inch flowers on compact, 10-inch early-blooming plants. Available in orange or yellow or a mix of these colors with apricot. 'Gypsy Festival' (or 'Fiesta Gitana') has orange or yellow flowers on 12-

inch plants. 'Pacific Beauty' bears 3-inch flowers on 20-inch plants.

Growing conditions. Sow seeds indoors four to six weeks before the last expected frost. Seeds may also be sown outdoors where plants are to grow, in midspring—about four weeks before the last frost. Germination takes 10 to 14 days. Move hardened seedlings or purchased bedding plants to the garden two weeks before the last frost. Space them 12 to 15 inches apart. As calendula does best where temperatures remain below 80° F, it is used as a spring or fall plant in hot climates, and as a summer plant where summers are cool. It prefers full sun but will grow in light shade. Soil should be rich in organic matter, fertilized with 5-10-5 before planting and kept well watered. Cut off flowers as they fade.

Note: if you use calendula in tea or as a garnish for food, avoid spraying your garden with any pesticide not recommended for vegetables.

—

California bluebell see *Phacelia*
California poppy
see *Eschscholzia*
Calliopsis see *Coreopsis*

—

Callistephus (kah-LISS-tih-fuss)
China aster

A midsummer- and fall-blooming aromatic plant native to China, with oval leaves and solitary flower heads.

Selected species and varieties. *C. chinensis,* China aster: bears blue, white, lavender, purple, yellow, pink or red flower heads atop long stems. Has basal foliage; comes in many different flower types, including single and double as well as pompon, chrysanthemum, peony, cactus and plumed forms. Plants reach from 6 to 36 inches in height. Use them in beds and borders and as cut flowers. Medium-sized (18 to 24 inches) cultivars include: 'Crego', with ostrich-feather flowers; 'Early Charm', very early, fluffy double flower; 'Fluffy Ruffles', 4½-inch plumed flowers; 'Powder-puff' (also called 'Bouquet'), 3-inch double flowers, wilt-resistant; 'Rainbow', both single and double varieties. Dwarf (6 to 18 inches) cultivars include: 'Color Carpet', 2-inch double flowers, wilt-resistant; 'Dwarf Queen', 3-inch double flowers; 'Milady', early 4-inch double blooms.

Growing conditions. Sow seeds indoors six to eight weeks before the

CALENDULA OFFICINALIS

CALLISTEPHUS CHINENSIS

CAMPANULA MEDIUM

CAPSICUM ANNUUM 'MASQUERADE'

CATANANCHE CAERULEA

last frost date, or outdoors after all danger of frost has passed. Germination will take 10 to 14 days. Move seedlings or purchased bedding plants outdoors after danger of frost has passed. Space plants from 6 to 15 inches apart, depending on their ultimate height, in full sun and a rich, well-drained sandy soil that is kept well watered. Fertilize with 5-10-5 prior to planting and again every month during growth. China asters are shallow-rooted; mulch with dried grass clippings, compost or straw to prevent drying of soil and roots. Once the flowers have been cut or have faded, the plants will not bloom again. To ensure a continuous supply of cut flowers, start new plants every two weeks. Planting early-blooming types of China aster with late-blooming types will also extend the flowering season. To reduce the risk of disease, avoid planting China asters near marigolds or in the same location two years in a row.

Campanula (kam-PAN-u-lah)
Bellflower

The bellflowers that are grown as annuals produce spikes of 2-inch white, blue, lavender, purple and pink flowers in summer; blooms are elongated and bell-shaped. Bellflowers make good accent or back-of-the-border plants and long-lasting cut flowers.

Selected species and varieties. *C. medium,* Canterbury bells: a biennial grown as an annual; grows 2 to 3 feet tall and blooms in mixed colors. *C. medium* 'Calycanthema', cup-and-saucer: has double flowers. *C. spicata:* also a biennial grown as an annual; has blue flowers on an 18- to 24-inch plant.

Growing conditions. Start seeds indoors six to eight weeks before planting outdoors in midspring. Seed is very fine and should not be covered during the 10- to 14-day germination period. In warm climates, seeds may be sown in fall for growth and flowering the following spring and summer. Set plants 12 to 15 inches apart in full sun or light shade. Soil must be rich, well drained and kept well watered. Feed with 5-10-5 at planting time and again monthly until flowering is finished. Encourage reblooming by snipping off faded flower spikes.

Campion see *Silene*
Canary bird flower
see *Tropaeolum*

Candytuft see *Iberis*
Canterbury bells see *Campanula*
Cape daisy see *Venidum*
Cape marigold
see *Dimorphotheca*
Caper spurge see *Euphorbia*

Capsicum (KAP-sih-cum)
Pepper

The genus of tropical woody plants that yield edible peppers used for food seasoning. Ornamental peppers are excellent annuals for beds, borders or containers, but beware: although they are edible, many of these plants produce fruit that is too hot to eat.

Selected species and varieties. *C. annuum,* ornamental pepper: tiny white, star-shaped flowers are followed by small fruits. Depending on the cultivar, fruit may be round, tapered or cone-shaped and go through shades of white, cream, chartreuse, purple, red or orange as it matures. The cheery peppers, more colorful than many flowers, sit atop bright green leaves on 4- to 12-inch plants. 'Fireworks' bears cone-shaped fruit on 6- to 8-inch spreading plants that are excellent for hanging baskets. 'Holiday Flame' produces slim fruit on 12-inch plants. 'Holiday Time' plants are petite (4 to 6 inches); cone-shaped peppers develop in a central crown along the main stem. 'Masquerade' bears long, thin peppers on 8- to 10-inch plants. 'Red Missile' has 2-inch tapered fruit on a 10-inch plant.

Growing conditions. You can buy bedding plants, or start your own plants from seeds sown indoors six to eight weeks before the last frost date. Don't cover the seeds, as they need light during the 21- to 25-day germination period. Set plants in full sun or very light shade, 6 to 9 inches apart. Ornamental peppers like a long, hot, humid summer to flourish, and are very heat- and drought-resistant. Soil should be rich and well drained. Feed lightly with 5-10-5 before planting and do not feed again; overfertilizing leads to lush foliage but no peppers. Keep soil evenly moist. To grow ornamental peppers for the winter holidays, start plants on May 1, let them summer outdoors in pots and bring them inside in fall.

Cardinal climber see *Ipomoea*
Carnation see *Dianthus*
Castor bean see *Ricinus*

Catananche (kat-ah-NAN-kee)

Crisp flowers borne on long, wiry stems over woolly swordlike leaves.

Selected species and varieties. *C. caerulea,* Cupid's dart: has lavender-blue, 2-inch flowers with darker blue centers. The petals are flat, but each has a toothed tip that gives the flower a lacy appearance. Makes an excellent cut or dried flower. A perennial, but can be grown as an annual if started early enough.

Growing conditions. Start seeds indoors six to eight weeks before setting plants into the garden. Germination takes 21 to 25 days. Plants may be safely moved outdoors in early spring as soon as the soil can be worked. Where winters are mild, seeds can be sown outdoors in late summer or early fall. Set plants 10 to 12 inches apart in a light to average soil and full sun. Grow on the dry side, and fertilize little, if at all. To prolong bloom, remove flowers as they fade.

—

Catchfly see *Silene*

—

Catharanthus
(kath-ah-RAN-thus)
Periwinkle

Leathery green leaves and waxy, five-petaled flowers of white or rose are borne abundantly on spreading or upright plants. A tender perennial grown as an annual.

Selected species and varieties. *C. roseus,* rose periwinkle, Madagascar periwinkle: erect, 2-foot plant with showy 1½-inch flowers in pink or white. Carpet series cultivars are ground-hugging plants, reaching 3 inches in height but spreading to 24 inches. Flowers are white, pink, rose or pink with a dark-rose eye. The Little series cultivars are upright, nonspreading plants, reaching 10 inches in height. Cultivars include 'Little Blanche' (white), 'Little Bright Eye' (white with red eye), 'Little Delicata' (white with pink eye), 'Little Pinkie' (rosy pink), 'Little Rosie' (deep rose) and 'Little Linda' (violet rose). 'Polka Dot' is a ground-hugging cultivar, 4 to 5 inches tall, with white flowers with a red eye.

Growing conditions. Rose periwinkle plants should be set into the garden after all danger of frost has passed; seeds sown outside will not reach maturity before frost. You can use purchased bedding plants, or grow your plants from seeds sown indoors 12 weeks before the last frost. Cover the seeds, which need darkness for the 15- to 20-day germination. Plant rose periwinkles in full sun or part shade in any well-drained garden soil. Plants prefer to be kept moist but will tolerate drought, heat and urban pollution. Fertilize with 5-10-5 before planting; no further feeding is needed. Faded flowers of periwinkle fall cleanly and need not be removed.

—

Cathedral bells see *Cobaea*

—

Celosia (sell-OH-see-ah)

A large genus of brightly colored tropical plants grown for their exotically shaped flower heads. One form is crested and has tightly convoluted flowers; the other is plume-shaped, with loose and feathery blooms. Dwarf cultivars, growing 6 inches high, are used for borders and edgings; tall cultivars work well at the back of a border and also make good cut flowers and dried flowers.

Selected species and varieties. *C. cristata,* plumed celosia, crested celosia, cockscomb: flower heads may be any of several bright reds, pinks or yellows, or cream, apricot, orange, gold or salmon. Plumed forms include 'Apricot Brandy', which bears feathery 7-inch, apricot-colored spikes on 16- to 18-inch, weather-tolerant plants. Century series cultivars bloom early and bear brighter and longer-lasting plumes than many other cultivars of celosia; the spikes are 12 inches long on 24-inch plants. 'Forest Fire' has 15-inch plumes of fiery scarlet, with maroon foliage on 30-inch plants. Kewpie series cultivars are the smallest of the plumed types, with bushy, 7-inch plumes on 10-inch plants. Crested cultivars include the Jewel Box series, bearing combs that are 4 to 5 inches across and come in the full range of colors.

Growing conditions. Celosia seeds may be sown outdoors where the plants are to grow after all danger of frost has passed, but for best results start with bedding plants or your own seedlings. Sow seeds indoors four weeks before the last frost date and transfer outside after frost danger has passed. To minimize transplant shock, sow seeds in peat pots and transfer pot and all into the garden. Germination takes 10 to 15

CATHARANTHUS ROSEUS

CELOSIA CRISTATA (CRESTED FORM)

CELOSIA CRISTATA (PLUMED FORM)

CENTAUREA CYANUS

CENTRATHERUM INTERMEDIUM

CHEIRANTHUS CHEIRI

days. These plants prefer warm weather; if set into the garden too early, they will flower prematurely, go to seed, and die without producing the large blooms and showy summer display for which they are grown. Plant celosias in full sun, 6 to 18 inches apart, in a rich and well-drained soil. Water when the ground becomes dry. Fertilize with 5-10-5 before planting; no further feeding is needed. Celosia is very tolerant of heat and drought, and will add color to the garden until frost.

—

Centaurea (sen-TAW-ree-ah)

These popular garden plants produce double, frilly, ruffled or tufted blooms, primarily blue but also in shades of pink, rose, lavender, yellow and white. Blooms are borne atop wiry stems with long, thin foliage. Centaureas work well in a border, and they make long-lasting cut flowers and excellent dried flowers.

Selected species and varieties. *C. americana,* basket flower: grows 4 to 6 feet tall and has 4- to 5-inch violet flowers. *C. cineraria,* dusty miller: grown for its foliage of broad, oak-shaped leaves. 'Silverdust' foliage is deeply lobed and silvery white. *C. cyanus,* cornflower, bachelor's button: grows up to 36 inches tall with 1½-inch blooms that are usually blue, sometimes purple or pink. 'Blue Boy' bears clear, purplish blue flowers on 30- to 36-inch plants. 'Polka Dot' produces all possible cornflower colors on bushy 16- to 20-inch plants. 'Jubilee Gem' grows only 12 inches tall and has dark blue flowers. *C. moschata,* sweet sultan, grows 24 inches tall, has fringed, sweetly scented 2-inch flowers in blue, pink, white and yellow. 'Imperialis' has 4-inch flowers in white, pink and purple, and may reach 4 feet.

Growing conditions. Basket flower, cornflower and sweet sultan are all very hardy and will withstand frost, so seeds or well-hardened plants may be put into the garden in midspring as soon as the soil can be worked. For earlier bloom, start seeds indoors four weeks before the outdoor planting date. Germination will take seven to 14 days, and seeds must be completely covered because they require darkness to germinate. Where winters are mild, seeds can be sown in autumn for early-spring bloom. Cornflowers are not long-blooming plants; for a continuous supply of color, sow seeds every two weeks through spring and sum-

mer. To prolong blooming, remove spent flowers.

For best results with dusty miller, purchase bedding plants, or start seeds indoors eight to 10 weeks before the last frost date, and plant them outdoors only after all danger of frost has passed. Germination takes 10 to 14 days. If plants get leggy as summer wears on, shear them back.

—

Centratherum (sen-TRA-the-rum)

A genus of 30 species of freely branching plants having terminal thistle-like flower heads.

Selected species and varieties. *C. intermedium,* manaos beauty: crinkled and serrated blue-green foliage with tiny fluffy lavender flowers. Neat and uniform, 18 to 24 inches tall, this plant is useful for edgings, low borders, rock gardens or bedding.

Growing conditions. Seeds may be sown outdoors where plants are to grow, after all danger of frost has passed. For best results, however, sow seeds indoors four to six weeks before the last frost date and then transplant seedlings outdoors after the last frost. Germination takes 10 to 14 days. Space plants 12 to 15 inches apart in full sun or light shade in light, sandy, well-drained soil. Do not overwater; fertilize little if at all. Manaos beauty tolerates heat and drought.

—

Cheiranthus (kae-RAN-thus)
Wallflower

Fragrant flowers borne in clusters on bushy 12- to 30-inch plants. Leaves are narrow and bright green.

Selected species and varieties. *C. cheiri,* English wallflower: yellow, orange or mahogany-colored 1-inch blooms borne in erect, showy clusters. Wallflower is a perennial, but does not tolerate heat and can survive only in areas—such as the Pacific Northwest—with cool, moist summers; elsewhere it is therefore treated as an annual. Used in beds, borders and rock gardens.

Growing conditions. Sow seeds indoors in midwinter, six to eight weeks before transplanting outdoors. Germinate wallflowers at a cool (60° F) temperature; seedlings will appear five to seven days after sowing. Hardened seedlings or purchased bedding plants may be set in the garden in early spring as soon as soil can be worked. Where winter temperatures do not drop below 20° F, seeds may also be sown in late summer for bloom the following spring; move plants into place two months before the first fall frost. Space plants 12 to 15 inches apart in full sun or light shade in an average, well-drained soil, and use a protective mulch against possible frost damage. Fertilize with 5-10-5 before planting. Keep soil well watered and mulched.

—

China aster see *Callistephus*
Chinese-houses see *Collinsia*

—

Chrysanthemum
(krih-SAN-the-mum)

Chrysanthemums are among the most popular garden plants. Although the fall-blooming perennial is probably best-known, it has many annual relatives that can brighten the summer border. These colorful plants have single or double daisy-like blooms in all colors except blue and purple. The flowers range from large and showy to diminutive and button-like; foliage is generally divided and strong-smelling. One species is grown not for its flower heads but for its silver-gray foliage.

Selected species and varieties. *C. carinatum,* tricolor chrysanthemum: 24 to 36 inches tall, with deeply cut foliage and single or double flower heads. White, red, gold, yellow or maroon ray florets surround large purplish centers; the ray florets often have one or more contrasting hues at their base, creating one or more rings of color around the dark center. *C. coronarium,* crown daisy, garland chrysanthemum: a 1- to 4-foot plant with fernlike foliage; its 1½-inch daisy-like flower heads can be double or single, and golden or light yellow. 'Tom Thumb', a dwarf cultivar, grows only 1 foot tall. *C. frutescens,* white marguerite, Paris daisy: a bushy, 3-foot plant with lacy gray-green leaves and 2-inch white or pale yellow flowers with dark yellow centers. A tender perennial that can be grown as an annual. *C. multicaule:* bears masses of tiny single blooms on 4- to 6-inch plants. A good choice where a ground cover, rock-garden plant or edging is needed. *C. paludosum:* bears tiny white daisy-like flower heads above deeply lobed foliage. A 6-inch plant that grows in a mounded carpet, does best in a low border and has a long blooming peri-

od. *C. parthenium,* feverfew: a perennial that can become invasive because of its prolific reseeding, so is often grown as an annual; to prevent reseeding, remove flowers as they begin to fade. The tiny flower heads are borne in clusters and are either daisy-like, with short white ray florets surrounding yellow centers, or button-like with yellow centers. Plants grow 2 to 3 feet in height, and the foliage is aromatic. *C. ptarmiciflorum,* dusty miller: grown for its attractive foliage. 'Silver Lace' has finely cut, almost fernlike silver-gray leaves.

Growing conditions. Annual chrysanthemums do best where summers are mild and moist, though they will tolerate moderate heat and drought. Sow seeds of most species outdoors after all danger of frost has passed, or indoors eight to 10 weeks before the last frost date; dusty miller, however, must be sown indoors 14 weeks before the last frost date. Germination takes eight to 18 days, depending on species. Do not cover seeds of feverfew, because they need light to germinate. Annual chrysanthemums are also generally available in spring as bedding plants, which can be set in the garden after all danger of frost is past. Set plants 4 to 18 inches apart, depending on the ultimate size of the species, in full sun and a well-drained, average soil. Fertilize at planting time and again every month during the growing season. To ensure continuous bloom, pick flowers as they fade.

—

Cigar flower see *Cuphea*

—

Clarkia (CLARK-ee-ah)
Clarkia, godetia, Rocky Mountain garland, garland flower

A plant that bears showy 1- to 3-foot spikes of delicate, frilled flowers that may be single or double. Colors range from white to pink, salmon, red, lavender and purple. Suitable for wildflower gardens and for beds and borders, clarkias also make long-lasting cut flowers.

Selected species and varieties. *C. amoena,* satin flower, farewell-to-spring: bears single, 1½-inch flowers with pink or lavender petals that usually have bright red markings. The plants are 36 inches tall. *C. concinna,* red ribbons: bears single, 1-inch flowers of deep, bright pink on 16-inch plants. *C. purpurea* produces single, 1-inch flowers of lavender,

CHRYSANTHEMUM FRUTESCENS

CLARKIA AMOENA

CLEOME HASSLERANA

COBAEA SCANDENS

COLEUS × HYBRIDUS

pink, purple or red on 30-inch plants. *C. unguiculata* (sometimes listed in seed catalogs as *C. elegans)* bears single or double, ¾-inch flowers of pink, lavender, salmon or purple on 36-inch plants.

Growing conditions. Sow seeds outdoors where plants are to grow as soon as the soil can be worked in the spring. In frost-free areas, sow in fall for bloom the following spring. Clarkias prefer full sun or light shade in a light, sandy soil with excellent drainage. Do not try to start seeds indoors, as clarkias do not transplant well. Seeds are very fine and should be barely covered during the five- to 10-day germination period. Thin the seedlings to 8 to 10 inches apart, and do not fertilize at all or the plants will not blossom. Water very lightly. Clarkias do best in areas that share the cool summers and dry, sandy soil of their native Pacific Northwest mountains. Where summers are hot, clarkias can be grown in spring.

—

Cleome (klee-OH-me)

More than 300 species of tropical plants, only one of which is useful to the gardener.

Selected species and varieties. *C. hasslerana,* spider flower: strong-scented white, rose, pink or lavender florets; the protruding clusters of 2- to 3-inch stamens look somewhat spidery. Seedpods are conspicuously long and slim. Spider flower is perfect for the back of a border, where its waving 3- to 6-foot stems are most attractive. 'Pink Queen' is the best-known cultivar, growing 3½ feet tall and producing pink flowers. White-flowered cultivars are available.

Growing conditions. Sow seeds where plants are to grow after all danger of frost has passed, or sow them indoors four to six weeks before last frost. Germination will take 10 to 14 days. Space plants 2 to 3 feet apart in a warm spot with full sun and average soil. They will withstand high summer heat and are very drought-resistant. Feed very lightly, if at all, and do not overwater. In the South, spider flower will reseed itself from year to year.

—

Cobaea (koe-BEE-ah)

A tropical climbing vine that has showy flowers.

Selected species and varieties. *C. scandens,* cup-and-saucer vine,

Mexican ivy, monastery bells: has 2-inch cup-shaped flowers that open a pale green and darken to purple as they mature. Foliage is dark green. 'Alba': a cultivar with white flowers. Cup-and-saucer vine, a very fast-growing plant, can reach 20 feet in a year and is very suitable for use on screens and trellises. In frost-free areas it is a perennial, but it can be grown in the North as an annual.

Growing conditions. Start seeds indoors in peat pots six to eight weeks before the last frost date. Set the large, flat seeds on edge, barely covering the top edges with soil. Germination takes 15 to 20 days. After all danger of frost is past, transplant to a location with full sun or light shade, a rich, moist, well-drained soil and a support on which the vine will climb. Cup-and-saucer vine tolerates wind, but in areas with hot summers, it prefers afternoon shade.

—

Cockscomb see *Celosia*

—

Coleus (KO-lee-us)
Coleus, flame nettle

A popular, shade-loving plant grown for its striking foliage. Use coleus in shady beds, borders or containers.

Selected species and varieties. *C.* × *hybridus:* foliage is edged, blotched or patterned in splashy combinations of green, chartreuse, white, gold, bronze, scarlet, ivory, orange, rose, copper, yellow and purple. Leaf edges may be lacy, smooth, fringed, wavy or toothed. Dragon series cultivars bear large heart-shaped serrated leaves on 12-inch plants that have a ridged texture and an exotic look. Saber series cultivars have lobed, sword-shaped leaves that cascade and look well in hanging baskets.

Growing conditions. Either purchase bedding plants or start seeds indoors six to eight weeks before the last frost date. When sowing, do not cover seeds; they need light for germination, which takes 10 to 15 days. Coleus can also be propagated by stem cuttings. Take cuttings in fall before the first frost or in spring from plants overwintered indoors. Move plants to the garden after all danger of frost has passed. Coleus prefers partial to deep shade and should be spaced 10 to 12 inches apart. Plants will survive in full sun if they are adequately watered, but foliage color will fade. Soil should be rich in organic matter, and kept moist. Fertilize with 5-10-5 before planting and repeat during the season. Flowers may be left on the plants as they form, but removing them will help maintain bright foliage color.

—

Collinsia (kol-LIN-see-ah)

Spring-blooming annuals native to the western United States, having whorled leaves and snapdragon-like flowers with two distinct lips. Choose them for mixed borders, beds and containers.

Selected species and varieties. *C. grandiflora,* bluelips: grows 15 inches tall, has flowers ¾ inch long. The lower lip is deep purple or violet, the upper lip purple or white. *C. heterophylla,* Chinese-houses: grows to 24 inches. Flowers are 1 inch long, with a violet or purple lower lip and a white upper lip.

Growing conditions. After danger of frost is past, sow seeds outdoors where plants are to bloom; germination will take 10 to 20 days. Seeds may also be sown outdoors in fall for bloom early the following spring. Thin plants to stand 6 to 10 inches apart, in part shade and a dry soil. Water and fertilize sparingly. These plants prefer a cool climate—especially cool nights—and will not withstand heat.

—

Coneflower see *Rudbeckia*

—

Consolida (kon-SO-lih-dah)
Larkspur

Stately 1- to 5-foot flower spikes covered with beautiful 1- to 3-inch flowers. Flowers are white, blue, purple, pink or yellow and appear throughout spring and early summer. Use them for the back of a border or against a fence. They make fine cut flowers and dried flowers.

Selected species and varieties. *C. ambigua,* rocket larkspur (sometimes incorrectly sold as *Delphinium ajacis):* has erect branches, most growing to 2 feet, but some reaching 5 feet. *C. orientalis* (sometimes incorrectly sold as *D. orientale* or *D. consolida)* is similar, but the branches are more horizontal. 'Giant Imperial' is a mixture of plants that produce double, closely spaced feathery flowers on low-branching plants 4 to 5 feet tall.

Growing conditions. Larkspur does best in cool climates, and is a good choice for spring in warm areas. Seeds may be sown outdoors where plants are to grow in early spring; in mild areas, sow outdoors in fall. Indoors, start six to eight weeks before the last frost date, but sow in peat pots, since plants do not transplant well. The seeds need darkness during their eight- to 15-day germination period, so cover them with a thin layer of soil. Since the seeds are short-lived, plant only fresh seeds and do not store seeds for later use. Space plants 12 to 36 inches apart in full sun and rich, loose, slightly alkaline soil. Fertilize at planting time and again monthly during the growing season. Larkspurs will reseed themselves from year to year. Water and mulch to keep soil moist and cool. To extend bloom, remove flowers as they fade. If plants grow tall, they may need to be staked.

—

Convolvulus (con-VOL-view-liss)
Glorybind, bindweed

A genus having more than 200 species in the morning glory family.

Selected species and varieties. *C. tricolor,* dwarf or bush morning glory: an old-fashioned garden favorite that, unlike its vining relatives, is an erect, mound-shaped plant reaching 1 foot in height. Its species name, *tricolor,* derives from the fact that each of the 1½-inch blue to purple flowers has a yellow throat circled with a white margin. Each blossom opens for only a day, but the plants bloom so abundantly that they provide color all summer long. Use dwarf morning glory for edging a bed, in window boxes or in hanging baskets.

Growing conditions. Dwarf morning glories bloom best in dry, sunny locations but will tolerate almost any kind of soil. In areas with long, hot summers, sow seeds in the ground where the plants are to grow. Elsewhere, sow seeds indoors in peat pots five to six weeks before the last frost date. To speed germination, nick the hard seed coats with a nail file before sowing. Space plants 12 inches apart in the garden after all danger of frost has passed.

—

Copperleaf see *Alternanthera*

—

Coreopsis (core-ee-OP-sis)

A genus of about 100 species, a dozen of which are grown for their showy blooms.

COLLINSIA HETEROPHYLLA

CONSOLIDA AMBIGUA

CONVOLVULUS TRICOLOR

COREOPSIS TINCTORIA

COSMOS BIPINNATUS 'SENSATION MIXED'

COSMOS SULPHUREUS 'SUNNY RED'

CUPHEA IGNEA

Selected species and varieties. *C. tinctoria,* calliopsis, golden coreopsis: flower heads to 1¼ inches across, with centers of red or purple and rays of yellow, brown or red-purple. Blooms may be bright red, yellow, pink or purple. The blooms, solid-colored or banded, are borne atop slender, wiry stems 8 to 36 inches tall. With their long flowering season, calliopsis are perfect for borders; they are also excellent cut flowers.

Growing conditions. Sow seeds outdoors in early spring where plants are to grow; then thin seedlings to 6 to 8 inches apart. Or purchase bedding plants; or start seeds indoors six to eight weeks before the last frost date. Seeds germinate in five to 10 days and need light to germinate, so do not cover them. When transplanting, take care not to disturb their roots. Calliopsis likes full sun, a light sandy soil with excellent drainage, little or no fertilizer and sparse watering. To keep plants neat and encourage them to produce more flowers, clip flowers as they fade.

■

Cornflower see *Centaurea*

■

Cosmos (KOS-mos)

Cosmos will fill the garden from early summer until frost with clusters of single or double daisy-like flower heads in white, gold, yellow, orange, pink or crimson. Ray florets are wide and serrated, on slender stems 4 to 6 feet in height. Taller types are excellent for the back of a border; use shorter ones in the middle of a border and in massed plantings. All make excellent cut flowers.

Selected species and varieties. *C. bipinnatus,* garden cosmos, common cosmos: tall, with lacy foliage and brightly colored 1- to 2-inch flowers. 'Sensation Mixed': grows 36 to 48 inches tall and bears single flowers that are 3 to 6 inches across in a mix of lavender, pink, red and white. *C. sulphureus,* yellow cosmos, orange cosmos: has denser, broader foliage and generally shorter plants than *C. bipinnatus.* 'Bright Lights' has semidouble flowers of flame red, bright yellow, gold or orange on 30- to 36-inch plants. 'Diablo' has scarlet-orange 2- to 3-inch flowers on 24- to 36-inch plants. 'Sunny Red' has bright orange-red single 2-inch blooms that fade to scarlet as they age. It is the first truly dwarf cosmos, growing only 12 to 14

inches tall, and is very heat-resistant. 'Sunny Red' has yielded a series of dwarf cultivars: 'Sunny Gold', 'Sunny Orange' and 'Sunny Yellow'.

Growing conditions. Cosmos seeds may be sown outdoors where plants are to grow after all danger of frost has passed. Use purchased bedding plants, or start seeds indoors five to seven weeks before the last frost date. Germination takes five to 10 days. Space plants 9 to 24 inches apart, depending on their ultimate size, in full sun and a warm spot. Soil should be dry and infertile; rich soil will produce foliage but no flowers. Do not overwater or overfertilize. To keep plants trim, cut off faded flowers. Tall types may need some wind protection.

■

Cotton thistle see *Onopordum*

Creamcups see *Platystemon*

Creeping gloxinia see *Asarina*

Creeping zinnia see *Sanvitalia*

Crown daisy see *Chrysanthemum*

Cup-and-saucer bells see *Campanula*

Cup-and-saucer vine see *Cobaea*

Cupflower see *Nierembergia*

■

Cuphea (KU-fee-ah)

A compact tender perennial that is usually grown as an annual. The brightly colored, tubular 1-inch flowers resemble small cigars or firecrackers and are borne in the leaf axils. Plants grow 12 to 18 inches high, and are well suited for bedding or hanging baskets.

Selected species and varieties. *C. ignea,* cigar flower, firecracker plant: bears fiery red tubular flowers, each with a ring of violet or black near the tip and an ash white mouth. *C. × purpurea:* has flowers of bright rose or red, tinged with violet or purple. 'Firefly' has clusters of crimson blooms.

Growing conditions. Seeds of both species may be sown outdoors after all frost danger has passed, but for best results, start seeds indoors six to eight weeks before the last frost date. Germination takes eight to 10 days. Plant 9 to 12 inches apart in sun or light shade in a light, well-drained soil. Keep well watered. Fertilize with 5-10-5 before planting; no further feeding is needed. These plants do best in hot climates with high humidity.

—

Cupid's dart see *Catananche*

—

Cynoglossum
(sigh-no-GLOS-sum)

A genus of about 90 species of plants, many having small flowers arranged in arching clusters.

Selected species and varieties. *C. amabile,* Chinese forget-me-not: bears ¼-inch flowers of blue, purple, pink or white in spraylike clusters on 2-foot plants. The tiny blooms are five-lobed or star-shaped. The plant is a biennial grown as an annual for use in a flower border, in beds and as cut flowers. 'Firmament' bears blue flowers over gray-green leaves on 16-inch plants.

Growing conditions. Sow seeds outdoors in early spring as soon as the soil can be worked. For earlier bloom, start seeds indoors six to eight weeks before planting outside. Cover the seeds; they need darkness during the five- to 10-day germination period. In mild areas, sow seeds in fall for early spring bloom. Space plants 9 to 12 inches apart in full sun or light shade and an average, well-drained soil. Chinese forget-me-nots are not fussy and can be grown wet or dry, warm or cool. Fertilize with 5-10-5, at planting time only.

—

Cypress vine see *Ipomoea*
Dahlberg daisy see *Dyssodia*

—

Dahlia (DAL-yah)

Dahlias are tender, tuberous-rooted perennials usually grown as annuals. They range in size from less than 1 to 6 feet tall, but the dwarf species (from 10 to 15 inches) are generally used for massed displays of color in annual beds, borders and containers. They bloom in all colors except blue, and generally come in mixtures.

Selected species and varieties. *D.* hybrids: 'Dahl Face' has masses of single blooms on 10-inch plants. 'Figaro' has mostly double 3-inch flowers on a 12- to 14-inch plant. 'Fresco' is earliest-blooming dwarf hybrid and bears semidouble and double flowers on 10- to 12-inch plants. 'Redskin' has bronze foliage that contrasts with 3-inch semidouble

to fully double blooms on 15-inch plants. 'Rigoletto' has early, semi-double 3-inch flowers on 14-inch plants. Sunny series cultivars are the first dahlia from seed to be available in separate colors, red and rose. These cultivars have double flowers on 14-inch plants.

Growing conditions. Dahlias are propagated by two methods: seeds and tubers. Which you choose depends on how fussy you are about color and economics. Many gardeners start dahlias from seed, grow them all season and let frost kill them in fall. Others save tubers at the end of the growing season, store them over the winter in a cool, dry place and replant them the following year. The advantage of planting tubers is that you will get the same plant, year after year. If you have a favorite type or color, you should grow dahlias from tubers.

Dahlias started from seed are a little less predictable. Flower form and plant size can be known in advance, but usually color cannot. Start seeds indoors four to six weeks before the last frost, then move plants outdoors after the last frost. Germination takes only five to 10 days.

Space dwarf dahlia plants 8 to 24 inches apart, in a light, rich soil with excellent drainage. Fertilize with 5-10-5 before planting and again every month during the growing season. Dahlias prefer full sun but will grow and bloom well in a light shade. Water heavily, never letting the ground dry out completely. Mulch to conserve moisture. Dahlias look better and bloom more if faded flowers are removed. If you want very large blooms, remove side buds.

To store tubers over the winter, wait until frost has blackened the plant tops. Dig up the tubers, shake off excess soil and store them in a cool, dry place. Check periodically to make sure they are not drying out. If they start to grow, they are receiving too much light or heat, or both.

—

Daisy see *Arctotis; Bellis; Brachycome; Chrysanthemum; Dorotheanthus; Dyssodia; Felicia; Gerbera; Machaeranthera; Rudbeckia; Venidum; Xanthisma*

—

Datura (da-TOOR-ah)
Thorn apple

Members of this genus are annuals or short-lived perennials with lobed, unpleasantly scented leaves and trumpet-shaped flowers resembling

CYNOGLOSSUM AMABILE

DAHLIA HYBRID

DATURA METEL

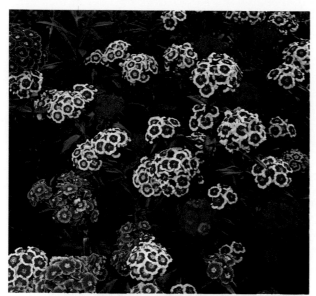
DIANTHUS BARBATUS

DIGITALIS PURPUREA

DIMORPHOTHECA SINUATA HYBRID

large petunias. Blooms, which are often fragrant, open at sunset and last only one day. The plants are large and can be used as fillers at the back of a border or as accents.

Note: the leaves and seeds of these plants contain a poisonous alkaloid; do not consider planting them where there are small children.

Selected species and varieties. *D. inoxia,* angel's trumpet: a 3-foot, spreading plant with 10-inch leaves and pink, white or lavender pendant flowers 8 inches long and 5 inches wide. *D. metel,* horn-of-plenty: grows to 5 feet, with 8-inch leaves and single or double white, yellow or purple upright flowers 7 inches long and 4 inches wide. 'Huberana' has blooms of blue, yellow or red.

Growing conditions. Start seeds indoors 12 to 16 weeks before the plants' outdoor planting date, which is several weeks after frost danger has passed. Germination takes 21 to 40 days, and plants develop slowly. Transplant into full sun and rich, moist soil. Keep well watered. Fertilize with 5-10-5 before planting and feed monthly thereafter. Thorn apples do best in hot climates.

—

Dianthus (die-AN-thus)

The dianthus genus is a large one, with members known as pinks, sweet William and carnation. The name "pinks" comes not from the flowers' color, but from their serrated petals, which look as if they might have been cut with pinking shears. Most dianthus have a delicious fragrance reminiscent of cloves; plant them where their aroma can be enjoyed, in rock gardens, rock walls, beds or borders.

Selected species and varieties. *D. armeria,* Deptford pink: a biennial grown as a hardy annual, grows 16 inches tall and has dense clusters of tiny red toothed and bearded flowers. *D. barbatus,* sweet William: a biennial or perennial often grown as an annual; grows to 12 inches. Pinked blooms are red, white, pink or rose-purple, many with a contrasting "eye"; they appear in dense round clusters over green leaves. 'Roundabout' has mixed colors on dwarf, spreading plants. 'Wee Willie' is only 3 inches high and colorful all season. *D. chinensis,* China rainbow pink, grows from 6 to 18 inches tall, has single or double flat-topped, frilled flowers of red, white, pink, rose or lilac. Blooms are 1 inch across, some in solid colors, others two-toned.

Foliage is grasslike and gray-green. 'China Doll' produces clusters of double flowers in a wide color range, on 12- to 15-inch plants. Magic Charms series cultivars bear large, abundant blooms on dwarf plants; available in five separate colors: crimson, scarlet, coral, pink and white. Princess series cultivars are among the most reliable for compactness, neatness and all-summer flowering; colors include ruby, salmon, crimson, scarlet, white. 'Snowfire': a dwarf cultivar bearing snow white blooms with cherry red centers; is rain- and heat-tolerant. 'Telstar' is a cheerful mix of crimson, pink, rose, scarlet, white and bicolors; withstands light frost and heat.

Growing conditions. Sow seeds indoors six to eight weeks before the last frost date; germination takes five to 10 days. Set seedlings or purchased bedding plants into the garden after danger of frost has passed. Space plants 6 to 9 inches apart in full sun and a light, rich, well-drained soil. Dianthus prefers alkaline conditions, so check soil and raise pH with lime if necessary. Incorporate 5-10-5 into the soil before planting, and feed monthly thereafter. Cut back plants after they bloom to encourage further flowering. Dianthus perform best in areas with a cool to moderate climate and high humidity. Some of those sold as annuals, particularly the newer hybrids, may be perennial in areas where winter temperatures do not go below 0° F.

—

Digitalis (didge-ih-TAL-iss)
Foxglove

A dramatic plant that grows up to 6 feet tall and bears spikes of nodding 1- to 3-inch bell-shaped flowers of white, yellow, pink, purple or red. The blooms resemble the end of a glove finger, and many have spots of contrasting colors inside. Leaves may be round or tapered. Use foxglove as a bold accent plant or in the back of a flower border. Although a biennial or perennial, it can be grown as an annual.

Selected species and varieties. *D. purpurea* 'Gloxiniiflora': robust and large-flowered, has flower spikes longer than those of other cultivars. 'Excelsior' hybrids bear their large, showy flowers all around the stem, and so are attractive from any angle. 'Foxy' is bred to bloom the first year.

Growing conditions. To grow foxgloves as annuals, start them indoors 10 to 12 weeks before the last frost, and move them to the garden two weeks before the last frost date. To grow them as biennials, set plants or seeds in the garden in late summer, two months before the first expected frost. Germination takes 15 to 20 days. Plant foxgloves in part shade, 15 to 24 inches apart, in rich, loose, well-drained soil. Avoid excessive heat. Water well, without making soil soggy and never let it dry out. Fertilize at planting time with 5-10-5, and again as blooming begins. Apply mulch in fall after the ground freezes. To propagate as biennials, divide plants in early spring.

—

Dimorphotheca
(die-more-foe-THEE-kah)
Cape marigold, star-of-the-veldt

Cape marigolds are cheerful-looking 4- to 16-inch plants with 1½- to 3-inch daisy-like flowers of white, yellow, orange, salmon or pink. The undersides of the petals are blue or lavender; centers are a contrasting dark color or yellow. During the day, they make a bright addition to any bed, border or ground cover. The flowers close at night.

Selected species and varieties. *D. pluvialis* bears 2½-inch flowers of white with violet to purple undersides and yellow centers; plants grow to 16 inches. *D. sinuata* grows 12 inches tall. Its 1½-inch flowers are orange-yellow with violet at the base and yellow centers.

Growing conditions. After all danger of frost has passed, sow seeds outdoors where plants are to grow. For earlier bloom, purchase bedding plants or start seeds indoors four to five weeks before the outside planting date. Germination takes 10 to 15 days. To ensure success, use only fresh seeds. Set plants 4 to 8 inches apart in full sun and a light, sandy, well-drained soil. Cape marigolds prefer dry soil, so water them lightly. Fertilize the plants every other month. Cape marigolds are easy to grow, preferring cool weather, but tolerating heat and drought.

—

Dorotheanthus
(door-oh-the-AN-thus)
Livingstone daisy

Low-growing, spreading succulent plant (formerly classified as *Mesembryanthemum*) that grows to 3 inches tall. Excellent for the seashore, as it tolerates drought and salt spray.

Selected species and varieties. *D. bellidiformis,* Livingstone daisy: has showy, 2-inch daisy-like flowers in pinks, reds, orange, pale yellow or white, sometimes bicolored.

Growing conditions. Sow seeds indoors 10 to 12 weeks before the last frost. Seeds are fine, and should be only lightly covered with soil; but they need darkness to germinate, so cover the flat with black plastic during the 15 to 20 days when the seeds are germinating. Set plants 2 to 6 inches apart in full sun, in average, dry garden soil, and do not overwater. Fertilize with 5-10-5 at planting and again every other month during the growing season.

—

Dusty miller see *Centaurea; Chrysanthemum; Senecio*

—

Dyssodia (diss-OH-dee-ah)

A genus of about 30 species in the daisy family, with single flowers that bloom atop stalks or in clusters along one side of a stem.

Selected species and varieties. *D. tenuiloba,* Dahlberg daisy: single daisy-like 1-inch flowers with yellow or yellow-orange ray florets around yellow centers. Plants grow only 4 to 6 inches tall; stems are slender; foliage is very fine and threadlike. Blooming plants form a low, dense carpet sprinkled with gold flecks, lending a cheery brightness to low borders, edgings, rock gardens and rock walls.

Growing conditions. Sow seeds indoors six to eight weeks before the last spring frost and transplant seedlings outdoors after all danger of frost has passed. Set plants 4 to 6 inches apart, in full sun and in average soil with good drainage. Water sparingly; plants prefer dry soil. Fertilize little if at all. Although Dahlberg daisies prefer cool temperatures, they tolerate heat and drought well.

—

Echium (EK-ee-um)
Viper's bugloss

Two biennial species of viper's bugloss are grown as annuals for their erect spikes of small five-lobed flowers of blue, purple, red, pink or white. The 1- to 3-foot plants have broad, hairy, tongue-shaped leaves and hairy stems. Best used in borders and rock gardens.

DOROTHEANTHUS BELLIDIFORMIS

DYSSODIA TENUILOBA

ECHIUM VULGARE

ESCHSCHOLZIA CALIFORNICA

EUPHORBIA MARGINATA

EUSTOMA GRANDIFLORUM

Selected species and varieties. *E. lycopsis:* grows to 2 feet, bears red flowers that change to bluish purple as they age. *E. vulgare,* blueweed, blue devil: grows to 3 feet, has blue flowers. 'Blue Bedder' reaches only 12 inches in height, is covered with ½-inch, cup-shaped blooms.

Growing conditions. Sow seeds outdoors in early spring as soon as the soil can be worked, or start them indoors four to six weeks earlier. Germination takes seven to 14 days and requires a temperature of about 60° F. In the garden, space plants 12 to 15 inches apart in full sun and in dry, well-drained, poor soil. Avoid overwatering and fertilize little, if at all; in rich soil, the buglosses produce few flowers.

▬

English daisy see *Bellis*

▬

Eschscholzia (es-SHOLE-ze-ah)
California poppy

A popular member of the poppy family, having four-petaled flowers in yellow, orange and reds. Native to the North American West Coast, this California spring wildflower is said to have been used by the American Indians for toothache. Good in wildflower gardens, borders, massed plantings and containers. The blossoms close at night, but in daytime provide excellent color in fall, winter and spring.

Selected species and varieties. *E. californica,* California poppy: silky-looking cup-shaped flowers 2 to 3 inches across, single or double, many with a crinkled texture. Colors include gold, yellow, bronze, orange, scarlet, rose and white. Stems grow 12 to 24 inches tall above very finely cut spreading foliage. 'Aurantiaca': an old cultivar; single flowers of rich orange; useful for accents. 'Ballerina': mixture of fluted double and semidouble flowers up to 3 inches across, some marked with two contrasting colors. 'Mission Bells': semidouble flowers in very bright color range of rose, gold, cherry, scarlet, copper, orange and pink.

Growing conditions. Sow seeds outdoors in early spring where the plants are to grow. Seeds can be started indoors four to six weeks before outdoor planting time, but transplanting may disturb the roots and is not recommended. Germination takes 10 to 12 days. Space plants 6 to 8 inches apart in full sun; soil should be light, sandy and well drained, but

not too rich. California poppies tolerate cold, heat and drought. In warm climates, they self-sow readily. To ensure bloom throughout the summer, remove faded flowers.

▬

Escobita see *Orthocarpus*

▬

Euphorbia (you-FOR-bee-ah)
Spurge

A large genus of plants that includes succulents, the popular Christmas poinsettia and a number of commonly grown annuals. These plants produce brilliantly colored, showy, petal-like bracts and insignificant flowers. They are useful in beds, in borders and as cut flowers.

Note: make sure that you are careful when handling these plants, because their stems have milky juices that can irritate eyes and skin.

Selected species and varieties. *E. cyathophora,* fire-on-the-mountain, annual poinsettia: grows 3 feet tall and has upper bracts of bright red, like those of the holiday plant. *E. lathyris,* caper spurge: pointed leaves on a 3-foot plant with small, yellow-green bracts. *E. marginata,* snow-on-the-mountain: bracts are white or white-edged green; leaves are glossy and green.

Growing conditions. Use purchased bedding plants, or start plants from seed. Sow seeds outdoors where plants are to grow, after danger of frost is past, or sow them indoors six to eight weeks before the last frost date. Transplant seedlings or purchased bedding plants outdoors after danger of frost has passed. Germination takes 10 to 15 days. Space plants 10 to 12 inches apart in full sun or light shade. Average soil is quite adequate; spurge grows well in even the poorest soil. Water the plants very sparingly, and do not fertilize them. All spurges tolerate drought and high heat.

▬

Eustoma (yew-STO-mah)

Formerly named (and sometimes sold as) lisianthus, eustoma is a member of the gentian family and bears single or double 3-inch flowers of white, pink, blue or lavender. The blossoms are cup-shaped and upward-facing, appearing in clusters on strong, stiff stems. Plants can grow to 30 inches in height, but they flower more abundantly and are therefore more attractive if kept at 12 inches by early pinching. Use them in beds, borders and containers, and as cut flowers; they are long-lasting.

Selected species and varieties. *E. grandiflorum,* prairie gentian: Lion is a double-flowered series of cultivars with blue, white or pink blooms. Yodel series bears single blooms in all colors, accented by silvery green foliage.

Growing conditions. It takes seven months from the time seeds are sown until these plants blossom, so it is easiest to begin with purchased plants. If you do start your own seeds indoors, give them a warm spot for the 15-day germination and following growth. Barely cover the seeds, as they are very fine. Space plants 12 inches apart in full sun and in garden soil that has excellent drainage. The soil must be moderately fertile, so incorporate 5-10-5 before planting and fertilize again every other month during the growing season. To keep prairie gentians compact, pinch the plants back as soon as they are set in the ground and again when they have grown to 2 or 3 inches in height. Without pinching, plants will grow too tall and will need to be staked. They tolerate heat, drought and rain, and prefer warm summers.

—

Everlasting see *Ammobium; Helichrysum; Helipterum*

—

Evolvulus (ee-VOLV-you-lus)

A low-growing tropical plant of the morning glory family.

Selected species and varieties. *E. glomeratus,* blue daze: produces single 1-inch blue flowers on spreading plants 12 inches tall. Blue daze is useful in the front of a border, in containers or as an annual ground cover, especially where soil erosion needs to be controlled. As it tolerates salt spray, it is excellent for the seaside.

Growing conditions. Start with purchased plants or propagate your own with stem cuttings; seeds are not widely available. Plant in full sun, 12 to 18 inches apart, in a well-drained sandy soil. Fertilize with 5-10-5 before planting and again every month during the growing season. Blue daze prefers dry climates and low humidity. In containers, give the plants plenty of room; they deteriorate if root-bound.

Exacum (EX-ah-cum)

Exacum forms a compact mound and is covered with fragrant, star-shaped flowers. Used frequently as a house plant, it also grows well outdoors as an edging and in hanging baskets.

Selected species and varieties. *E. affine,* Persian violet, German violet: plant is 9 inches tall; blooms are ½ inch across and may be purple, blue or white, with prominent yellow stamens. 'Midget' bears generous quantities of wonderfully fragrant, Oxford blue flowers, each with a royal purple ring around its yellow stamen. Grows very well in the South. 'Rosendal', a ball-shaped plant, is free-flowering and compact; flowers are blue or white.

Growing conditions. Start with potted plants for early bloom, or sow seeds indoors four to six weeks before the last frost. Do not cover seeds, which need light during the 15- to 20-day germination period. After the last frost, transplant seedlings carefully; growth will be slowed if roots are disturbed. Space plants 9 inches apart, in a warm, partly shaded spot. Soil must be rich and have excellent drainage. Keep soil evenly moist at all times and feed every two weeks.

Farewell-to-spring see *Clarkia*

—

Felicia (fe-LEE-she-ah)

Two species of felicia are grown for their daisy-like ¾- to 1½-inch flower heads, consisting of blue ray florets around yellow centers. Stems and leaves are hairy and the plants have a loose growing habit.

Selected species and varieties. *F. amelloides,* blue daisy or blue marguerite: a small, bushy shrub grown as an annual. It grows 3 feet wide and high and has 1½-inch flower heads. It is a fine plant for beds or the middle of a border. *F. bergerana,* kingfisher daisy: a bushy 6- to 8-inch annual with 1-inch flower heads. It is used as an edging or at the front of a border.

Growing conditions. Seeds of either of the two species above can be sown outdoors in early spring as soon as the soil can be worked. For starting seeds indoors 10 to 12 weeks before planting outdoors, various methods are used. Blue daisy must be germinated at 55° F and will benefit from three weeks' chilling in the re-

EVOLVULUS GLOMERATUS

EXACUM AFFINE

FELICIA AMELLOIDES

FUCHSIA × HYBRIDA

GAILLARDIA PULCHELLA

GAURA LINDHEIMERI

frigerator before sowing. Kingfisher daisy is sown at room temperature. Both take 30 days to germinate. Space plants a distance apart equal to their mature height. Plant in full sun and dry, sandy, well-drained soil. Water and fertilize sparingly. Both species do best in a cool climate.

—

Fennel flower see *Nigella*

Feverfew see *Chrysanthemum*

Firecracker plant see *Cuphea*

Fire-on-the-mountain see *Euphorbia*

Five spot see *Nemophila*

Flax see *Linum*

Fleece flower see *Polygonum*

Floss flower see *Ageratum*

Flowering maple see *Abutilon*

Flowering tobacco see *Nicotiana*

Forget-me-not see *Anchusa; Cynoglossum; Myosotis*

Fountain plant see *Amaranthus*

Four-o'clock see *Mirabilis*

Foxglove see *Digitalis*

—

Fuchsia

(FEW-sha or FEWKS-ee-ah)
Fuchsia, lady's eardrop

Fuchsias bear delicate drooping flowers shaped like hoop skirts, generally two-toned and having long, showy stamens. They are splendid in hanging baskets.

Selected species and varieties. *F. × hybrida:* blooms, usually single but sometimes double, come in shades of pink, red, white, lavender, blue, orange, yellow and fuchsia.

Growing conditions. Fuchsia plants are generally sold in baskets ready to use, but it is possible to grow them from seeds or cuttings. Sow seeds indoors six months before desired blooming time. Do not cover seeds, as they need light during the 21- to 28-day germination period. Stem cuttings may be taken at any time and rooted. Grow fuchsia in full or partial shade in rich soil with excellent drainage. Keep soil well watered and mist the plants frequently; they need high humidity and cool temperatures to perform adequately. Either work a slow-release fertilizer into the soil at planting time, or fertilize every two weeks thereafter. The plants benefit from regular pinching, which

keeps them compact. In fall, you can lift the plants from the garden, let them dry out and then store them, dormant, in a cool, dry spot for the winter. For more reliable results, however, start afresh each year with new seeds, cuttings or plants.

—

Gaillardia (gah-LAR-dee-ah)
Gaillardia, blanket flower

Showy 2½-inch flower heads on plants from 10 to 24 inches tall. Blooms have ray florets of red, bronze, butterscotch and maroon, often tipped with yellow. Use them in beds and borders and as cut flowers indoors. They are also heat- and drought-tolerant and therefore especially useful in seaside gardens.

Selected species and varieties. *G. pulchella:* plants are neat and covered with flowers until frost. Some of the flowers are double; those of newer cultivars are almost ball-shaped. 'Lollipops': a 10- to 12-inch mounded cultivar covered with ball-shaped flowers in solids and bicolors.

Growing conditions. Sow seeds outdoors where plants are to grow, after all danger of frost has passed. For earlier bloom, start with bedding plants or sow seeds indoors four to six weeks before outdoor planting date. Germination takes 15 to 20 days. Gaillardias grow as wide as they are tall, so plant them 10 to 24 inches apart, depending on the ultimate height of the species you grow. Soil should be light, sandy and well drained. These annuals are an excellent choice where hot sun beats on the garden, because they prefer full sun, heat and dry soil. Fertilize little, if at all, and to keep plants in best condition, remove flowers as they fade.

—

Garland flower see *Clarkia*

—

Gaura (GAW-rah)

A perennial often grown as an annual. Flowers may be white, pink or yellow; plants reach 3 to 5 feet in height and width. Gaura look best in an informal border or a wildflower garden.

Selected species and varieties. *G. lindheimeri* has loose, informal 1-inch flowers with four petals and prominent stamens. Blooms are white, darkening to rose as they age.

Growing conditions. Seeds may be sown outdoors after all danger of frost has passed, or started indoors four to six weeks before the last frost. Germination takes 15 to 20 days. Space plants 2 feet apart; water and fertilize sparingly. Gaura does best in hot climates and is easy to grow in full sun and average, well-drained soil.

—

Gazania (ga-ZANE-ee-ah)

A showy member of the daisy family, native to South Africa. Gazania is a tender perennial grown as an annual, and can be used as edging, bedding and ground cover, as well as in containers. The flowers, however, close up at night and on cloudy days.

Selected species and varieties. *G. rigens,* treasure flower: blooms have an interesting combination of stripes and contrasting centers along with solid colors. Flower heads are single and daisy-like, with ray florets of yellow, gold, orange, cream, pink or red. Some centers are yellow, others dark. The 8- to 10-inch stems rise above 6- to 9-inch dark green basal leaves with felty white or silver undersides. 'Chansonette': grows to 10 inches high, has 2½-inch flowers in bright shades of rose, bronze, salmon, red, orange and yellow with contrasting rings or dark centers; a very free-flowering early-blooming cultivar. Daybreak series cultivars are available in bright orange and yellow, and mixtures of those colors together with bronze, pink and white. Flowers bloom early in the season and also open earlier in the day than most varieties. Mini Star series has cultivars with white, tangerine, yellow and a mixture; the 3-inch flowers, some with contrasting rings, are borne on 8-inch plants. 'Sunshine': plants that bear giant 5-inch flowers in shades of chestnut, bronze, brown, ruby, gold, salmon, red, orange or yellow.

Growing conditions. Start seeds indoors four to six weeks before the last expected frost and transfer the seedlings to the garden when frost danger has passed. You can also use purchased bedding plants, or sow seeds outdoors where they are to grow, after the last frost date. Cover seeds, as they need darkness during the eight- to 14-day germination period. Space plants 8 to 10 inches apart in full sun and a light, sandy soil. Fertilize with 5-10-5 before planting. Gazanias do best where summer temperatures are high; they also tolerate drought. To keep plants tidy and encourage blooming, cut flowers as they fade. Gazanias can be dug out

of the garden in late summer, potted up and brought indoors for several more months of color. Inside, give them full sun and sparse watering.

—

Geranium see *Pelargonium*

—

Gerbera (JER-ber-ah)

A slow-growing plant that is a perennial in the warm areas of its native South Africa and Asia, but an annual in most parts of the United States. Use it in beds, borders and containers and for cut flowers; blooms can last two weeks.

Selected species and varieties. *G. jamesonii,* Transvaal daisy: bears one daisy-like flower head, up to 5 inches across, on each leafless stem and comes in orange, red, pink, yellow, white, salmon or lavender. Foliage, dark green and deeply lobed, with white woolly undersides, hugs the ground. 'Double Parade Mix' bears 4½-inch double flowers on dwarf plants 6 to 7 inches high; the blossoms are yellow, cream, red, pink, plum or salmon, or red-and-yellow bicolor. 'Happipot' is best in containers, but it is also good for beds and borders. Plants grow to 12 inches in height, with 4-inch flowers of red, rose, pink, salmon, orange, yellow or cream.

Growing conditions. Start seeds indoors 20 weeks before the last expected frost date. Or purchase plants in spring for use outdoors in summer. Plants will bloom for about two months. Gerberas are also good flowering houseplants in winter, and can be lifted from the garden in autumn for wintering indoors. Seeds are short-lived; sow them as soon as possible after purchase. When sowing, place the pointed end of the seed down. Do not cover the seeds completely as they need light to germinate, which takes 15 to 25 days. Space plants 12 to 15 inches apart in full sun and a moist, very rich, slightly acid soil. Make sure the crowns are not planted below soil level. For best results, incorporate large amounts of peat moss or other organic matter into the soil before planting. Fertilize with 5-10-5 before planting and again monthly during growth and flowering. To keep the plants healthy and blooming heavily, remove all faded flowers.

—

German violet see *Exacum*

GAZANIA RIGENS 'SUNSHINE'

GERBERA JAMESONII

GILIA CAPITATA

GLAUCIUM FLAVUM

GOMPHRENA HAAGEANA

GYPSOPHILA ELEGANS 'COVENT GARDEN'

Gilia (JIL-ee-ah)

A group of plants native to California, Oregon and Washington, with blue, yellow, pink or white flowers that generally grow in clusters.

Selected species and varieties. *G. capitata,* globe gilia, Queen Anne's thimble: tiny five-petaled light blue flowers in fluffy, ball-shaped heads above 4-inch lobed leaves. Plants grow to 3 feet and are suitable for borders, for wildflower gardens and for cutting.

Growing conditions. Gilia seedlings do not transplant well, so sow seeds outdoors in early spring where the plants are to grow, as soon as the soil can be worked. Plant in full sun and a light, sandy, well-drained soil. In areas with mild winters, seeds may be sown in fall for spring bloom. Germination takes 10 to 20 days. Thin the seedlings to 10 to 15 inches apart. Water heavily. Fertilize prior to sowing and repeat monthly. Gilia does best in cool climates.

—

Glaucium (GLAW-see-um)
Horned poppy

Horned poppies are grown for their single 2-inch showy flowers. Blooms are red, yellow or orange; many have dark spots at the bases of the four petals. Plants have leafless stems, finely cut basal foliage and large, bristly seedpods. Use in borders.

Selected species and varieties. *G. corniculatum:* grows 18 inches tall, has red or orange flowers spotted at the base with black. *G. flavum,* a biennial grown as an annual, bears golden yellow flowers on a 3-foot plant; has foot-long seedpods.

Growing conditions. Sow seeds outdoors in early spring where plants are to grow. Where winters are mild, sow seeds in fall for bloom the following spring. Germination takes 15 to 20 days. Grow in full sun and a dry, sandy, well-drained soil, spacing the plants a distance apart equal to half their mature height. Fertilize little if at all and water sparingly.

—

Globe amaranth see *Gomphrena*
Gloriosa daisy see *Rudbeckia*
Godetia see *Clarkia*

—

Gomphrena (gom-FREE-nah)

A genus of about 100 tropical plants having dense, chaffy heads. Use in massed plantings and borders, and for cut flowers and dried flowers.

Selected species and varieties. *G. globosa,* globe amaranth: bears round, mounded, papery, clover-like 1-inch flower heads; grows 30 inches tall. Blooms come in a range of colors, from purple through lavender, rose, pink, orange, yellow and white. *G. haageana*: has red bracts and yellow flowers.

Growing conditions. For earliest bloom, start with bedding plants, or use seedlings started from seed sown indoors six to eight weeks before the last frost date. Germination takes 15 to 20 days. To speed germination, soak the seeds in water three to four days before sowing; then cover the sown seeds well, as they need darkness to germinate. Set plants in the garden 10 to 15 inches apart, after all danger of frost has passed. Seeds also can be sown outside, after the last frost date. Gomphrena likes full sun and tolerates drought and heat. Soil should be sandy, light and well drained. Water lightly and feed monthly with 5-10-5 fertilizer. To dry, cut flowers before they are fully open and hang them upside down in a dry, cool, airy spot.

—

Gypsophila (jip-SOF-ih-lah)

A genus of 125 plants, mostly Eurasian, bearing profusions of small pink or white flowers.

Selected species and varieties. *G. elegans,* baby's breath: has a delicate, airy, light appearance. Multi-branched, mound-shaped plants grow 15 to 18 inches tall. Their thin stems are covered with clouds of tiny white, pink or red flowers. Although baby's breath is usually grown for use as a dainty filler in fresh and dried flower bouquets, it can be used in the rock garden, beds, borders or rock walls. 'Covent Garden' is the largest flowered white annual baby's breath. 'Rosen' has deep pink flowers. 'Shell Pink' has light pink flowers.

Growing conditions. Sow seeds outdoors where plants are to grow in early spring as soon as the soil can be worked. Or start plants indoors from seed four to six weeks before planting outside; germination takes 10 to 15 days. For best effect and for a continuous supply of flowers, sow seeds every two weeks from early spring to early summer. Space plants 18 inches apart in a loose, well-drained alkaline soil. If liming is necessary, take care not to get lime on the plants. Avoid overwatering, and allow the soil to dry out between waterings. Full sun is a must. Fertilize with 5-10-5 before planting and again monthly during the growing season. To dry, pick when the flowers are fully open and dry upside down in a cool, dark, dry area.

Helianthus (heel-ee-AN-thus)
Sunflower

Large, coarse, hairy, somewhat sticky leaves on stalks topped with very large flower heads. Traditional sunflowers are yellow, but newer cultivars have yellow-orange, white or bronze ray florets and dark red, purple, yellow or brown centers; some bear double flowers. Traditional sunflowers reach 4 to 12 feet, but modern dwarf forms grow to only 15 inches. Very attractive to birds. Easy to grow, good for cutting, fun for young gardeners because it grows so fast they will see results soon.

Selected species and varieties. *H. annuus,* common sunflower: grows 12 feet high; flowers, in white, yellows, oranges, browns and bi-colored, may be 1 foot or more across. 'Italian White' has 4-inch cream-colored ray florets with a ring of yellow around a black center on a 4-foot plant. 'Sunburst Mixed': deep crimson, lemon, bronze or gold 4-inch blooms on a 4-foot plant. 'Teddy Bear': an 8- to 12-inch cultivar, bears golden yellow flower heads with hundreds of ray florets on a sturdy 2-foot plant.

Growing conditions. Sow seeds outdoors in the spring where the plants are to grow, after all danger of frost has passed. Seeds can be started indoors and will germinate in 10 to 14 days, but sunflowers grow so fast that indoor sowing is not necessary. Space plants 2 to 4 feet apart in full sun and a light, dry, well-drained soil. Fertilize sparingly, keeping soil fertility low. Do not overwater. Sunflowers thrive in hot temperatures. Taller cultivars require staking.

Helichrysum (hel-ee-CRY-sum)
Helichrysum, everlasting

More than 300 species of plants having stiff, papery bracts that hold their color long after drying.

Selected species and varieties. *H. bracteatum,* strawflower: grows 12 to 30 inches tall, with narrow leaves and wiry stems. Showy flower heads, composed of colorful bracts, not petals, around centers of tiny disc florets. The bracts may be bright red, salmon, yellow, pink or white; the centers come in these colors plus purple. May be used in beds or for cut flowers, but is usually grown for drying. *H. petiolatum,* licorice plant: grown for its oval, woolly foliage; may bear 2-inch creamy white flower heads, but seldom blossoms.

Growing conditions. Although seeds can be sown outdoors where plants are to grow, after all danger of frost has passed, better results will be achieved by using bedding plants or by starting seeds indoors four to six weeks before planting outside. Do not cover the seeds, which need light during the seven- to 10-day germination. Space plants 9 to 15 inches apart, in full sun, in a porous, well-drained soil. Fertilize every two weeks during the growing season. Strawflower thrives where summers are hot and dry. To dry flowers, cut them just before the center petals open, strip off the foliage and hang the flowers to dry upside down in a shaded area.

Heliotrope see *Heliotropium*

Heliotropium
(he-lee-oh-TRO-pee-um)
Heliotrope

A mainly tropical or subtropical genus with more than 200 species, one of which is widely cultivated for its fragrant flowers.

Selected species and varieties. *H. arborescens:* can grow as tall as 6 feet, but generally only reaches 24 inches. Bears tiny white, dark blue or purple flowers in flat 6-inch clusters. Foliage is dark green and textured. 'Marine': bushy, compact cultivar bearing large flower heads of deep purple up to 15 inches across, over dark green foliage. Pretty as bedding plants, heliotropes are often used in pots and hanging baskets, placed where their alluring fragrance can be enjoyed. Also used to attract bees to vegetable gardens and orchards.

Growing conditions. Start with purchased plants or sow seed started indoors 10 to 12 weeks before the last frost date. Germination takes 21 to 25 days. Heliotropes are very sensitive to frost, so wait until two weeks after the last average frost date to set plants outside. Space plants 12 inches apart in full sun and a rich, well-

HELIANTHUS ANNUUS

HELICHRYSUM BRACTEATUM

HELIOTROPIUM ARBORESCENS 'MARINE'

HELIPTERUM MANGLESII

HIBISCUS MOSCHEUTOS

HUNNEMANNIA FUMARIIFOLIA

drained soil. Fertilize with 5-10-5 before planting and feed again every other month. Keep well watered. When grown in containers, heliotropes do best in light shade.

—

Helipterum (he-LIP-ter-um)
Everlasting, strawflower

As the common names of the genus suggest, helipterums are grown for their durable paper-like flowers. The blooms of these daisy-family members are dense heads of tiny yellow disc florets surrounded by showy, petal-like bracts of yellow, white or pink. Blooms are borne on long stalks above felty white leaves. Helipterums dry very well; they also make good bedding plants and good cut flowers.

Selected species and varieties. *H. manglesii,* Swan River everlasting: 18 inches tall, with long, slender stems and 1½-inch flowers of pink, silver-white or violet with golden centers. 'Maculatum' is taller and more vigorous and has pink flowers. *H. roseum,* sometimes incorrectly sold as *Acrolinium roseum,* is a branching 24-inch plant with 2-inch single or double daisy-like flowers of pink, salmon, apricot or white.

Growing conditions. Everlasting seed may be sown outdoors where plants are to grow, after frost danger has passed. However, for best results, use purchased bedding plants or start seeds indoors six to eight weeks before outdoor planting time. Germination takes 14 to 21 days. Transplant after all danger of frost has passed, working very gently, as everlastings dislike transplanting. Space plants 8 to 12 inches apart, in full sun and an average, dry, sandy soil with excellent drainage. Do not overwater. Fertilize with 5-10-5 at planting time and again every other month. To dry, cut stems before the flowers are fully opened, tie in bunches and hang with blossoms upside down in a dry, shady, well-ventilated area. In areas with long growing seasons, make several plantings at two-week intervals to lengthen the harvest period.

—

Hibiscus (hi-BIS-kus)
Hibiscus, mallow

Shrubby plants of varying heights that are filled during summer with large, usually single, five-petaled flowers, whose prominent stamens protrude in a tubular formation. Many hibiscus are perennials and some are woody shrubs; others are annuals or grown as annuals. Many are useful as hedges or accents; they bring an exotic, tropical look to the garden.

Selected species and varieties. *H. acetosella*: grown for its foliage; its stalks and leaves are red and shiny, and may be either unlobed or deeply lobed and maple-like. Grows to 5 feet, bears insignificant flowers of purple-red or yellow and is the most heat-resistant hibiscus. 'Red Shield' has vivid burgundy leaves with a metallic sheen. *H. moscheutos,* rose mallow: a perennial that can be grown as an annual. Varies in height from 18 inches to 6 feet, has downy stems and hairy leaves, and 4-inch flowers of pink, red or white; flowers in summer if started early indoors. 'Dixie Belle' grows to 24 inches tall, with 8- to 9-inch flowers of rose, red, pink and shell pink with a red eye; an early bloomer. 'Disco Belle' series cultivars are available in white, rosy red and a mixture, with all flowers having dark red eyes. Plants grow to 20 inches; flowers are 10 inches across. 'Southern Belle' grows 4 to 6 feet, with 10-inch flowers of red, rose, pink, pink-and-white, and white with a red eye. *H. trionum,* flower-of-an-hour: an annual that grows to 4 feet, with 1½-inch flowers of white, cream or yellow with a red base.

Growing conditions. Annual hibiscus seeds may be sown outdoors where they are to grow, after all danger of frost has passed, or sown indoors six to eight weeks before the outside planting date. The seeds are hard-coated; score each one with a knife or scissors before planting, or soak them all in water. They will sink when they are ready for planting. Germination takes 15 to 30 days. Set seedlings or purchased bedding plants into the garden after frost danger is past. To grow perennial hibiscus as an annual, buy bedding plants, or start seeds indoors three months before the outside planting date for mid- to late-summer bloom. Space dwarf hibiscus a distance apart equal to their ultimate height, as they are very bushy plants. Taller hibiscus should be planted a distance apart equal to about two-thirds of their ultimate height; for example, hibiscus that will grow to 6 feet should be planted 4 feet apart. Hibiscus like full sun or light shade and a rich, well-drained, moist soil. Plants tolerate heat in summer as long as they are kept well watered. Native to swampy areas, they do well in wet spots. Fertilize with 5-10-5 before planting; no further feeding will be necessary.

Where winter temperatures drop below 20° F, protect perennial hibiscus with a 6-inch mulch of straw if you wish to keep it over the winter.

—

Hollyhock see *Alcea*
Honesty see *Lunaria*
Horn-of-plenty see *Datura*
Horned poppy see *Glaucium*

—

Hunnemannia
(hun-nee-MAN-ee-ah)
Mexican tulip poppy

A member of the poppy family that is native to Mexico.

Selected species and varieties. *H. fumariifolia,* Mexican tulip poppy: a tender perennial grown as an annual. Flowers are 3 inches across, yellow and have ruffled edges. Leaves are bluish green, finely divided and fernlike. Plants reach 2 feet in height. Can be used in flower borders and also for cutting. 'Sunlight' has canary yellow, semidouble flowers.

Growing conditions. Sow seeds outdoors where plants are to grow, after all danger of frost has passed; or start seeds indoors four to six weeks before the outside planting date. Germination takes 15 to 20 days. Mexican tulip poppy dislikes transplanting, so grow it in individual peat pots to lessen transplanting shock. Set plants 9 to 12 inches apart in a warm location and full sun. Soil should be light, dry, well drained and slightly alkaline. Do not overwater; Mexican tulip poppy is quite drought-resistant. Feed lightly if at all.

—

Iberis
(eye-BEER-iss)
Candytuft

Annual candytufts, like their perennial cousins, generally bear flat-topped clusters of four-petaled flowers in white, pink, red or lilac; leaves are narrow and dark green. Excellent for borders, edgings and rock gardens.

Selected species and varieties. *I. amara,* rocket candytuft: grows 18 to 20 inches tall, bears large, upright, cone-shaped spikes of fragrant, glistening white flowers. Grown as a florists' crop; excellent as a cut flower. Coarsely toothed leaves are 3 to 4 inches long. *I. pinnata* grows 12 inches tall and has fragrant, white to lilac flowers. *I. umbellata,* globe can-

dytuft: mound-shaped, 8 to 10 inches tall, with uniform flowers of pink, crimson, rose, carmine, lavender or white and no fragrance; leaves are 2 to 3 inches long and narrow.

Growing conditions. Sow seeds outdoors where plants are to grow, after all danger of frost has passed. For earlier bloom, purchase bedding plants or start seeds indoors six to eight weeks before the last frost date. Germination takes 10 to 15 days. Space plants 6 to 10 inches apart in full sun and an average, well-drained garden soil. Fertilize with 5-10-5 before planting, and water when dry. Candytuft does best in cool climates. Shear faded blooms to encourage further flowering.

—

Iceland poppy see *Papaver*
Ice plant see *Mesembryanthemum*
Immortelle see *Xeranthemum*

—

Impatiens
(im-PAY-shens)
Balsam, jewelweed

Showy plants, primarily from the African and Asian tropics, bearing bright, spurred flowers in their leaf axils. Flowers come in shades of pink, red, purple, lavender, yellow and white, and may be single or double. Except for one group grown for its brightly variegated foliage, impatiens have simple green leaves. Especially valuable for their tolerance of shade. Use them in beds, borders or planters.

Selected species and varieties. *I. balsamina,* garden balsam: a favorite in Victorian gardens; bears waxy blooms close to the stem. Flowers can be single but most are double; some new cultivars have double blooms resembling camellias. Flowers come in white, pink, red, purple, lavender, salmon or yellow, sometimes solid colors, sometimes spotted. Plants grow 10 to 36 inches tall and have toothed, pointed, 6-inch leaves. 'Tom Thumb' is a drought-tolerant compact cultivar 10 to 12 inches tall, with ruffled flowers at the top of the plant.

I. × 'New Guinea': a special strain discovered in the 1970s by botanists visiting New Guinea and brought back to the United States; many cultivars have been developed from it. Grown not so much for its flowers as for its showy, often red-veined leaves of maroon or of variegated green, yellow and cream. Plants grow 12 to 24

IBERIS UMBELLATA

IMPATIENS BALSAMINA

IMPATIENS × 'NEW GUINEA'

109

IMPATIENS WALLERANA

IPOMOEA TRICOLOR 'HEAVENLY BLUE'

IPOMOPSIS RUBRA

inches high and bloom moderately, with flowers resembling those of garden impatiens in lavender, orange, pink, red, salmon and purple. The Sunshine series cultivars have large flowers and compact plants, most with variegated foliage. 'Sweet Sue', the first New Guinea impatiens that can be grown from seed, bears flaming orange flowers 2 to 3 inches across; its foliage is lance-shaped and deep green and has a touch of bronze.

I. wallerana, garden impatiens, busy Lizzie, patience plant: one of the most popular annuals, beloved for its rainbow of colors, variety of sizes, nonstop bloom from spring to frost, easy care, shade tolerance, uniform habit and dependability. Varieties of garden impatiens range from short ground covers to tall, mounded plants reaching 18 inches. Most flowers are flat, 1 to 2 inches across, five-petaled and single, although there are double-flowered cultivars. Flower colors divide into seven shades: pink, white, salmon, orange, scarlet, red and violet. There are also bicolors, with white, starlike centers. 'Accent': at 6 to 8 inches, a flat-growing, ground-hugging plant with early-blooming flowers 2 inches across. 'Blitz': the largest flowering impatiens, with 2½-inch blooms on a 12- to 18-inch plant. Very tolerant of heat and sun, excellent for containers. 'Duet' blooms are 25 percent double, the rest semidouble, in bicolors of red, orange, scarlet or deep rose with white. Flowers are 1¼ inches across on 10- to 12-inch plants.

This is only a small sampling of the wide variety of garden impatiens cultivars available; new ones are introduced every year. To select the best plants for your garden, consider height, recommended use, heat- and sun-tolerance, flower color and bloom type, and consult a garden center or the latest seed catalogs.

Growing conditions. All impatiens are planted outside in spring after all danger of frost has passed. Either grow your own seedlings indoors, or use purchased bedding plants. Do not sow garden impatiens seeds outdoors; start them indoors 10 to 14 weeks before outdoor planting and expect germination to take 14 days. Balsam seeds may be sown outdoors where plants are to grow, after all danger of frost has passed, or started indoors six to eight weeks before the outdoor planting date; germination takes eight to 14 days. All New Guinea impatiens (except 'Sweet Sue') are propagated by stem cuttings in a mixture of peat moss and perlite. Start seeds of 'Sweet Sue'

New Guinea impatiens indoors 12 to 16 weeks before the last frost. Temperatures must be very warm during the 14- to 28-day germination period. Normally, only about half of the seeds will germinate, so sow more heavily than usual.

Space plants 6 to 15 inches apart, depending on their ultimate height. Plant balsam in full sun or part shade in a rich, well-drained soil. Fertilize with 5-10-5 before planting and again monthly. Balsam loves heat and should be watered heavily. Plant New Guinea impatiens in partial to full sun and a very rich, well-drained soil. Keep well watered; dryness causes plant stress and may produce leaf burn and defoliation. Mulch plants at planting time; they need cool soil for best growth. Fertilize at planting time with 5-10-5 and again every other month during the season. Over-fertilizing will discourage flowering.

Garden impatiens will perform well in a wide range of temperatures including high heat, especially when the humidity is high. Soil should be rich in organic matter to retain moisture, and fertilized lightly with 5-10-5 before planting. Feed garden impatiens only sparingly; if overfed, they stop blooming. Water all impatiens when the ground starts to become dry. In extreme heat or sun, impatiens foliage will wilt during the day, but this does not necessarily mean the plants need watering. If the foliage perks up when the sun goes down, do not water. If the foliage stays limp or starts to turn yellow, more water is necessary. A mulch will help retain water and keep the ground cool. Although impatiens is known as a shade plant, thriving in anything from four hours of direct light to all-day dappled light, it can be grown in part or full sun if it is heavily watered. Faded flowers fall cleanly, so impatiens plants do not require deadheading.

━━

Ipomoea (ip-oh-MEE-ah)
Morning glory

A large group of fast-growing annual and perennial vines, some growing as much as 30 feet per year, with showy tubular flowers. They are excellent for covering fences, trellises or other areas where privacy is needed, and good in hanging baskets.

Selected species and varieties. *I. alba,* moonflower, moon vine: a tender perennial grown as an annual; climbs to 15 feet and has handsome, bright green, shiny leaves. Fragrant, trumpet-shaped white flowers open in the evening. *I. coccinea,* red morning glory or star ipomoea: has 1½-inch scarlet flowers with yellow throats; vines grow to 10 feet. *I. × multifida,* cardinal climber: grows fast to 30 feet, with finely cut foliage and 2-inch tubular red flowers. *I. quamoclit,* cypress vine: reaches 25 feet, with threadlike leaves and 1½-inch red, pink or white flowers. *I. nil, I. purpurea* and *I. tricolor:* three species of common morning glory. All grow to 10 feet, with heart-shaped leaves and tubular single or double flowers. Colors include blue, purple, pink, red and white; flowers open in the morning and fade by afternoon, to be replaced by others the next day. Blooms are solid-colored, striped, bicolored or tricolored. *I. tricolor* 'Heavenly Blue' has intense blue flowers with lighter blue centers. *I. leptophylla,* bush moonflower, man-of-the-earth: a morning glory that does not climb, but produces a 3-foot bush with 3-inch flowers of rosy pink deepening to purple.

Growing conditions. To sow indoors, plant seeds four to six weeks before the last frost date; for best results, start them in individual pots. Germination takes only five to seven days; to hasten germination, nick the hard seed coats with a file or a tiny pair of scissors before sowing, or soak the seeds in water for 24 hours. Transplant gently, so as not to disturb roots. To plant seeds directly outdoors, wait until all danger of frost has passed, and set seeds 12 to 18 inches apart in full sun and a sandy, light, well-drained soil. Too-rich soil will produce all vine and no flowers. Water very moderately, and provide a trellis or other support for all but the bush types. Some tying may be necessary, as not all morning glories are natural climbers.

Ipomopsis (ip-oh-MOP-sis)

Flowers are very long, tubular and slim, opening into five-pointed stars at the tips. Plants grow 2 to 6 feet tall and are clothed in dainty, feathery foliage. Most ipomopsis are biennials, but two species can be grown as annuals if started early enough.

Selected species and varieties. *I. aggregata,* skyrocket: has flowers of red, yellow, pink or white on 24-inch plants; used in beds or in the middle of a border. *I. rubra,* standing cypress: flowers are scarlet outside, with red dots on a creamy yellow inside. Can grow to 6 feet and is used as an accent plant, in hedges or in the back of a border.

Growing conditions. Sow seeds outdoors in early spring as soon as soil can be worked, or in late summer for growth the following spring. Germination takes 10 to 15 days. Seeds may be started indoors, but must be kept at 65° F or below during germination, and seedlings do not transplant well. Set plants 12 to 24 inches apart in full sun and a dry, light, well-drained soil. Water and fertilize sparingly. Taller plants may need to be staked.

Iresine (eye-res-EYE-nee)
Iresine, bloodleaf

Primarily grown for its ornamental foliage, but sometimes bears clusters of tiny flowers.

Selected species and varieties. *I. herbstii,* chicken gizzard: a tender perennial used as an annual bedding plant. Has blood-red foliage, some with purple tinge and prominent veining; seldom flowers. 'Aureo-reticulata' has green or greenish red leaves with yelow veins. Used in borders, as an edging plant and especially in designs.

Growing conditions. Bloodleaf is grown from cuttings, since foliage color does not come true from seeds. Bedding plants can be purchased. To grow your own plants, take stem cuttings in late winter and root them in a mixture of perlite and peat moss. Transfer the rooted cuttings outside after all danger of frost has passed. Set the plants 12 to 15 inches apart in a warm location with full sun and an average garden soil. Water them well; iresine thrives in soil too wet for many other plants. Fertilize with 5-10-5 at planting time; no further feeding is needed.

Johnny-jump-up see *Viola*

Joseph's-coat see *Alternanthera; Amaranthus*

Kingfisher daisy see *Felicia*

Kiss-me-over-the-garden-gate see *Polygonum*

Knotweed see *Polygonum*

Kochia (KOE-kee-ah)

A genus of 80 species, all having narrow leaves and insignificant flowers. Used as a hedge or garden novelty. However, the blooms are thought to cause hay fever.

IRESINE HERBSTII 'AUREO-RETICULATA'

KOCHIA SCOPARIA TRICHOPHYLLA

LANTANA CAMARA

LATHYRUS ODORATUS

LAVATERA TRIMESTRIS

Selected species and varieties. *K. scoparia trichophylla,* summer cypress, burning bush: a globe-shaped, 3-foot plant with dense, narrow, feathery leaves and greenish flowers that are all but invisible. Looks like a conifer from a distance; in early autumn, however, it turns a bright cherry red and becomes a real attraction.

Growing conditions. Start from bedding plants or seeds. Sow seeds outdoors after all danger of frost has passed, where plants are to bloom. To start seeds indoors, sow them in individual peat pots four to six weeks before the outdoor planting date. Do not cover seeds; they need light during the 10- to 15-day germination period. Space kochia plants 18 to 24 inches apart in full sun and a dry soil with excellent drainage. Hot weather is preferred; in fact, the plant is slow to develop when weather is cool. Shear to keep plants symmetrical. Fertilize with 5-10-5 before planting and monthly thereafter. Seeds drop easily and sprout quickly, which can be something of a nuisance. Keep well weeded.

Lantana (lan-TAN-ah)
Lantana, shrub verbena

Subtropical or tropical shrubs or perennials grown for their dense, 2-inch clusters of tiny flowers. Foliage is gray-green; flower colors include pink, yellow, orange and red, changing as flowers age. Grown as perennials in the South, and used in the North as annuals or greenhouse plants. Good as bedding, border or container plants, small hedges or ground covers.

Selected species and varieties. *L. camara,* common lantana, yellow sage: the most popular species for garden use. As a perennial shrub in frost-free areas, it can grow to 4 feet tall; used as an annual, it grows to 2 feet. Flowers open orange-yellow and change to red or white as they age. 'Alba' has white flowers; other cultivars are available in many colors. *L. montevidensis,* weeping lantana: trailing, vinelike stems reach 3 feet and bear pink or lilac blooms.

Growing conditions. For best results, look for bedding plants; these have been propagated from either cuttings or seeds. You can start your own seeds, but sow 12 weeks before the last frost date and be prepared for a six-week germination period. Or take stem cuttings in the fall, to be rooted and grown over win-ter for use the following summer. Plant seedlings outside after all danger of frost has passed. Lantanas prefer warm weather, so do not set out until the weather is consistently warm. For bedding-plant use, space lantana 12 to 15 inches apart in full sun and a rich, loamy, well-drained soil. Fertilize with 5-10-5 prior to planting, and feed again regularly. Water lightly, as dry soil is preferred. Lantana takes well to pruning and can be shaped extensively. Container-grown plants can be brought indoors for the winter and then set out again in the spring. Weeping lantana makes a good seashore plant because it roots easily and helps control erosion.

Larkspur see *Consolida*

Lathyrus (LATH-ih-rus)

A group of more than 100 species belonging to the pea family. Most are vinelike and bear tendrils.

Selected species and varieties. *L. odoratus,* sweet pea: may be either tendril-bearing vines that climb to 6 feet, or bushy dwarf plants reaching 2½ feet. The pealike, 2-inch flowers of this old-fashioned garden favorite are deliciously fragrant and come in purple, rose, red, white, pink and blue; solid or bicolored. 'Bijou Mixed' has large ruffled flowers on dwarf, 16-inch plants. 'Royal Family': 6-foot heat-resistant vines bear large flowers that make excellent cut flowers. 'Supersnoop' is an early-flowering dwarf strain with a long blooming season; very bushy 2-foot plants.

Growing conditions. Sow seeds outdoors in early spring as soon as the soil can be worked; in mild areas, sow seeds in fall for early color the following spring. Even for spring sowing, prepare the seedbed the previous fall. Soil should be deeply prepared, rich in organic matter and slightly alkaline. Before sowing seeds, soak them in water for 24 hours, or file the hard seed coat, to shorten germination time to 10 to 14 days. Cover seeds completely; they need darkness to germinate. Seeds can also be started indoors four to six weeks before outdoor planting; sow in individual peat pots, because sweet peas don't like to be transplanted. Be sure to harden seedlings off by gradually exposing them to cool spring air before transplanting outdoors. Plant dwarf sweet peas 15 inches apart;

vining types should be planted 6 to 8 inches apart. Sweet peas do best where it's cool, and will not tolerate drying winds. Provide a trellis or other support for the climbers, and give both types full sun. Feed with 5-10-5 when planting and feed again monthly during the growing season. Water heavily, and mulch to keep soil cool and damp. Keep faded flowers picked to prolong flowering.

Lavatera (Lav-ah-TER-ah)
Lavatera, tree mallow

Grown for their cuplike, 2½- to 3-inch blooms, which form in the upper leaf axils and resemble the hollyhock's. Flowers come in pink, red or white; the dark green, serrated leaves often turn bronze in cool weather. Reaching 2 to 10 feet, the hairy-stemmed plants work well in borders, hedges, backgrounds and screens.

Selected species and varieties. *L. arborea,* tree mallow: purple-red flowers with dark veins on a shrubby plant that grows to 10 feet. A biennial that sometimes blooms the first year when grown as an annual. *L. trimestris,* herb tree mallow: a true annual; grows 2 to 3 feet tall, with 4-inch white, pink or red flowers. The cultivars 'Mont Blanc' and 'Mont Rose' are white and rose-colored respectively.

Growing conditions. Although lavatera seeds can be started indoors six to eight weeks before planting outside, seedlings are hard to transplant, so outdoor sowing is preferred. Sow seeds of herb tree mallow outdoors in early spring as soon as the soil can be worked, where plants are to grow. Sow seeds of tree mallow in late summer for bloom the following year, or sow indoors in late winter and transplant after frost, for bloom the first year. Germination takes 15 to 20 days. Space plants 15 to 24 inches apart, in full sun, in average, well-drained soil. Fertilize with 5-10-5 before planting and feed monthly thereafter. Do not overwater tree mallows, which prefer a slightly dry soil. To prolong bloom, keep faded flowers picked. Plants perform best where nights are cool.

Layia (LAY-ee-ah)

A California wildflower having flower heads that consist of eight to 20 yellow or white rays.

Selected species and varieties. *L. platyglossa,* tidy tips: 2-inch flower heads with bright yellow centers surrounded by a single row of yellow ray florets edged with white. Plant grows in a solid mound 12 to 24 inches high with narrow, grasslike, grayish foliage. Fits well into beds and borders.

Growing conditions. Sow seeds outdoors where plants are to grow, in midspring, several weeks before the last frost. Or start them indoors six to eight weeks before the outside planting date. Germination takes eight to 12 days. Space plants 10 to 12 inches apart in full sun and a light, well-drained soil rich in organic matter. They will withstand light frost, both spring and fall. Fertilize with 5-10-5 at planting time, and feed again every second month during the growing season. Tidy tips prefers cool weather and a well watered soil. Mulch will improve the plants' growth by keeping the soil cool and moist. Remove flowers as they fade.

Licorice plant see *Helichrysum*

Limnanthes (lim-NAN-thees)
Meadow foam

A low-growing flower that is native to California and southern Oregon. Use it in a rock garden, as edging or at the front of a border. Prefers cool climates.

Selected species and varieties. *L. douglasii:* grown for the fragrant five-petaled, 1-inch blooms that smother the 6- to 12-inch plants. The blooms, in yellow, pink, white or yellow tipped with white, appear over deeply cut compound leaves.

Growing conditions. Seeds may be sown outdoors in early spring as soon as the soil can be worked. In areas with mild winters, sow outdoors in late fall. Space plants 4 to 6 inches apart in full sun and a rich, moist soil. This is a marsh plant and must be watered heavily. Fertilize with 5-10-5 at planting time and again during the flowering period.

Limonium (lih-MOWN-ee-um)
Statice, sea lavender

A genus of 150 species that grow on sea coasts of all seven continents.

Selected species and varieties. *L. sinuatum:* an everlasting grown for its delicate panicles of tiny, papery, funnel-shaped flowers in

LAYIA PLATYGLOSSA

LIMNANTHES DOUGLASII

LIMONIUM SINUATUM

LINARIA MAROCCANA

LINUM GRANDIFLORUM

LOBELIA ERINUS

shades of purple, blue, yellow, red or white. Plants grow to 30 inches tall on winged stems. A biennial grown as an annual, the plant makes an attractive temporary hedge as well as excellent dried or cut flowers.

Growing conditions. Sow seeds outdoors where plants are to bloom, after all danger of frost has passed. Or sow seeds indoors, using peat pots to minimize the shock of transplantation, eight to 10 weeks before the last frost date. Germination takes 15 to 20 days. Move seedlings or purchased bedding plants to the garden after danger of frost has passed. Space the plants 18 to 24 inches apart in full sun and a sandy, light, well-drained soil. Statice tolerates drought, high temperatures and salt spray. Fertilize at planting time with 5-10-5, and water moderately. To dry, cut when flowers are fully open and hang in bunches in a cool and dry area.

—

Linaria (lih-NARE-ee-ah)

A member of the snapdragon family that grows in northern temperate climates. It may be used in borders, edgings, beds or rock gardens, and for cut flowers.

Selected species and varieties. *L. maroccana,* Morocco toadflax: flowers of yellow, blue, lavender, pink, red, salmon and white, many with a yellow spot on the lower lip. Blooms are tiny, about ½ inch across. The 8- to 12-inch mounded plants have hairy foliage.

Growing conditions. Sow seeds outdoors where the plants are to grow, in late winter or very early spring. These direct-sown seedlings will be very small; when weeding the garden be careful not to disturb them. In areas with a mild climate, sow seeds in autumn for bloom the following spring. If you start your own seedlings indoors, sow them in a cool (60° F) room four to six weeks before outside planting time. Germination takes 10 to 15 days. Move plants to the garden in early spring, just as soon as the soil can be worked. Space them 6 to 10 inches apart in a rich, sandy, well-drained soil, in full sun to light shade. Water moderately, and mulch to keep the soil moist and cool. Linaria does best where summers are cool; in hot areas, grow it as a spring annual to complement bulbs and other early flowers. Fertilize with 5-10-5 before planting and again every other month during the growing season.

Linum (LY-num)
Flax

Two species of flax are grown for their delicate, single, blue or red flowers, which may last only one day but are quickly replaced by others. Flax is well suited for mass plantings or for the rock garden.

Selected species and varieties. *L. grandiflorum,* flowering flax: 2-foot plants bear 1½-inch flowers in colors ranging from bluish purple to scarlet to rose pink. *L. usitatissimum:* 4-foot plants bearing ½-inch flowers of blue or sometimes white. Its seeds yield linseed oil; its stems, linen thread.

Growing conditions. Sow seeds in clumps outdoors in early spring, where plants are to bloom. Where winters are mild, seeds may be sown outdoors in fall for spring bloom. Germination takes 10 to 12 days. Flax does not transplant well, and so should not be started indoors. Space plants 12 to 24 inches apart in full sun and a light, well-drained soil. Fertilize with 5-10-5 at planting time and again each month during the blooming season; water sparingly. Flax does best in cool climates.

—

Lisianthus see *Eustoma*
Livingstone daisy
see *Dorotheanthus*

—

Lobelia (loe-BEE-lee-ah)

An alternate-leaved plant that has conspicuous spires of brightly colored flowers.

Selected species and varieties. *L. erinus:* ½-inch flowers are blue or violet with yellow or white throats. Plants grow only 3 to 8 inches tall and spread to 10 inches across. Use for edgings, borders, ground covers, rock gardens and containers. 'Blue Moon', an early-blooming, heat-tolerant cultivar, bears bright blue flowers with green foliage. Cascade series cultivars are ideal trailing plants for containers; flowers come in shades of blue, red, ruby, white, purple and lilac. 'Crystal Palace' is the most popular lobelia, with eye-catching dark blue flowers and bronze leaves. 'White Lady' has sparkling snow white flowers.

Growing conditions. Ten to 12 weeks before the last frost, sow seeds indoors in vermiculite, and do not cover them. Provide a warm (75° F) environment during germination, which takes 15 to 20 days, and water only from the bottom, as the species is vulnerable to damping off. You may prefer to use purchased bedding plants. Transfer plants to the garden after the last frost date; space them 8 to 10 inches apart in full sun or part shade in a rich, well-drained soil. Lobelias do best where summers are cool; in warm areas, keep them out of full sun. Fertilize with 5-10-5 before planting, and keep moist during the growing season. If plants get leggy, cut them back to encourage compact growth and heavier bloom. Flowers fall cleanly as they fade.

Lobularia (lob-you-LAIR-ee-ah)

A genus of plants native to the Mediterranean; most have white flowers. Used for borders, edgings or containers, especially where their fragrance can be appreciated.

Selected species and varieties. *L. maritima,* sweet alyssum: domed clusters of tiny, sweetly scented flowers of white, rose, lavender or purple, covering 3- to 4-inch plants that spread to 12 inches. Foliage is linear, almost needle-like. A perennial that is usually grown as a hardy annual, sweet alyssum reseeds itself readily. 'Carpet of Snow' is a very uniform cultivar with pure white flowers. 'Rosie O'Day': more heat-resistant than others, bears an abundance of nonfading, rose pink blooms. 'Royal Carpet': slightly taller than others; bears flowers in clusters that are deep violet at the edges and lighter toward the center. 'Snow Cloth': similar to 'Carpet of Snow' but earlier to flower, more compact, bears more flowers. 'Wonderland' is an early-blooming mixture of compact plants with cherry-rose, purple and white flowers.

Growing conditions. Sow seeds outdoors several weeks before the last expected frost. Or start seeds indoors four to six weeks before the last frost date. Do not cover seeds, as they need light for germination, which takes eight to 15 days. You may prefer to purchase bedding plants. Sweet alyssum seedlings are particularly prone to damping-off, so do not overmoisten the soil. Move plants into the garden after the last spring frost; only small plants transplant well. Space plants 10 to 12 inches apart, in full sun or partial shade and an average, well-drained soil. Fertilize with 5-10-5 before planting. Sweet alyssum tolerates drought but prefers to be kept moist. It prefers cool weather. While sweet

alyssum will grow in hot areas, it will not flower abundantly. Flowers fall cleanly as they fade. If plants become leggy, cut them back to encourage compact growth and further bloom.

Lonas (LOE-nas)

A Mediterranean plant having flat-topped flower heads. It adds brightness to a rock garden or border, and tolerates wind and salt spray; lonas is thus a good choice for a seaside garden. It also makes excellent cut or dried flowers.

Selected species and varieties. *L. annua,* yellow ageratum, African daisy: fluffy, button-like ¼-inch flower heads of bright golden yellow, borne in dense 2-inch clusters. Flowers appear over finely cut leaves on upright, spreading plants growing 10 to 18 inches tall.

Growing conditions. Seeds can be sown outdoors where the plants are to grow, after all danger of frost has passed; but for best results start seeds indoors six to eight weeks before the last frost date. Germination takes five to seven days, and seeds should be covered completely as they need darkness to germinate. Space seedlings or purchased bedding plants 6 to 8 inches apart, in full sun and average, well-drained soil. Incorporate 5-10-5 fertilizer into the soil before planting; no further feeding will be needed. Yellow ageratums will not withstand excessive heat. Plant as early as possible, so plants can become established before hot weather. Keep yellow ageratums well watered and mulched.

Love-in-a-mist see *Nigella*
Love-lies-bleeding
see *Amaranthus*

Lunaria (Lu-NARE-ee-ah)
Money plant, honesty

An erect plant with white to purple flowers. Grown for the translucent coinlike disc of silvery membrane within its seedpod, which is revealed when seeds and husks are removed after drying.

Selected species and varieties. *L. annua,* silver dollar: bears small, fragrant, pinkish purple, four-petaled flowers on 3-foot-long stems that are clothed in coarsely toothed, heart-shaped leaves. The cultivar 'Alba' has white flowers.

LOBULARIA MARITIMA

LONAS ANNUA

LUNARIA ANNUA

115

LUPINUS TEXENSIS

LYCHNIS COELI-ROSA

MACHAERANTHERA TANACETIFOLIA

MALCOLMIA MARITIMA

Growing conditions. Sow seeds outdoors in midspring where plants are to bloom, or start them indoors four to six weeks before the last frost date. Germination takes 10 to 14 days. If growing money plant as a biennial, start seeds outdoors in midsummer. Space plants 12 to 15 inches apart in full sun or light shade, in average garden soil with excellent drainage. Feed lightly and water when dry. When seedpods have matured, cut the branches, rub the coverings off the seedpods, and hang the branches to dry in a cool, airy place. If seedpods are allowed to fall onto the ground, seeds will sprout, giving a weedy look.

Lupinus (lu-PIE-nus)
Lupine

Graceful, dense spikes of five-petaled flowers. Foliage is compound and silky. Used in massed plantings and wildflower gardens.

Selected species and varieties. *L. subcarnosus,* bluebonnet: 10-inch plants bearing ½-inch-long blue flowers, each with a contrasting white or yellow spot. *L. texensis,* Texas bluebonnet: has ¾-inch flowers of darker blue, also spotted with white or yellow, on 12-inch plants. The state flower of Texas.

Growing conditions. Seeds are best sown outdoors in early spring, where plants are to grow, because they produce a long taproot that makes them difficult to transplant. Put seeds in warm water and soak them for 24 hours or nick the hard seed coats before sowing. Germination takes 15 to 20 days. Space plants 8 to 10 inches apart in full sun and an average, well-drained, slightly alkaline soil. Fertilize little if any. Keep well watered. Texas bluebonnet blooms best in cool and humid weather; in hot areas, use it as a spring-blooming flower. Mulch to keep the soil cool.

Lychnis (LIK-nis)
Campion, catchfly

A plant with white, pink, purple or red flowers, native to a broad range of regions, from the Arctic to the Mediterranean.

Selected species and varieties. *L. coeli-rosa,* rose-of-heaven: multi-branched plants 12 to 20 inches tall, with hairy stems and threadlike leaves. The five-petaled 1-inch blooms are white, red or rose; some

have a purple eye. Use as a bedding plant or in the front of a border.

Growing conditions. Sow seeds outdoors in early spring or, for best results, start them indoors in early spring and move seedlings outside when spring bulbs are blooming. Germination takes 21 to 25 days. Space plants 6 to 10 inches apart in full sun and average, well-drained soil. Protect plants from hard freezes, and avoid overwatering; fertilize lightly. Rose-of-heaven does best in warm climates.

Machaeranthera
(mah-kee-RAN-the-rah)

A small genus of taprooted plants related to the aster and native to western North America.

Selected species and varieties. *M. tanacetifolia,* Tahoka daisy: bears 2- to 2½-inch flower heads having yellow centers surrounded by slender, pointed lavender-blue ray florets. Plants grow 12 to 24 inches high and have bristly, fernlike leaves. Use Tahoka daisy as a bedding plant or in informal massed plantings.

Growing conditions. Sow seeds outdoors in early spring as soon as the soil can be worked. To start seeds indoors, place them in moistened peat moss in the refrigerator for two or three weeks before sowing, and transplant outdoors after all danger of frost has passed. Germination takes 25 to 30 days. In mild areas, seeds may be sown outdoors in fall for spring bloom. Space plants 9 to 12 inches apart in full sun and an average, well-drained soil. Water and fertilize sparingly. Tahoka daisy does best in a cool, dry climate.

Malcolmia (mal-KOE-me-ah)
Malcolm stock

Low-growing plants with grayish foliage and small flowers.

Selected species and varieties. *M. maritima,* Virginia stock: loose clusters of sweet-scented, four-petaled ½-inch flowers in white, red-violet or lavender. The spreading 4- to 8-inch plants are weak-stemmed with small gray-green leaves that cover the ground. Good for edgings or the front of a border; plant where the scent can be enjoyed.

Growing conditions. Sow seeds outdoors in midspring where plants are to bloom. Choose a location with full sun or light shade and a well-drained, average garden soil. Barely cover the fine seeds, and fertilize before planting with 5-10-5. Germination takes 10 to 14 days. Since Virginia stock blooms briefly, make successive sowings several weeks apart for continuous bloom. Thin seedlings to 3 to 6 inches apart, and do not overwater. This species does best in a cool climate.

Mallow see *Hibiscus; Lavatera; Malva*

Malva (MAL-vah)
Mallow

Tall, bushy plants with deeply lobed leaves and clusters of white, rose or purple flowers whose ½- to 1-inch petals are notched at the tips. Used as accent plants and at the middle to back of a border.

Selected species and varieties. *M. sylvestris,* high mallow: a biennial commonly grown as an annual; bears rose to purple flowers with darker veining, and grows to 3 feet. *M. verticillata crispa,* curled mallow: grows to 6 feet, has white or purplish flowers and crisp leaves; sometimes used as a salad plant.

Growing conditions. Sow seeds outdoors in midspring, where plants are to bloom; choose a location with full sun or light shade and an average garden soil with excellent drainage. Germination takes five to 10 days. Thin seedlings to 15 to 30 inches apart. Fertilize with 5-10-5 before planting and again every other month during the growing season. Keep well watered. Mallows do best in cool climates. Since they self-sow easily, they tend to become weedy.

Manaos beauty
see *Centratherum*

Marguerite see *Chrysanthemum; Felicia*

Marigold see *Calendula; Dimorphotheca; Tagetes*

Mask flower see *Alonsoa*

Matricaria (mat-rih-KAY-re-ah)
Matricary

A genus related to chrysanthemum, with finely cut leaves and terminal flower heads.

Selected species and varieties. *M. recutita,* sweet false chamomile: a multibranched 2½-foot annual with sweet-scented foliage and daisy-like 1-inch flower heads. Disc florets are yellow; white ray florets may or may not be present. Use sweet false chamomile in beds or borders where its fragrance can be appreciated.

Growing conditions. Sow seeds outdoors in early spring, where plants are to grow. Select a location with full sun and an average, well-drained soil. Germination takes 10 to 18 days. Thin seedlings to 12 to 15 inches apart. Water when the soil becomes dry and do not fertilize.

Matthiola (ma-thee-OH-la)
Stock

Spikes of cross-shaped, single or double flowers on 12- to 18-inch plants with blue-gray foliage. Stocks make pretty bedding plants and marvelous cut flowers, but are most valued for their fragrance, which is especially strong in the evening. Set them near windows and on patios.

Selected species and varieties. *M. incana,* common stock or gillyflower: bears stiff spikes of 1-inch white, blue, purple, reddish, pink or yellowish flowers. The columnar types, such as 'Giant Excelsior', produce only one bloom spike and are grown for florists' use. The multibranching, more compact cultivars include 'Trysomic 7-Week', 'Giant Imperial', 'Midget', 'Dwarf 10-Week' and 'Beauty of Nice'. ("Seven-week" or "10-week" in the cultivar name refers to the length of time between germination and blooming.) *M. longipetala,* evening stock: its loose clusters of small lilac or pink flowers are less showy than common stock's, but at night its fragrance is pervasive. Grows 12 to 18 inches tall.

Growing conditions. Purchase bedding plants or grow your own by sowing seeds indoors six to eight weeks before you expect to move them outdoors. Do not cover the seeds, as they need light for their seven- to 10-day germination. Stocks are cool-weather plants; set them in the garden in midspring, about four weeks before the last expected frost. Seeds can also be sown outside in early spring; in mild areas, they can be sown in fall for early-spring bloom. Space stock plants 12 to 15 inches apart in full sun and a light, sandy, rich, moist soil. Fertilize with 5-10-5 prior to planting and again every month during the growing season. Keep well watered.

MALVA SYLVESTRIS

MATRICARIA RECUTITA

MATTHIOLA INCANA

117

MENTZELIA LINDLEYI

MESEMBRYANTHEMUM CRYSTALLINUM

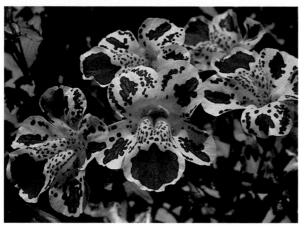
MIMULUS × HYBRIDUS

Meadow foam see *Limnanthes*

Mentzelia (ment-ZEE-lee-ah)

A genus of approximately 60 species of plants native to the desert areas of the western United States, with flowers that may be yellow, orange, red or white.

Selected species and varieties. *M. lindleyi*, blazing star: bears very fragrant, waxy, 3-inch blooms, each with five golden yellow petals. The 12- to 24-inch plants are also ornamental, with deeply divided fernlike leaves. Flowers open in the evening and last until the following noon. Use blazing star in beds or borders, especially those viewed at night.

Growing conditions. In early spring as soon as the ground can be worked, sow seeds outdoors where plants are to grow; seedlings do not transplant well. Select a location with full sun and a light, rich, sandy soil with excellent drainage. Seeds germinate in only five to 10 days. Thin plants to 8 to 10 inches apart. Keep well watered until plants bloom; then reduce watering. Fertilize at planting time with 5-10-5, and feed again every other month during the growing season.

Mesembryanthemum
(mez-em-bree-AN-the-mum)
Ice plant

A genus of low-growing succulent plants with fleshy stems and small flowers; it originally included a group now classified as *Dorotheanthus (see Dorotheanthus)*. Ice plant is excellent for the seashore, as it tolerates drought and salt spray.

Selected species and varieties. *M. crystallinum*, ice plant, sea fig, sea marigold: a prostrate plant that spreads to 2 feet across; its 1-inch white or pink flowers have spidery petals, and its fleshy leaves are covered with lumps that glisten like ice. A perennial in the warmest parts of the South and West, where it is used as a ground cover and rock-garden plant. In other areas, it is grown as an annual.

Growing conditions. Sow seeds indoors 10 to 12 weeks before the last frost. The seeds are fine and therefore should not be covered with soil; however, they need darkness to germinate, so lay a sheet of black plastic over the flat for the 15- to 20-day germination. Transplant seedlings or purchased bedding plants to the garden after danger of frost is past. Space plants 8 to 12 inches apart in full sun. Soil can be an average garden soil, but it must be dry; do not overwater. Fertilize with 5-10-5 at planting and again every other month during the growing season.

Mexican poppy see *Argemone; Hunnemannia*

Mexican sunflower see *Tithonia*

Miami-mist see *Phacelia*

Mignonette see *Reseda*

Mimulus (MIM-you-lus)
Monkey flower

A member of the snapdragon family having tubular, two-lipped flowers and narrow, glossy green foliage that is often sticky. A tender perennial usually grown as an annual. Use it in beds, borders or containers.

Selected species and varieties. *M. × hybridus:* 1- to 2-inch blooms in yellow, gold or red, often flecked with a contrasting color. Plants grow 6 to 10 inches high. Calypso series cultivars have 1½- to 2-inch flowers, in gold, clear red, or cream with dark red spots. Malibu series cultivars, more compact and freer flowering than other monkey flowers, are best for hanging baskets and containers; blooms are red, orange or yellow. Velvet series cultivars have exotic-looking 2-inch flowers; some have yellow blooms flecked with maroon, others maroon flecked with yellow.

Growing conditions. Start seeds indoors six to eight weeks before the last frost date. Light is necessary for germination, which takes seven to 14 days, so leave seeds uncovered when sowing, and use supplemental fluorescent light to provide a total of 13 hours of light each day. Plant seedlings or purchased bedding plants outdoors in spring as soon as the soil can be worked; monkey flowers tolerate frost. Space plants 6 inches apart in a rich, moist, well-drained soil in shade or part shade; they will tolerate full sun only if temperatures are cool. Keep plants well watered, especially if in the sun. Fertilize with 5-10-5 before planting, and feed again monthly. Mulch to keep the soil moist and cool.

Mirabilis (mi-RAB-ih-lis)

A genus of 60 species of tropical plants having tuberous roots. The genus is called *mirabilis,* meaning "miraculous," because flowers of several different colors appear on a single plant.

Selected species and varieties. *M. jalapa,* four-o'clock, marvel-of-Peru, beauty-of-the-night: A tender perennial grown as a tender annual; easy to grow, perfect for a child's first garden. Fragrant, trumpet-shaped 1- to 2-inch flowers in white, red, yellow, pink or violet; may be solid, mottled, striped, veined or splashed with contrasting colors. Flowers open in the afternoon and close the following morning, unless sky is overcast. Plants are heavily branched, and grow to 18 to 36 inches. Used in the back of a border or as a hedge.

Growing conditions. In mild climates, seeds can be sown outdoors where plants are to grow after all danger of frost has passed. Indoors, sow seeds four to six weeks before outside planting time; sow in peat pots to prevent transplant shock. Germination takes seven to 10 days. Space seedlings or purchased bedding plants 12 to 18 inches apart in full sun and a light, well-drained soil. Four-o'clocks tolerate poor soil and summer heat, although they will do well where temperatures are cool. Fertilize with 5-10-5 before planting and again monthly during the growing season. The fleshy roots can be dug up at the end of the growing season, stored in a cool, dry place over the winter and replanted the next spring.

—

Moluccella (mol-lew-SELL-ah)

An everlasting that is a member of the mint family, native to the Mediterranean and India. Use it in beds, for cut flowers and in dried arrangements.

Selected species and varieties. *M. laevis,* bells-of-Ireland: grown for its enlarged lime-green calyxes, the leaflike protective coverings at the base of these and most other flowers. The true flowers—white, fragrant, insignificant—appear in the centers of the calyxes, or "bells," in late summer. The 1-inch calyxes, crisp in texture and lightly veined, encircle the 2- to 3-foot stems, nearly hiding the oval, toothed 1-inch leaves.

Growing conditions. Sow seeds outdoors in early spring as soon as the soil can be worked. Do not cover the

seeds; they need light for the 25- to 35-day germination period. Seeds sown indoors should be started 8 to 10 weeks before the last frost date. Transplant after danger of hard frost is past. Space plants 12 inches apart in full sun or light shade in an average garden soil with good drainage. Water moderately, and fertilize monthly with 5-10-5 from planting until harvest. Stake plants to promote long, straight stems and prevent wind damage. Bells-of-Ireland self-sows readily; uproot unwanted seedlings as they appear.

—

Money plant see *Lunaria*
Monkey flower see *Mimulus*
Moon vine see *Ipomoea*
Morning glory see *Ipomoea*
Moss rose see *Portulaca*

—

Myosotis (my-oh-SOW-tiss)
Forget-me-not

Prostrate plants with hairy foliage and stems, and clusters of small flowers. Use forget-me-nots at the front of a border, as edging, or as ground cover to contrast with spring bulbs and early-blooming perennials.

Selected species and varieties. *M. sylvatica,* garden forget-me-not: profuse quantities of ¼-inch flowers, usually blue with a yellow eye, but may be rose, pink or white. Plants grow 6 inches high and 10 inches wide.

Growing conditions. For early-spring bloom, scatter seeds outdoors in early fall; they will germinate and bloom the following year. For fall bloom, sow seeds outdoors in early spring. Plants can be started indoors in winter for transplanting outside in early spring, but this is not an easy method, as the seeds must be kept at 55° F during the eight- to 14-day germination period. Cover them completely, as they also need darkness to germinate. Space plants 6 to 8 inches apart in a rich, very moist, well-drained soil. Grow in a cool spot with light shade. Fertilize every other month during the growing season, and keep plants well watered. Forget-me-not plants will die back in the heat of summer. They self-seed very easily, so if you want flowers to return, allow them to go to seed after they bloom.

MIRABILIS JALAPA

MOLUCCELLA LAEVIS

MYOSOTIS SYLVATICA

NEMESIA STRUMOSA

NEMOPHILA MENZIESII

NICOTIANA ALATA 'NICKI ROSE'

NIEREMBERGIA HIPPOMANICA VIOLACEA

Nasturtium see *Tropaeolum*

Nemesia (ne-MEE-see-ah)

Tubular, two-lipped flowers somewhat resembling snapdragons. They are useful in rock gardens, borders and containers.

Selected species and varieties. *N. strumosa,* pouch nemesia: 1-inch blooms of white, yellow, orange, pink, red and purple; may be solid-colored or marked with contrasting colors. Foliage is finely toothed and attractive; plants are 1½ to 2 feet tall. 'Carnival Mixed' is a dwarf cultivar 8 to 10 inches high.

Growing conditions. Must be grown where summers are cool, as plants do not tolerate high heat or humidity. Sow seeds indoors four to six weeks before the last frost date. Cover seeds completely, as they need darkness during the seven- to 14-day germination time. In the South, sow seeds outdoors where plants are to grow after all danger of frost has passed. Space plants 6 inches apart in full sun or light shade in rich, moist, well-drained soil. Pinch back when setting into the garden to induce bushiness. Fertilize with 5-10-5 at planting time, and feed again every two weeks. Keep well watered, and mulch the ground to keep roots cool and moist.

Nemophila (nee-MOF-il-ah)

A wildflower that blooms continuously through spring and summer in cool regions. Used in wildflower gardens, beds and rock gardens, and as ground cover.

Selected species and varieties. *N. maculata,* five spot: trailing plant that grows to 1 foot long and has fragrant, bell-shaped, 1¾-inch white flowers, each petal tipped with a purple spot. *N. menziesii,* baby-blue-eyes: has 1½-inch flowers, usually blue with white centers, but some solid blue and some solid white. Trailing stems with attractive, deeply cut leaves spread to fill a space 12 inches across and 6 inches high.

Growing conditions. Sow seeds outdoors in early spring as soon as the soil can be worked. In the warmest areas, seeds can be sown in fall for color the following spring. Seeds can also be started inside six weeks before the outside planting date, provided a 55° F temperature can be maintained during the seven- to 12-

day germination. Set plants 8 to 12 inches apart in full sun or, preferably, light shade. Soil should be light, sandy and well drained. Fertilize with 5-10-5 at planting time, and again every other month during the growing season. Baby-blue-eyes self-sows readily. It does best if sheltered from the wind.

Nicotiana (nih-koe-she-AN-ah)

An upright-growing plant with somewhat fuzzy, sticky foliage and fragrant, trumpet-shaped flowers.

Selected species and varieties. *N. alata,* flowering tobacco: a relative of the commercially grown tobacco plant, with loose bunches of flowers of yellow, purple, green, red, pink or white. 'Domino' is a compact cultivar that grows 10 to 14 inches tall and has early-blooming flowers of purple, pink with a white eye, red, lime green, crimson and white. Nicki series grows 16 to 18 inches tall, with pink, red, rose, white, yellow or lime green blooms.

Growing conditions. Flowering tobacco seeds can be sown outdoors where they are to grow, after all danger of frost has passed. For earlier bloom, buy bedding plants or sow seeds indoors six to eight weeks before the last frost date. Germination takes 10 to 20 days. Leave seeds uncovered; they need light to germinate. Flowering tobacco flourishes in full sun or part shade. Choose a rich, well-drained soil, fertilize with 5-10-5 before planting and space plants 10 to 12 inches apart. Plants will tolerate hot summer weather as long as the humidity is high and they are well watered. Keep them neat by cutting off dead flower stalks; new blooms will quickly replace old ones until frost. Flowering tobacco reseeds freely, so if you let the plants go to seed after blooming, they will return.

Nierembergia
(nee-ram-BER-gee-ah)
Cupflower

A summer-blooming plant with multiple branches and cup-shaped flowers of white, lilac or blue. Used in beds, borders, edgings and rock gardens. An annual in the North, a perennial in the South.

Selected species and varieties. *N. hippomanica violacea:* 1-inch yellow-centered violet blooms on mounded plants with hairy, fernlike leaves; height ranges from 6 to 15 inches. 'Purple Robe': a 6-inch cultivar that forms a dense mat; its purple-blue flowers have good heat resistance.

Growing conditions. Use purchased bedding plants, or start seeds indoors 10 to 12 weeks before the last spring frost. Germination takes 15 to 20 days. Seedlings can be moved outdoors after the last frost date, or, if they are hardened off by gradual exposure to cool spring air, two to three weeks before the last frost date. Space plants 6 to 9 inches apart in full sun to light shade in a light, moist, well-drained soil. Fertilize with 5-10-5 before planting, and feed again monthly during the growing season.

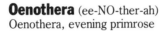

Nigella (neye-JEL-ah)
Nigella, fennel flower

A genus of about 20 species native to the Mediterranean. Leaves are feathery; flowers are mostly blue or white. The cut flowers are often used in fresh arrangements; the seedpods are used in dried arrangements.

Selected species and varieties. *N. damascena*, love-in-a-mist: grown for its blue, purple, pink, or white 1½-inch flowers, which sit atop collars of fine, threadlike foliage. Plants grow 12 to 24 inches high. 'Persian Jewels' is a sparkling mixture of white, blue, pink, red, mauve and purple blooms.

Growing conditions. Love-in-a-mist has a very short blooming period, so seeds must be sown successively outdoors every two or three weeks from early spring to early summer for continuous bloom. Seeds can be started indoors four to six weeks before transplanting outdoors, but as love-in-a-mist does not transplant well, sow in individual peat pots and transplant with care. Germination takes 10 to 15 days. Final spacing should be 8 to 10 inches apart. Plant in full sun and average garden soil with excellent drainage. Work 5-10-5 into the soil before planting and repeat monthly; keep soil moist but not too wet. Love-in-a-mist prefers cool weather and tolerates frost. In warm and hot areas, it is used as a spring and fall annual; in mild climates, seeds can be sown in fall to germinate early the following spring. To ensure development of seedpods for use in dried arrangements, leave blooms on the plant as they fade. However, if you leave pods on the plant after they mature, plants will self-sow.

Nolana (no-LAY-nah)

A plant native to the semidesert regions of Chile and Peru, with fleshy leaves and solitary flowers. A perennial grown in northern climates as a spring and early-summer annual.

Selected species and varieties. *N. napiformis*, blue bird: 2-inch flowers resembling morning glories, blue or purple with yellow-and-white centers. A dwarf, creeping plant that reaches 6 inches in height. Useful as an edging and as an annual ground cover.

Growing conditions. Seeds of blue bird germinate and grow quickly, so they can be sown outdoors where they are to grow, after all danger of frost has passed. Or, sow them indoors four to six weeks before the last frost date; germination takes seven to 10 days. Transplant carefully, to avoid disturbing the roots. Space plants 12 to 15 inches apart in full sun or light shade and an average garden soil. Water when dry, and fertilize little if at all.

Oenothera (ee-NO-ther-ah)
Oenothera, evening primrose

Showy, single flowers with four petals of golden yellow, white or pink. Many species are night-blooming. Use them in the front or middle of a border; plants look best when several are massed together.

Selected species and varieties. *O. biennis:* an evening-flowering plant with yellow to gold, 2-inch flowers above a rosette of basal leaves. A biennial that can be grown as an annual; reaches 3 to 6 feet. *O. deltoides,* desert evening primrose: an evening-flowering annual 2 to 10 inches high with 3-inch flowers that open white and turn pink as they age; leaves are often deeply cut. *O. primiveris:* an evening-flowering annual with yellow to orange 3-inch blooms and deeply cut, hairy leaves; reaches 6 to 9 inches. *O. speciosa*, white evening primrose, showy evening primrose: despite its name, a day-blooming plant; a perennial that can be grown as an annual. Plants reach 1 to 2 feet, with deeply cut leaves and 3-inch flowers that open pink or white and age to a darker pink.

Growing conditions. Sow seeds outdoors in early spring as soon as the soil can be worked, or sow indoors six to eight weeks before planting outside. Germination takes 21 to 25 days. Space plants 6 to 8 inches apart, in full sun or part shade in an

NIGELLA DAMASCENA

NOLANA NAPIFORMIS

OENOTHERA SPECIOSA

ONOPORDUM ACANTHIUM

ORTHOCARPUS PURPURASCENS

OXYPETALUM CAERULEUM

PAPAVER NUDICAULE

average, well-drained garden soil. Oenotheras are not fussy about care; they need no fertilizer and need watering only when dry. They spread quickly and can become weedy.

Onopordum (on-oh-POR-dum)

A plant with prickly, toothed or lobed leaves and flower heads that may be solitary or clustered. It is a biennial usually grown as an annual, and used at the back of a border or as a screen.

Selected species and varieties. *O. acanthium,* cotton thistle, Scotch thistle: has large, deeply cut, prickly leaves; flowers are bundles of threadlike petals, ½ to 2 inches across and reddish purple. The plant can grow from 6 to 9 feet tall.

Growing conditions. Sow seeds outdoors where plants are to grow, after all danger of frost has passed, or start them indoors six to eight weeks before moving outside. Germination takes seven to 10 days. Plant in full sun, 3 feet apart, in average garden soil. No special care is needed; water when dry and fertilize little, if at all.

Ornamental cabbage
see *Brassica*

Ornamental kale see *Brassica*

Ornamental pepper
see *Capsicum*

Orthocarpus (or-tho-KAR-pus)
Owl's clover

A genus of about 25 species, native to the western United States. Leaves may be smooth or cut; bracts are colored in many species. Especially effective in massed plantings and informal gardens.

Selected species and varieties. *O. purpurascens,* owl's clover, escobita: dense spikes of reddish purple snapdragon-like flowers borne over fine, threadlike foliage on 15-inch plants. Each bloom's lower lip is tipped with yellow or white.

Growing conditions. Sow seeds outdoors in early spring as soon as the soil can be worked. Germination takes 10 to 14 days. Space plants 6 to 8 inches apart in full sun and a light, rich, well-drained garden soil. Fertilize prior to planting and repeat monthly during the blooming season. Water when the soil starts to dry out. Owl's clover is a hardy annual and will tolerate summer heat.

Owl's clover see *Orthocarpus*

Oxypetalum (ox-ee-PET-ah-lum)

A genus of about 125 species, native to Central and South America, having dainty flowers on branched stems. A perennial in its native habitat but grown as an annual in the Northern Hemisphere.

Selected species and varieties. *O. caeruleum,* southern star: star-shaped, five-petaled 1-inch flowers appear in gracefully arching sprays along woody stems of shrubby, twining 15- to 18-inch plants with elongated, velvety leaves. From pink buds, blooms open silvery blue and darken to purple as they mature.

Growing conditions. Sow seeds outdoors where plants are to grow, after all danger of frost has passed. Or start seeds indoors six to eight weeks before the last frost date, then transplant after the last frost. Germination takes 10 to 15 days. Set plants 6 to 8 inches apart in a rich, well-drained soil. Fertilize with 5-10-5 at planting time, and again monthly; keep well watered. Though planted fairly early, southern star may not bloom until late summer, when other annuals are fading.

Painted tongue see *Salpiglossis*

Pansy see *Viola*

Papaver (pa-PA-ver)
Poppy

Annual poppies look just like their perennial cousins. They bear single or double 1- to 3-inch flowers in red, purple, white, pink, salmon or orange, with a texture like crepe paper. Stems are tall and emerge from deeply cut basal leaves.

Selected species and varieties. *P. nudicaule,* Iceland poppy: a perennial that can be grown as an annual; bears 1- to 3-inch white, pink, yellow-orange or red flowers and reaches 1 foot in height. *P. rhoeas,* corn poppy, Flanders poppy, Shirley poppy: grows to 3 feet, and bears 2-inch flowers of red, purple or white.

Growing conditions. Sow poppy seeds outdoors where the plants are to grow, either in late fall or as soon as the ground can be worked in spring. Seeds may also be started indoors, but they need cool temperatures (55° to 60° F) and the seedlings do not transplant well. Cover seeds completely, as they need darkness for germination, which takes 10 to 15 days. Sow Shirley poppy seeds successively every two weeks during spring and early summer for continuous bloom. They will do best before hot weather. Iceland poppy must be started early if it is to bloom the first year. Set plants 9 to 12 inches apart, in full sun and a rich soil with excellent drainage. Do not overwater. Fertilize with 5-10-5 before planting; no further feeding is recommended.

Pelargonium
(pel-ar-GOE-nee-um)
Geranium

Showy clusters of white, pink, salmon or scarlet flowers, above roundish, hairy, toothed and slightly ruffled foliage. Plants may be trailing or upright and somewhat woody. Good in garden beds, borders and containers of all kinds.

Selected species and varieties. *P. × domesticum*, Martha Washington, Lady Washington, regal geranium: has deeply lobed and serrated leaves, large flowers with dark blotches on the upper petals; can be grown only in cool areas of the northern United States. *P. × hortorum*, zonal geranium, bedding geranium: single or double flowers in 5-inch round clusters atop leafless stems. Leaves are heart-shaped with scalloped edges; some have brown or black markings called "zoning," some are solid green, others are variegated with white, yellow, bronze, purple, pink or orange. Flower colors include white, pink, rose, salmon, coral, lavender and red. Grown as annuals, plants reach 24 inches high. 'Didden's Improved Picardy' is light salmon pink with medium green zoned foliage. It is tall and tolerates part sun. Glacier is a series that comes in crimson, clear red, dark red, salmon and scarlet specifically bred for northern climates. It has medium green leaves on a compact plant. Sunbelt is a series specially bred for southern climates. It is medium to tall and comes in coral, dark red, hot pink, salmon and scarlet. Ringo is a series having mostly zoned leaves and a compact, uniform plant. Sprinter is a series of compact plants that bloom profusely; among its cultivars are 'Merlin' (crimson with an orange eye) and 'Bright Eyes' (red with a white eye). *P. peltatum*, ivy geranium, hanging geranium: trailing stems that reach 3 feet in length. Flowers range in color from white to deep pink and are borne in five- or seven-flowered clusters. The 2- to 3-inch leaves are ivy-shaped and may have a reddish zone. Ivy geraniums are used in pots and hanging baskets and as ground cover. 'Summer Showers' is the first ivy geranium cultivar that can be grown from seed. Flowers are single in pink, lavender, red, magenta and white.

Growing conditions. All geraniums can be propagated from cuttings, and this method ensures that flower color and leaf form remain the same. If you choose to propagate from seeds, sow them indoors 12 to 16 weeks before the last expected frost. Cover the fine seeds sparsely, and keep the flat in a warm spot (70° to 80° F) during the five- to 15-day germination period. Set seedlings in the garden after all danger of frost has passed. Space plants 8 to 12 inches apart in a very rich, slightly acid, well-drained soil. Zonal geraniums need full sun; ivy and Martha Washington geraniums benefit from dappled shade. Geraniums perform best when well fertilized, so incorporate 5-10-5 into the soil before planting and feed again monthly. Keep well watered, applying water to the ground only, and not to the foliage and flowers. In northern climates, geraniums may be dug up at the end of the growing season, stored indoors in a cool, dark place and replanted outdoors the following spring.

Geraniums that are grown in containers respond best to a rich, soil-less mixture and prefer to be potbound. To keep the plants neat and encourage further blooming, cut off faded flowers.

Penstemon (PEN-ste-mon)
Beard tongue

A wildflower native to the Midwestern and Rocky Mountain states, having tubular flowers on tall stems. Best used in the middle of a border.

Selected species and varieties. *P. gloxinioides*: spikes of 2-inch, two-lipped flowers in red, rose, pink, lavender or white; leaves are dark green and attractive; plants reach 2 to 3 feet in height.

Growing conditions. Beard tongue does best in cool climates. Seeds should be sown outdoors where plants are to grow, in late fall or early spring. Seeds can be started indoors, provided you maintain a temperature of about 55° F; sow them six to eight weeks before the last frost date. Germination will take

PELARGONIUM × DOMESTICUM

PELARGONIUM × HORTORUM

PELARGONIUM PELTATUM

PENSTEMON GLOXINIOIDES

123

PERILLA FRUTESCENS

PETUNIA × HYBRIDA 'ULTRA CRIMSON STAR'

PETUNIA × HYBRIDA
'PURPLE PIROUETTE'

PETUNIA × HYBRIDA 'RESISTO BLUE'

10 to 15 days. Set plants 12 to 18 inches apart in a light, rich, acidic soil with excellent drainage. Fertilize with 5-10-5 before planting. Do not allow the soil to dry out.

—

Perilla (peh-RIL-ah)

A member of the mint family, often having leaves of variegated colors. Used to add colorful foliage in borders and designs.

Selected species and varieties. *P. frutescens,* beefsteak plant: toothed, deep-reddish-purple leaves with a bronze metallic sheen, on an 18- to 36-inch plant. Bears pale lavender, pink or white flowers in 3- to 6-inch-long clusters in late summer, but is grown primarily for its foliage. 'Atropurpurea' has dark purple leaves. 'Crispa' has bronze or purple leaves with highly wrinkled margins.

Growing conditions. Sow seeds outdoors after all danger of frost has passed, or start them inside four to six weeks before moving them to the garden. Leave seeds uncovered, as they need light during the 15- to 20-day germination. Transplant seedlings carefully, to avoid disturbing their roots. Space plants 12 to 15 inches apart in full sun or light shade in an average to dry garden soil with good drainage. Pinch when 6 inches tall to encourage bushiness. If allowed to bloom, beefsteak plant self-sows readily and can become weedy. Fertilize with 5-10-5 before planting and repeat every month. Water when dry.

—

Periwinkle see *Catharanthus*
Persian violet see *Exacum*
Peruvian rock purslane
see *Calandrinia*

—

Petunia (pe-TOON-ee-ah)

A genus of approximately 30 species, nearly all from Argentina, having bright-colored flowers and small, fuzzy leaves. May be grown as a spreading or a cascading plant, and used in beds, borders, containers or hanging baskets.

Selected species and varieties. *P. × hybrida:* blooms in every color of the rainbow; blossoms are solid or splashed, starred, zoned, speckled, striped, veined or edged in white. Petunias come in two basic classes: grandiflora and multiflora. Grandi-

floras have flowers up to 5 inches across; multifloras produce greater numbers of smaller (2- to 3-inch) blossoms and are more disease-resistant. Blooms in both classes may be single and trumpet-shaped, perhaps with fringed or ruffled petals; or double, having extra petals in the center and somewhat resembling carnations. 'Cascade': a grandiflora with single flowers up to 4½ inches, on vigorous 12-inch plants that spread to 24 inches. 'Flash' is a very early-blooming and weather-tolerant grandiflora with 3-inch flowers on a compact, 10-inch plant. 'Picotee': a grandiflora with weather-resistant, wavy single flowers 3 inches wide on plants that grow to 10 inches; blooms have a white margin that does not fade in hot weather. Ultra series has many 3-inch flowers in various reds, white and blue, sometimes bicolored, on compact, very weather-tolerant 8-inch plants. 'Purple Pirouette': a grandiflora double with deep purple petals ruffled and edged in white; plants are 12 inches high and 18 inches across; blooms are 3½ to 4 inches. 'Comanche' is a multiflora single with 2½-inch crimson flowers that do not fade in heat. 'Madness' is a very popular, compact multiflora with flowers rather large for the class. Resisto series, also multiflora singles, were developed to withstand cool, wet summers; flattened by a heavy rain, the 12-inch plants will spring right back. 'Tart', a multiflora double, has early-blooming 2½-inch flowers on 12- to 15-inch plants; excellent for containers.

Growing conditions. Start these very fine seeds indoors 10 to 12 weeks before the last frost date. Do not cover them, as they need light for the 10-day germination; they also need warmth (70° to 85° F) to germinate. If you purchase bedding plants, choose ones not yet in bloom—they will grow better and bloom more vigorously. Set plants in the garden in spring after all frost danger has passed. Space petunias 8 to 12 inches apart in a sunny or lightly shaded spot. Average, well-drained garden soil with 5-10-5 incorporated before planting will suffice. Petunias do very well in sandy and dry soil. Where soil is heavy, poor or alkaline, choose singles over doubles. Petunias will benefit from pinching at planting time to encourage bushy growth. If plants become leggy, cut them back and they will soon rebloom. Grandiflora petunias are susceptible to botrytis, a disease that kills blossoms, especially in rainy, humid areas. The multiflora types are resistant.

Phacelia (fah-SEE-lee-ah)
Phacelia, scorpion weed

A plant with fragrant and somewhat hairy foliage and clusters of 1-inch, bell-shaped flowers in bright blue, violet or white appearing in spring and early summer. Individual blooms are not showy, but massed plantings are very effective. Use phacelias in rock gardens and for borders.

Selected species and varieties. *P. bipinnatifida*: a biennial grown as an annual; reaches 2 feet in height, bears violet or blue flowers over deeply cut leaves. *P. campanularia,* California bluebell: bright blue flowers and toothed leaves on a 20-inch plant. *P. purshii,* Miami-mist: pale blue flowers with white centers on a 1½- to 2-foot annual with deeply cut leaves.

Growing conditions. Sow seeds outdoors where plants are to grow, in late fall or early spring. Select a location with full sun and a dry, sandy, well-drained soil. Thin plants to 6 to 8 inches, to achieve a dense, massed look. Fertilize and water very little, as poor, dry soil is preferred. Phacelias do best where nights are cool.

Phaseolus (fay-zee-OH-lus)
Bean, phaseolus

A vine related to the snap bean and other beans grown in the vegetable garden for food.

Selected species and varieties. *P. coccineus,* scarlet runner bean: 1-inch, showy scarlet flowers on 8- to 12-foot vines. Edible foot-long beans follow the flowers, but scarlet runner bean is used in flower gardens for its quick growth and handsome flowers and foliage. Plant it against a wall or a trellis to provide a quick screen. Very attractive to hummingbirds.

Growing conditions. Sow seeds outdoors where plants are to grow, after all danger of frost has passed. Germination takes six to 10 days. Space plants 2 inches apart in full sun and a rich, moist, well-drained soil. Fertilize at planting time and repeat monthly. Keep well watered. To keep plants flowering, pick off spent blooms before beans can form.

Phlox (FLOCKS)

A genus of about 60 species, having lance-shaped leaves and terminal clusters of flowers.

Selected species and varieties. *P. drummondii,* annual phlox, Drummond phlox, Texan pride: compact, mounded 6- to 18-inch plant with long, thin leaves and round or star-shaped 1-inch flowers in white, pink, blue, red, salmon, lavender and sometimes yellow. Good for edging, bedding, borders, rock gardens and containers. 'Dwarf Beauty' is 12 inches tall; its blooms often have contrasting eyes. 'Globe': a compact, rounded, 6- to 8-inch cultivar; blooms in a variety of light and dark colors. 'Petticoat': a mix of star-shaped flowers in white, red, rose, salmon and pink with white highlights on 6-inch plants; the most heat- and sun-resistant annual phlox, a reliable summer bloomer. 'Twinkle, Dwarf Star': a ball-shaped, 8-inch plant covered with star-shaped blooms composed of pointed, fringed petals. Solids and bicolors in red, pink, salmon, rose, lavender, blue and white.

Growing conditions. Sow seeds outdoors where plants are to grow, in spring as soon as the ground can be worked. Indoors, start 10 weeks before the outside planting date and sow seeds in individual peat pots, because the seedlings do not transplant well. Cover seeds well, for they need darkness to germinate. Cool temperatures (55° to 65° F) are also critical for the 10- to 15-day germination period. To prevent killing by damping-off, take care not to overwater seedlings. Harden off seedlings or bedding plants by exposing them gradually to cool spring air, then transplant them to the garden two to three weeks before the last frost date. When transplanting, select some of the weaker seedlings; these tend to produce more interesting colors. Plant in full sun, 6 inches apart, in a rich, light, well-drained sandy soil. Fertilize with 5-10-5 before planting, and feed monthly throughout the blooming season. Keep soil moist but not wet, watering in the morning to reduce risk of disease. Keep faded flowers removed; shearing the plants back encourages compact growth and more flowers. Though phlox is fairly heat-tolerant, flowering may decline in midsummer.

Pimpernel see *Anagallis*
Pincushion flower see *Scabiosa*
Pinks see *Dianthus*

Platystemon (plat-ee-STEM-on)
Creamcups

A member of the poppy family, native to California.

PHACELIA PURSHII

PHASEOLUS COCCINEUS

PHLOX DRUMMONDII

PLATYSTEMON CALIFORNICUS

POLYGONUM CAPITATUM

PORTULACA GRANDIFLORA

PORTULACA OLERACEA HYBRID

Selected species and varieties. *P. californicus:* 1-inch cream or yellow flowers borne singly on 12-inch plants that are covered with long, slender leaves. Prominent stamens form a dense tuft in the center of each bloom. Use creamcups as an annual ground cover, in a rock garden or as a low edging.

Growing conditions. Sow seeds outdoors in early spring where plants are to grow, as soon as the ground can be worked. Germination takes 10 to 15 days. Space plants 10 to 12 inches apart in full sun and a sandy, well-drained soil. Water well but never let the ground become soggy. Fertilize with 5-10-5 prior to planting; no other feeding will be needed.

Pocketbook plant
see *Calceolaria*

Poinsettia see *Amaranthus; Euphorbia*

Polyanthus see *Primula*

Polygonum (poe-LIG-oh-num)
Knotweed, fleece flower

A diverse group of somewhat coarse and weedy plants with small, petal-less flowers, generally pink or white, borne in loose clusters. The common name "knotweed" refers to the knot-like swellings in the stems, at the joints where the leaf stems grow. Smaller species can be used as annual ground covers, taller ones as screens or at the back of a border.

Selected species and varieties. *P. capitatum:* a trailing plant 18 inches across, 6 inches high; bears tiny pink flowers in dense, ball-shaped, ¾-inch heads, and has 1½-inch black-striped leaves. *P. orientale,* kiss-me-over-the-garden-gate, prince's feather: grows 6 feet high and has 3½-inch hanging clusters of pink flowers at the ends of thin, wiry stems. Both of these species are perennials sometimes grown as annuals.

Growing conditions. Sow seeds outdoors where plants are to grow, after all danger of frost has passed, or start seeds indoors six to eight weeks before the last frost date. Germination takes 20 to 25 days. Space plants 18 to 36 inches apart in full sun or light shade and a rich, light, well-drained soil. Water well, but do not fertilize. Knotweeds self-sow and root freely, and can become invasive.

Poor man's orchid
see *Schizanthus*
Poor-man's-weatherglass
see *Anagallis*
Poppy see *Argemone; Eschscholzia; Glaucium; Hunnemannia; Papaver*

Portulaca (por-tu-LAK-ah)
Portulaca, moss rose

Low-growing, ground-hugging plants 4 to 6 inches tall, with fleshy stems and leaves and generally showy flowers. Most flowers close up at night, in shade and on cloudy days. Best used as edgings, borders, ground covers or in containers.

Selected species and varieties. *P. grandiflora:* 1- to 2-inch ruffled flowers in pink, red, gold, yellow, cream, orange, white or salmon. Single flowers are wide-open and cup-shaped; semidouble and double flowers resemble tiny full-blown roses. Leaves are needle-like. 'Calypso', 'Double', 'Sunnyboy' and 'Sunnyside' are mixes, producing mostly double flowers in a variety of colors. 'Sundance' is a cultivar with 2-inch flowers in mixed colors; its flowers stay open longer than most other varieties. *P. oleracea:* has 18-inch-long trailing stems and bright yellow ⅜-inch flowers; hybrids come in mixed colors. *P. pilosa,* shaggy garden portulaca: bears ¾-inch red-purple flowers and has tufts of hair on the stems.

Growing conditions. Sow moss rose seeds outdoors where plants are to grow, after all danger of frost has passed. Sow seeds indoors eight to 10 weeks before the last frost date. Germination takes 10 to 15 days. Transplant seedlings or bedding plants after danger of frost has passed. Space plants 12 to 15 inches apart, in full sun and a dry, sandy, well-drained soil. Fertilize with 5-10-5 before planting and do not feed again. Moss rose withstands heat and drought and should be watered very lightly. Moss rose is a low-maintenance plant; its flowers fall cleanly as they fade, and plants self-seed from year to year.

Pot marigold see *Calendula*
Prickly poppy see *Argemone*
Primrose see *Oenothera; Primula*

Primula (PRIM-you-lah)
Primrose

A large genus of perennials and annuals bearing bright flowers in many colors, some with interesting contrasts and markings. The single flowers appear in clusters atop leafless stems. Good for containers, formal beds, borders or shade gardens.

Selected species and varieties. *P. malacoides,* fairy primrose: an annual that bears loose clusters of ½-inch flowers in rose, lavender or white. 'Alba' is a white-flowered cultivar. 'Rosea' has bright pink blooms. *P. obconica,* German primrose: a tender perennial grown as an annual; its 1-inch blooms are purple, pink, red or white. *P. × polyantha,* polyanthus: a short-lived perennial that can be grown as an annual; bears 1- to 2-inch flowers of white, purple, blue, red, pink or yellow, many with contrasting centers.

Growing conditions. To grow seedlings of transplantable size, seeds must be sown indoors up to six months before outdoor planting. Germination takes 21 to 40 days and seeds benefit from three weeks' chilling in moistened medium in the refrigerator before indoor sowing. Leave these tiny seeds uncovered, as they need light to germinate. However, since growing primroses from seed takes so long, you may prefer to start with purchased plants. These can be set outside in early spring as soon as the ground can be worked, if plants are well hardened off—that is, gradually acclimated to outdoor conditions. Space plants 8 to 10 inches apart in partial shade and a rich, slightly acid, well-drained soil. Keep well watered. Mulch to help keep the soil cool and moist. Fertilize with 5-10-5 prior to planting and again every month during the flowering season.

—

Prince's feather
see *Amaranthus; Polygonum*

—

Proboscidea
(proe-boe-SEE-dee-ah)
Unicorn plant

A spreading plant grown for its unusual seedpods, which can be pickled and eaten, or dried for decorative use.

Selected species and varieties. *P. louisianica,* unicorn flower, devil's claw, proboscis flower: spreads to 18 inches, bears tubular 2-inch flowers of yellow, lavender, pink or white, and produces 4- to 12-inch fruit that curves like a bird's beak. The plant has a strong odor that is offensive to many people; grow it in an out-of-the-way place where it will not overwhelm the fragrance of sweeter-smelling plants.

Growing conditions. Sow seeds outdoors after all danger of frost has passed, or start them inside six to eight weeks before the last frost date. Germination takes 20 to 25 days. Grow in full sun in a light, rich, well-drained soil. Fertilize with 5-10-5 before planting, and keep well watered. Unicorn plant does best in hot climates.

—

Purple ragwort see *Senecio*
Red-ribbons see *Clarkia*

—

Reseda (re-SEE-dah)
Mignonette

A genus of more than 50 species, native to the Mediterranean region, having small flowers that grow in long spikes.

Selected species and varieties. *R. odorata,* common mignonette: a 12- to 18-inch plant bearing thick 6- to 10-inch spikes of small, highly fragrant flowers that are yellowish green, yellowish brown or yellowish white, sometimes touched with red. Use mignonette in borders and beds, or as a pot plant on a deck or a patio where its fragrance can be appreciated; or plant it under windows to fill the house with its sweet scent.

Growing conditions. Sow seeds outdoors in the spring as soon as the ground can be worked. Seeds can be started indoors four to six weeks before the outdoor planting date, but mignonette is hard to transplant and not much is gained by starting it early. Do not cover the seeds because they need light for germination, which takes five to 10 days. In mild climates, seeds can be sown outdoors in fall for germination early the following spring. Space plants 10 to 12 inches apart. Select a location with soil that is rich and well drained. Mignonette likes sun but will thrive in light shade as well. Water well to keep soil moist, and mulch to keep it cool. Mignonette will flourish in warm climates; where summers are hot, it should be treated as a spring and fall plant.

PRIMULA MALACOIDES

PROBOSCIDEA LOUISIANICA

RESEDA ODORATA

127

RICINUS COMMUNIS

RUDBECKIA HIRTA

SALPIGLOSSIS SINUATA

Ricinus (rye-SIGN-nus)

A single species of fast-growing plant that is native to Africa; produces a bean that yields castor oil and a poison. Used as an accent plant, background or screen; adds a tropical look to the garden.

Selected species and varieties. *R. communis,* castor bean: a shrubby 5- to 8-foot plant grown for its deeply lobed leaves. Young leaves have a red or bronze tinge; as they mature, they darken to green and eventually reach 3 feet in width. The plant produces reddish brown or white flowers, but these are insignificant.

Growing conditions. Sow seeds outdoors after all danger of frost has passed or start seeds indoors six to eight weeks before the last frost date. Germination takes 15 to 20 days. Space plants 4 to 5 feet apart in full sun and a rich, well-drained, sandy or clay soil. Plants do best where climate is hot and humid; they like to be heavily watered. Fertilize with 5-10-5 before planting and again monthly during the summer. In mild climates, castor bean will grow as a perennial.

Rocky Mountain garland
see *Clarkia*

Rose-of-heaven see *Lychnis*

Rudbeckia (rude-BEK-ee-ah)
Coneflower

A genus of about 25 species native to North America; flower heads are usually yellow. Coneflowers work well in a border, but are especially effective in a wildflower garden. Excellent for cut flowers.

Selected species and varieties. *R. hirta,* 'Gloriosa daisy': developed from the black-eyed Susan that blooms along rural roadsides in the summer. The daisy-like flower heads are 3 to 6 inches across; their yellow or black cone-shaped centers, consisting of tiny disc florets, are surrounded by a single or double row of petal-like ray florets of gold, yellow, bronze, orange, brown or mahogany, often with zones or bands of contrasting colors. Plants reach 8 to 36 inches in height. Although gloriosa daisies can be perennial in many parts of the country, they are easily grown from seed to bloom the first year and thus make good annuals. 'Goldilocks' bears 3- to 4-inch semidouble flower heads on 8- to 10-inch plants. 'Mar-

malade' is wind-resistant. It grows to 2 feet and has 3-inch flowers of bright gold with contrasting dark centers.

Growing conditions. Sow seed indoors six to eight weeks before the last frost date or outdoors as soon as the soil can be worked; germination takes five to 10 days. Or purchase bedding plants. Seedlings should be moved to the garden after danger of frost has passed; space them 12 to 24 inches apart, in full sun or light shade. Any well-drained garden soil will do. Although gloriosa daisies do best in a rich soil kept evenly moist, they will tolerate drought and heat. Fertilize with 5-10-5 at planting time. No further feeding is needed. Gloriosa daisies freely reseed, so plants will probably reappear from year to year if spent blooms are not removed.

Sage see *Salvia*

Salpiglossis (sal-pee-GLOS-sis)

A plant of Chilean origin, having trumpet-shaped flowers that grow in loose terminal clusters from small leafy bracts. Used in borders and backgrounds, it also makes an excellent cut flower.

Selected species and varieties. *S. sinuata,* painted tongue: bears velvety flowers of purple, red, yellow, blue and rose. Blooms are 2½ inches across; their broad throats are often heavily veined in contrasting colors. Plants grow from 24 to 36 inches tall; foliage and stems are slightly hairy. 'Bolero' and 'Emperor' are cultivars with a range of colors and veining patterns; they grow to 30 inches. 'Splash' is bushier, with more stems and more flowers; also blooms earlier than other cultivars and is more tolerant of heat and drought.

Growing conditions. Sow seeds indoors at least eight weeks before the last frost date. Seeds are very fine and should not be covered with soil. Since darkness aids germination, cover the seed flats with black plastic until germination occurs, in 15 to 20 days. Set plants in the garden in midspring, several weeks before the last expected frost, as painted tongue is slightly frost-resistant. The larger the plants are when they are set out, the better they will grow and bloom. Space plants 8 to 12 inches apart in full sun. Soil should be light, alkaline and rich in organic matter, and have excellent drainage. Water well to keep the soil evenly moist, and mulch to keep it cool. Incorporate 5-10-5 into the soil before planting; no further feeding will be necessary. Painted tongue does best where summers are cool. The taller cultivars may need to be staked.

—

Salvia (SAL-vee-ah)
Salvia, sage

Salvia is a large genus of plants used in both flower gardens and herb gardens. The flowers are two-lipped and generally red, but may be purplish blue, white, reddish purple, deep purple or rose. Blooms are borne in showy terminal spikes; leaves are borne in pairs. Most salvias are perennials grown as annuals. Use them in massed plantings, beds, borders, containers and as cut flowers.

Selected species and varieties. *S. argentea,* silver sage: has small off-white flowers, but the species is grown for its silver-gray, hairy foliage. *S. coccinea,* scarlet sage: bears vivid red flowers on 3-foot stems. *S. farinacea,* mealy-cup sage: has narrow spikes profusely covered with violet-blue or white flowers. Leaves are gray-green; plants grow to 24 inches. *S. patens,* gentian sage: an unusual blue-flowered salvia with 2-inch clawlike flowers. Spikes are upright and very loose, and grow to 24 inches. The roots of this perennial salvia can be dug up, stored over the winter and replanted the following spring. *S. splendens,* scarlet sage: grown primarily for its spikes of red flowers borne over dark green leaves; plants reach 6 to 24 inches in height. 'Bonfire' is tall, to 24 inches, and bears scarlet blooms. 'Carabiniere' comes in orange, scarlet, purple and white, as well as reds. 'Hotline' series cultivars are very early and very compact. The flowers, available in red, salmon, white and violet, are the most heat-resistant of all salvias. 'Red Hot Sally' is very early to flower, and reaches only 10 inches in height. *S. viridis* grows 18 inches tall and bears masses of lilac, purplish red or purple flowers in loose spikes.

Growing conditions. Start seeds indoors eight to 10 weeks before the date of the last spring frost. Do not cover seeds of *S. splendens* as they need light to germinate. Germination takes 10 to 15 days. *S. farinacea* needs to be started indoors 12 weeks before transplanting outdoors. Salvia transplants best before it comes into bloom, so don't start seeds too early. Space plants 8 to 12 inches apart; dwarf cultivars can be planted closer

together. Salvias like full sun or part shade and a rich, well-drained soil. Although plants will tolerate dry soil, they do better if kept evenly watered. Salvia is very sensitive to fertilizer burn, so feed lightly but often throughout the summer. Salvia will reseed, but self-sown plants rarely reach blooming size during the summer except in the South.

—

Sanvitalia (san-vi-TAL-ee-ah)

Single or double daisy-like blooms having yellow or orange ray florets and brown or purple centers.

Selected species and varieties. *S. procumbens,* creeping zinnia: Blooms are ½ to ¾ inch across, on plants that grow only 4 to 8 inches tall but spread to cover an area 10 to 16 inches wide. Use creeping zinnia in borders, beds, edgings, containers and hanging baskets, and as a ground cover. 'Gold Braid' bears golden yellow flower heads on plants 4 to 6 inches tall, spreading to 16 inches. 'Mandarin Orange' has orange flower heads on plants that grow 8 inches tall and 15 inches wide.

Growing conditions. Creeping zinnia seeds may be sown outdoors where they are to grow, after all danger of frost has passed. Or, sow seeds indoors in individual pots four to six weeks before the last frost date. Do not cover the seeds, which need light to germinate. Germination takes 10 to 15 days. Take great care not to disturb the roots when transplanting seedlings and purchased bedding plants. Space plants 5 to 6 inches apart in full sun and a light, open, well-drained soil. Fertilize with 5-10-5 before planting. Plants will tolerate drought but should be watered when dry. Creeping zinnia is a low-maintenance plant; flowers fall cleanly as they fade.

—

Satin flower see *Clarkia*

—

Scabiosa (ska-bee-OH-sah)
Pincushion flower

Bears round, terminal clusters of white, dark purple, rose, blue or rose-violet blooms on long stems; individual flowers are small and tubular. Used in borders. Pincushion flowers make long-lived cut flowers, and one species makes an excellent dried flower.

SALVIA FARINACEA

SALVIA SPLENDENS

SANVITALIA PROCUMBENS

SCABIOSA ATROPURPUREA

SCABIOSA STELLATA

SCHIZANTHUS PINNATUS

SENECIO CINERARIA 'CIRRUS'

Selected species and varieties. *S. atropurpurea,* sweet scabious, mourning bride: bears 2- to 4-inch flower heads in pink, dark purple, rose, white or red. Silvery white or yellow stamens protrude beyond the blooms like pins. The fragrant, double blooms are borne atop slender 18- to 36-inch stems. 'Dwarf Double': a compact 18-inch plant with dense round flower heads of blue, white, rose or lavender. 'Giant Imperial Mix' grows 24 to 36 inches tall and bears ball-shaped, 3-inch flowers of pink, white, salmon, scarlet, deep red, lavender or blue. *S. stellata,* star-flower: bears 1¼-inch blue or rose-violet flowers; grown for its value as a dried flower. Dries to a light brown ball of little florets with maroon or brown starlike centers atop a stiff 24-inch stem. 'Ping Pong' has flowers that dry to the size of a ping-pong ball.

Growing conditions. Sow seeds outdoors after all danger of frost has passed, or start them indoors four to five weeks before the last frost date. Germination takes 10 to 15 days. After danger of frost has passed, transplant to a location in full sun, spacing plants 10 to 15 inches apart. Soil should be rich, well-drained and alkaline. Fertilize with 5-10-5 before planting and repeat monthly through the growing season. Water when soil is dry, but do not overwater. To prevent mildew, water in the morning. Tall varieties may need to be staked.

—

Scarlet runner bean
see *Phaseolus*

—

Schizanthus (ski-ZAN-thus)
Poor man's orchid, butterfly flower

Exotic flowers that look something like an orchid and something like a butterfly with its wings spread, hence the two common names. Borne in loose clusters, the showy 1½-inch blooms come in shades of purple, lavender, white, rose, yellow and red; many are marked or striped with contrasting colors. Plants are free-branching, grow 12 to 24 inches tall and have finely cut fernlike, fringy foliage. Poor man's orchid is generally used in containers or window boxes, but it makes a good bedding plant as well.

Selected species and varieties. *S. pinnatus:* 4 feet tall with lilac or purplish flowers, many marked with yellow on the lower lip. Cultivars with white, red or rose flowers are availa-

ble. *S. × wisetonensis:* only 1 to 2 feet tall, bears white, blue, pink, yellow, red and magenta flowers, many marked with contrasting colors. 'Angel Wings' and 'Hit Parade' both grow 10 to 14 inches tall, with a large array of flower colors and yellow throat markings. 'Star Parade', 6 to 8 inches high, is pyramidal and compact.

Growing conditions. Sow seeds indoors 12 weeks before the last frost. Seeds are very fine and should not be covered with soil during the 20- to 25-day germination period. However, they must have darkness to germinate, so lay black plastic over the planting medium. Transplant seedlings or purchased bedding plants to the garden after danger of frost is past. Space plants 12 inches apart, in full sun to light shade, in a rich, moist soil with excellent drainage. Fertilize with 5-10-5 before planting and feed again monthly during the growing season. At planting time, pinch the plants to encourage bushiness. When grown in a container, plants bloom best if potbound. Poor man's orchid thrives only in areas where night temperatures drop below 65° F. In the South and the West, it cannot survive the hot summers but does very well as a winter bedding plant.

—

Scotch thistle see *Onopordum*
Scorpion weed see *Phacelia*
Sea lavender see *Limonium*

—

Senecio (se-NEE-shee-o)

A large genus of 2,000 to 3,000 species. Many have showy flower heads borne in clusters; some have decorative foliage.

Selected species and varieties. *S. cineraria,* dusty miller: produces flowers of yellow or cream in small terminal clusters, but is grown primarily for its foliage, woolly and white with rounded lobes. Grows 2½ feet high and is used in beds and borders. 'Cirrus' has broad, oak-shaped, very white leaves and is heat-, rain- and frost-tolerant. *S. × hybridus,* florist's cineraria: hairy, heart-shaped leaves and dense clusters of 2-inch single or double flower heads in white, pink, red, purple, violet or blue, many with contrasting rings. The 1- to 3-foot plant is often used as a houseplant, but can be successfully grown outdoors in the cool, mild climate of the Northwest. *S. elegans,* purple ragwort: bears loose clusters of 1-inch flower heads having purple ray florets around yellow centers. Plants are 2 feet tall, with deeply cut foliage.

Growing conditions. For dusty miller, sow seeds indoors eight to 10 weeks before the last frost date. For purple ragwort, sow indoors six to eight weeks before the last frost date. Germination for both takes 10 days to two weeks. Florist's cineraria may be sown indoors and will germinate in 10 to 15 days, but the plant will not bloom for five to six months; sow seeds in late summer or early fall for blooming the following spring. Or start with purchased bedding plants. Either way, set plants in the ground when they are just coming into bud; plants already in flower will not adjust to the outdoors. All senecio plants should be set in the ground after the last frost, spaced 12 inches apart, and fertilized with 5-10-5 at planting time. Dusty miller likes full sun or light shade, a sandy, light and well-drained soil, and light watering when soil has dried out. If plants start to get leggy, they can be sheared back. Purple ragwort needs full sun and a rich, moist, well-drained soil—but only occasional watering. Florist's cineraria needs partial shade to full shade, a soil that is rich, moist and well-drained, and mulching and frequent watering. It should be fertilized monthly during the blooming season, and flowers should be picked off as they fade.

Silene (sy-LEE-nee)
Catchfly, campion

A genus of approximately 500 species distributed throughout the world. The stems of some species are sticky and trap flies; hence the common name catchfly.

Selected species and varieties. *S. armeria,* sweet William catchfly, none-so-pretty: a tufted plant that bears loose clusters of ½-inch five-petaled flowers in shades of pink. Grows 16 to 18 inches tall, is used in rock gardens, rock walls or borders.

Growing conditions. Sow seeds outdoors where plants are to grow, in late fall or as soon as the soil can be worked in early spring. Seedlings do not transplant well, so starting seeds indoors is not recommended. Germination takes 15 to 20 days. Plant in full sun, 12 to 15 inches apart, in average garden soil. Water when dry. Fertilize with 5-10-5 before planting; no

further feeding is necessary. Sweet William catchfly reseeds itself from year to year.

Skyrocket see *Ipomopsis*

Sleepy daisy see *Xanthisma*

Snapdragon see *Antirrhinum*

Snow-on-the-mountain see *Euphorbia*

Southern star see *Oxypetalum*

Spider flower see *Cleome*

Spurge see *Euphorbia*

Standing cypress see *Ipomopsis*

Starflower see *Scabiosa*

Star-of-Texas see *Xanthisma*

Star-of-the-veldt see *Dimorphotheca*

Statice see *Limonium*

Stock see *Malcolmia; Matthiola*

Strawflower see *Helichrysum; Helipterum*

Sunflower see *Helianthus; Tithonia*

Swan River daisy see *Brachycome*

Sweet false chamomile see *Matricaria*

Sweet pea see *Lathyrus*

Sweet sultan see *Centaurea*

Sweet William see *Dianthus*

Sweet William catchfly see *Silene*

Tagetes (ta-JEE-tees)
Marigold

A member of the daisy family, native to Mexico; the common name is a translation of the Spanish conquistadors' term for it, "Mary's gold." Showy flower heads of yellow, gold, orange or maroon, strongly scented foliage and deeply cut leaves. Used in beds, borders, massed plantings, edgings and containers; for cut flowers; and sometimes in vegetable gardens, because they are thought to repel certain beetles and nematodes.

Selected species and varieties. *T. erecta:* African marigold, American marigold, Aztec marigold: generally the tallest of marigolds, most varieties growing from 12 to 36 inches tall, but there are some dwarf

SENECIO × HYBRIDUS

SILENE ARMERIA

TAGETES ERECTA 'PRIMROSE LADY'

131

TAGETES PATULA × ERECTA (NUGGETS SERIES)

THUNBERGIA ALATA (SUSIE SERIES)

varieties that reach only 6 inches. Flowers are very full, double or carnation-like, and up to 5 inches across. Crush series, the smallest of the dwarf African marigolds, with 4-inch, flattened flowers on 6- to 8-inch plants, includes 'Pumpkin' (orange), 'Papaya' (gold) and 'Pineapple' (yellow). A mixture of all three colors is called 'Guys and Dolls'. Inca series includes 'Yellow', 'Gold' and 'Orange'; 16- inch plants are covered with solid, fully double, early-blooming, carnation-like flowers with good resistance to heat and rain. Blooms, up to 5 inches across, are larger than most others in this height range. Jubilee series includes 'Orange', 'Golden' and 'Diamond' (primrose yellow) varieties. Round, 4- to 5-inch, carnation-like flowers are weather-resistant and cover the tops of the plants, which grow to 24 inches tall. Lady series cultivars come in pale and golden yellows, and orange. The curved petals form a 3½-inch ball on a 20-inch rounded plant. Monarch series cultivars have yellow, gold and orange, intricately spaced petals on a slightly flattened, 4-inch double flower. Plants reach 20 inches and are exceptionally weather-tolerant. *T. patula,* French marigolds: 6- to 16-inch plants with a profusion of small flower heads in various shapes. Some are crested, having a tufted center surrounded by a collar of ray florets; others have broad, flat petals; still others are carnation-like. Aurora is the largest-flowered French marigold of the flat-petaled type, bearing 2½-inch double blossoms. Early-blooming, 10 to 12 inches tall, it comes in two varieties, 'Gold' and 'Fire' (a glowing red-and-orange bicolor). Bonanza series has 2-inch crested, heat-resistant blooms on 8- to 10-inch plants. Varieties include 'Gold', 'Yellow', 'Orange', 'Spry' (yellow crest with mahogany rays), 'Harmony' (orange crest with maroon rays) and 'Flame' (maroon petals bordered with gold). Janie series includes 'Gold,' 'Janie Bright Yellow', 'Flame' (red-and-orange bicolor) and 'Harmony' (mahogany with gold-orange centers); blooms are double, crested, and 1½ inches across on an 8-inch heat-resistant plant. 'Red Marietta' bears single, gold-edged red flowers, which stay red all summer when many others soften in color. Flowers are 2½ inches across on 16-inch plants. *T. patula × erecta:* unlike other marigolds, blooms all summer, even in the hottest part of the country. The plant is sterile and does not set seed. Nuggets series comes in yellow, orange and red, sometimes bicolored, bearing 2-inch double flowers on 10-inch plants. *T. tenuifolia,* signet marigold, dwarf marigold: has fine, lacy, lemon-scented foliage on 12-inch plants with tiny, single flowers in gold, lemon yellow or orange. *T. filifolia,* Irish lace: also has fine, fernlike foliage; flowers are white to slightly green and almost insignificant.

Growing conditions. Sow seeds indoors four to six weeks before the last frost date. Germination takes five to seven days. Seeds of most marigolds can also be sown outdoors where they are to grow, after danger of frost has passed. Two exceptions are African marigold, which takes longer than other marigolds to bloom, and sterile types, which have such a low germination rate that you can control them better by starting indoors. Transplant seedlings or purchased bedding plants to the garden after danger of frost has passed. Space plants a distance apart about half their ultimate height; for example, African marigolds expected to grow to 24 inches should be spaced 12 inches apart. Marigolds thrive in full sun and relatively high temperatures, but some will stop flowering when temperatures exceed 90° F. They generally bloom until fall frost and will do well in any average, not-too-rich garden soil. Fertilize with 5-10-5 prior to planting, and repeat monthly through the blooming season. Water when the soil is dry. To promote continuous bloom, pick off faded flowers regularly; this, of course, does not apply to sterile types, which do not set seed.

—

Tahoka daisy see *Machaeranthera*
Tampala see *Amaranthus*
Tassel flower see *Amaranthus*
Texas bluebonnet see *Lupinus*
Thorn apple see *Datura*
Throatwort see *Trachelium*

—

Thunbergia (thun-BER-gee-ah)

A genus of about 100 species, many of them vines, having showy flowers.

Selected species and varieties. *T. alata,* black-eyed Susan vine: a tender perennial that can be grown as an annual. Trumpet-shaped, 1½-inch flowers in white, yellow or orange, with dark purple or black throats in most cultivars. Vine grows fast and will reach 5 or 6 feet; bears dense, dark green, arrowhead-shaped leaves. Used for ground cover, on trellises, or in hanging baskets or containers. Susie series cultivars come in mixed and separate colors of white, yellow and orange.

Growing conditions. Sow seeds indoors, six to eight weeks before the last frost date; germination takes 15 to 20 days. In mild climates, seed can be sown outdoors where plants are to grow, when danger of frost has passed. Bedding plants are also readily available. Plant in full sun or very light shade in a light, rich, moist, well-drained soil. Set plants about 6 inches apart, and provide a support, such as a pole, lamp post or trellis, if you wish the plants to climb. Where summers are cool, black-eyed Susan vine has a long growing season. Do not prune plants during the growing season, but pick off flowers as they fade to keep the plants trim and productive. Water when the ground starts to become dry.

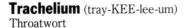

Tidy tips see *Layia*

Tithonia (teye-THO-nee-ah)
Mexican sunflower

Ten species of tall flowering plants that are native to Mexico and Central America.

Selected species and varieties. *T. rotundifolia:* 3-inch daisy-like flower heads of orange-red or yellow and 6- to 12-inch gray, velvety leaves, on plants that grow 4 to 6 feet tall and 2 to 3 feet wide. Mexican sunflowers bloom from midsummer to late fall; use them in a border, for cut flowers, as background plants or in a hedge. 'Goldfinger': the most compact of Mexican sunflowers; grows to 3 feet tall, with 3-inch scarlet-orange flowers. 'Yellow Torch' has chrome yellow blooms on plants that reach at least 3 feet but may grow to 6 feet.

Growing conditions. Sow seeds indoors six to eight weeks before the last frost date and do not cover seeds, as light aids germination. Seeds can also be sown where they are to grow, after frost danger has passed. Germination takes five to 10 days. Move bedding plants or seedlings into the garden after all danger of frost has passed. Space plants 2 to 3 feet apart in full sun and in average garden soil with good drainage. Mexican sunflowers are quite heat-resistant and will withstand drought; be careful not

to overwater. Fertilize lightly each month. For the longest-lasting cut flowers, cut when flowers are in the tight-bud stage.

Toadflax see *Linaria*

Torenia (tow-REE-nee-ah)
Wishbone flower

A genus of more than 40 species native to Africa and Asia, having many-branched stems and flowers in clusters. Used in edging, beds, borders and containers.

Selected species and varieties. *T. fournieri:* bushy dwarf plants that grow 8 to 12 inches tall, with toothed oval leaves. Each 1-inch bloom has a light violet upper lip, a dark purple lower lip and, in its yellow or white throat, a pair of stamens resembling a wishbone.

Growing conditions. Start seeds indoors 10 to 12 weeks before the last expected frost. Germination takes 15 to 20 days. Move plants outside after all frost danger has passed. Wishbone flower prefers a rich, moist, well-drained soil, and full or partial shade; it can withstand full sun only in cool climates, where night temperatures fall below 65° F. Space plants 6 to 8 inches apart and fertilize lightly.

Trachelium (tray-KEE-lee-um)
Throatwort

A genus of about eight species native to the Mediterranean region. Commonly grown as a pot plant, but can also be used in borders and for cut flowers.

Selected species and varieties. *T. caeruleum:* has ½-inch tubular flowers opening at the tip in the shape of a star. The flowers are borne in terminal 5-inch clusters on 2- to 3-foot plants.

Growing conditions. Sow seeds indoors eight to 10 weeks before the last frost date. In areas with long growing seasons, sow seeds outdoors after all danger of frost has passed. Germination takes 10 to 14 days. Space plants 12 to 15 inches apart in full sun or part shade and a moist, well-drained garden soil. Keep well watered. Fertilize with 5-10-5 at planting time and again monthly.

TITHONIA ROTUNDIFOLIA

TORENIA FOURNIERI

TRACHELIUM CAERULEUM

TRACHYMENE COERULEA

TROPAEOLUM MAJUS

VENIDIUM FASTUOSUM

Trachymene (tra-KIM-en-ee)

A genus of about a dozen species native to Australia, having compound leaves and minute flowers that radiate from a single point like the ribs of an umbrella. Used in borders and as cut flowers.

Selected species and varieties. *T. coerulea,* blue lace flower: tiny sweet-scented light-blue or lavender flowers borne in clusters on 24- to 30-inch plants.

Growing conditions. Sow seeds indoors in peat pots six to eight weeks before the last frost date, or outdoors directly in the soil after all danger of frost is past. Seeds must be fully covered; they need darkness for germination, which takes 15 to 20 days. Space plants 8 to 10 inches apart; a bit of crowding improves bloom. Plant in full sun and in a light, sandy, well-drained soil rich in organic matter. Fertilize with 5-10-5 when planting, and keep the ground moist and cool with mulch. Blue lace flower does poorly in extreme heat.

—

Transvaal daisy see *Gerbera*
Treasure flower see *Gazania*
Tree mallow see *Lavatera*

—

Tropaeolum (tro-pee-OH-lum)
Nasturtium

A genus of plants that come in three basic forms: bushy, growing to 12 inches; semitrailing, to 24 inches; and vining, to 8 feet. All grow rapidly and bear single, semidouble or double funnel-shaped flowers in tones of red, yellow and orange, each with a spur extending from the back. The flowers generally droop; some are fragrant. Foliage is round or lobed; stems are fleshy and curl around trellises and other objects. Depending on plant habit, nasturtiums may be used as bedding plants, in containers and hanging baskets, on a trellis or to overhang a wall. Easy to grow, they are often included in children's gardens. Sometimes they are planted in vegetable gardens, as they are thought to repel squash bugs and some beetles.

Selected species and varieties. *T. majus,* the common garden nasturtium, has showy yellow, orange, scarlet or mahogany blooms 2 to 2½ inches across. The round, 2- to 7-inch leaves are often used in salads; flower buds and unripened seeds are used as substitutes for capers, and the flowers are an edible garnish. 'Gleam': a semitrailing plant with large, semidouble or double, fragrant flowers in mixed colors. 'Jewel' is a bushy dwarf, growing 12 inches high with double and semidouble flowers of gold, mahogany, scarlet, pink, yellow, rose, orange and red. 'Whirlybird' has spurless, open and upward-facing flowers on an upright 12-inch plant. Blooms are gold, mahogany, tangerine, orange, scarlet and cream. *T. peregrinum,* canary bird flower, canary bird vine: has yellow flowers on 8-foot vines; makes a good screen.

Growing conditions. Sow seeds outdoors where they are to grow, after all danger of frost has passed. Seeds may be started indoors, but seedlings do not transplant well. Space plants 8 to 12 inches apart in full sun or light shade, in soil that is light and well drained. Do not fertilize; rich soil produces lush foliage but no flowers. Water when soil is dry, but do not overwater. Nasturtium does best where temperatures are cool; in warm climates, the bush types outperform the vining types. Where vines are grown, they need to be tied to their supports.

—

Unicorn plant see *Proboscidea*

—

Venidium (ve-NID-ee-um)

A genus of about 25 species of South African origin, having deeply cut grayish green foliage and daisy-like flower heads.

Selected species and varieties. *V. fastuosum,* cape daisy: bears 4- to 5-inch flower heads of orange-yellow ray florets; each ray floret has a splotch of purple-black near its base, creating a ring of color around the shiny black center. Plants reach 2 feet tall and are used in beds, borders and massed plantings.

Growing conditions. Sow seeds outdoors after all danger of frost has passed, or start them indoors six to eight weeks before the last frost date. Do not cover seeds; they need light for the 15- to 25-day germination period. Space plants 12 inches apart in full sun, in a light, sandy, well-drained soil. Do not overwater and feed little, if at all. Cape daisy does best in heat, drought, and sun.

Verbena (ver-BEE-nah)

Verbenas bear stunning brightly colored flowers in red, white, violet, purple, blue, cream, rose or pink. The individual flowers are small and tubular, but they appear in clusters 2½ to 4 inches across on spreading or upright plants. Use for edgings, beds, ground covers, rock gardens, in hanging baskets; they also make fine cut flowers.

Selected species and varieties.
V. × hybrida, common garden verbena: the most popular species in the genus. Upright or slightly creeping plants grow to 24 inches tall. Flowers come in all verbena colors, many with a contrasting white eye; leaves are deeply quilted or textured. 'Ideal Florist': a mixture with flowers in many colors; plants are 12 inches high, spreading and vigorous. Romance series cultivars: 8-inch plants that form a dense carpet; flowers come in scarlet, white, carmine, burgundy with a white eye, and violet with a white eye. Showtime series is heat-tolerant; its seeds also have a better germination rate than most other verbenas. The 10-inch-tall plants spread to 18 inches and bear flowers in all verbena colors, most with a white eye. Springtime series cultivars: seeds exhibit high germination rate; they are very early-flowering plants with a spreading habit. 'Trinidad': an upright grower, 10 inches tall, with shocking pink flowers. *V. peruviana*, Peruvian verbena: a spreading plant with clusters of scarlet or red flowers and long, toothed leaves; an excellent annual ground cover. *V. tenuisecta*, moss verbena: a spreading plant 12 inches tall, with blue, violet or purple flowers in 2½-inch clusters.

Growing conditions.
Verbena seeds are small and take a long time to germinate, so do not sow them outdoors. Buy bedding plants in spring, or sow seeds indoors 10 to 12 weeks before the last expected frost. Refrigerate seeds for seven days before sowing, and sow extra heavily, because verbena seeds' germination percentage is usually low, especially with the older cultivars. Cover the seed flat with black plastic until germination occurs, after 20 to 25 days. Verbena is particularly prone to damping-off, so make sure the medium is not overly wet. Plants are also easy to root from stem cuttings. Move plants outside after all danger of frost is past; select a spot with full sun and a rich, light, well-drained soil. Space spreading types 12 to 15 inches apart, and upright types 8 to 10 inches apart. Fertilize with 5-10-5 at planting time and feed monthly. Verbena is one of the best annuals to use where weather is hot and dry and soil is poor.

Viola (vie-OH-lah)
Violet, viola

Dainty, flat, single flowers with five round petals; foliage is usually round to heart-shaped. Depending on species and cultivar, flowers are ½ to 4 inches across, and plants grow 6 to 15 inches tall. Most are biennials grown as annuals. All prefer cool weather; in hot climates they are generally grown as spring and fall plants, to be replaced in summer by more heat-resistant annuals. Used in massed plantings, edgings, rock gardens and containers, and for spot color.

Selected species and varieties.
V. cornuta, horned violet, tufted pansy: a perennial grown as a hardy annual; grows 8 inches tall and has 1½-inch flowers of lavender, purple, red, pink, apricot, yellow, orange or white. *V. odorata*, sweet violet, English violet: the violet sold by florists; a perennial sometimes grown as an annual. Plants grow 12 inches high; flowers are ¾ inch across, fragrant, usually violet in color. *V. rafinesquii*, field pansy: grows to 15 inches, with tiny blooms of cream or light blue. *V. tricolor*, Johnny-jump-up: a perennial grown as a hardy annual; its ¾-inch flowers are purple, white and yellow. *V. × wittrockiana*, pansy, heartsease: flower colors are red, white, blue, pink, bronze, yellow, purple, lavender or orange. Some blooms are solid-colored, others have the lower three petals a different color from the top two; in many blooms the lower three petals bear a blotchy or facelike marking in a contrasting color. Pansies are classified as multiflora or grandiflora types; the multifloras have a greater number of smaller flowers. Crystal Bowl is a multiflora series highly resistant to heat and rain; the 2½-inch flowers are all clear-colored, with no blotches. Imperial series has uniform 3-inch, heat-resistant, clear and blotched flowers: 'Red' (blotched), 'Blue' (lavender-blue with a violet face), 'Yellow', 'Orange', 'Silver Princess' (creamy white with a deep rose blotch), 'Pink Shades' (lavender-pink with a rose blotch), and 'Orange Prince' (blotched apricot). Majestic Giant series has 4-inch flowers of blotched whites, blues, blotched yel-

VERBENA × HYBRIDA 'TRINIDAD'

VIOLA CORNUTA

VIOLA TRICOLOR

VIOLA × WITTROCKIANA

XANTHISMA TEXANA

XERANTHEMUM ANNUUM

low, blotched reds and purple. Roc series is even more cold-tolerant than many other pansies. Springtime series is among the most heat-tolerant pansies; it is an early bloomer with 3-inch flowers. Universal series has a low, mounded growing habit and 2- to 3-inch blooms; it is early-flowering and very winter-hardy.

Growing conditions. Sow seeds indoors 14 weeks before the last frost date. Be sure to cover the seeds completely as they need darkness for germination, which takes 10 to 20 days. Seeds benefit from several days' refrigeration in a moist medium before sowing. Purchased bedding plants and seedlings that have been hardened off—that is, gradually acclimated to outdoor conditions—can be set in the garden as soon as the ground can be worked in spring. In the South and warm parts of the West, where winter temperatures do not drop below 20° F, pansies planted and mulched in fall will survive the winter and bloom again the following spring. Pansy plants can also be overwintered in cold frames and transplanted in early spring. Space plants of all species 6 to 8 inches apart in a moist, rich soil. Except for sweet violet, all prefer full sun but will grow in part shade. Sweet violet needs part shade in most areas and full shade in very hot climates. Fertilize with 5-10-5 before planting and again every month during the blooming period. Water well; mulch to keep the soil moist and cool. In coastal areas where days are hot but nights are cool, pansies are long-lived; where nights are hot, they seldom thrive. To extend pansies' bloom time, pick flowers before they go to seed. If plants become leggy, pinch them back to keep them compact.

Violet see *Exacum; Viola*
Wallflower see *Cheiranthus*
Wishbone flower see *Torenia*

Xanthisma (zan-THIS-mah)
Sleepy daisy

A long-stemmed plant with single flower heads that close at night.

Selected species and varieties. *X. texana,* star-of-Texas: 18 to 30 inches tall, multibranched, with 2- to 3-inch daisy-like yellow flower heads. Foliage is narrow and gray-green. Star-of-Texas is a fine bedding plant and a good cut flower; it blooms well until frost.

Growing conditions. Sow seeds outdoors in midspring or late fall, or sow indoors eight weeks before the last frost. Germination takes 25 to 30 days. Move seedlings outside after the last frost date, spacing them 8 to 12 inches apart in full sun and a dry, sandy, well-drained soil. Water sparingly and do not fertilize. Star-of-Texas prefers cool weather.

Xeranthemum
(zer-AN-the-mum)

A small group of Mediterranean plants, some species of which are among the oldest and best-known everlastings. Attractive border plants, good cut flowers and excellent dried flowers.

Selected species and varieties. *X. annuum,* immortelle: flower heads are fully double, 1½ to 2 inches across, in purple, red, rose, white, pink or lilac. Plants grow from 18 to 24 inches tall, with silvery green foliage on wiry stems. A cut stem of immortelle dries quickly to a very crisp, papery texture.

Growing conditions. Sow seeds outdoors where plants are to grow, after all danger of frost has passed. Seeds can be started indoors six to eight weeks before outdoor planting time, if sown in individual peat pots for ease in transplanting to the garden. Germination takes 10 to 15 days. Plant in full sun in a light, rich, well-drained soil. It may be necessary to stake plants to keep them growing straight. Water well and fertilize monthly.

Yellow ageratum see *Lonas*

Zinnia (ZIN-ee-ah)

Flowers of these popular garden annuals range from tiny button-like heads to large double-petaled flower heads with quill-like ray florets. The flower heads come in pink, rose, red, cherry, lavender, purple, orange, salmon, gold, yellow, white, cream and light green—virtually every color except true blue. Plants range in size from 6-inch dwarfs to varieties almost 4 feet high. Use zinnias in edgings, borders or beds; they also make excellent cut flowers and good container plants. Plants start to bloom when still very short and continue blooming as they grow, until frost.

Selected species and varieties.
Z. angustifolia, formerly called *Z. linearis:* bears single, golden orange flower heads with yellow stripes. Plants grow to heights of 8 to 12 inches and have very narrow leaves. *Z. elegans,* common zinnia: heights up to 3 feet with stiff single or double flower heads from 1 to 7 inches across. Blooms in all colors. Some are solid-colored, others multi-colored or zoned. Some are round, domed or ball-shaped; others are shaped like dahlia or chrysanthemum flowers. Border Beauty series has 3½-inch, dahlia-like flowers that are semidouble to fully double, on 20-inch bushy plants. Peter Pan series cultivars: very large, slightly curled double flowers, up to 5 inches wide, on compact 12-inch plants. Ruffles series makes good cut flowers; the 2½-inch flower heads are ball-shaped, petals are ruffled, stems are upright and stiff. Plants grow 24 to 30 inches tall and are disease-resistant. *Z. haageana,* Mexican zinnia: grows from 12 to 18 inches high and bears 1½- to 2-inch, single or double flower heads in tones of red, mahogany, yellow and orange; some blooms are solid-colored; others are two-toned. 'Old Mexico' has fully double, 2½-inch blooms of deep, rich mahogany high-lighted with yellow-gold, on bushy, compact, 18-inch plants. 'Persian Carpet' bears 2-inch double, bi-colored flower heads of gold, maroon, purple, chocolate, pink or cream on a 15-inch plant.

Growing conditions. Sow zinnia seeds outdoors after all danger of frost has passed, where plants are to grow. Or sow seeds indoors four weeks before the last frost. Germination takes five to seven days. Move seedlings or purchased bedding plants to the garden after danger of frost has passed. Space plants from 6 to 24 inches apart—whatever their height will be at maturity. Do not crowd plants; they are susceptible to mildew, which is warded off by good air circulation. For maximum growth and flowering, incorporate 5-10-5 into the soil at planting time and feed again twice monthly. Zinnias like full sun and a rich, fertile, well-drained soil. Encourage bushiness by pinching plants when they are young. Cutting flowers for indoor use and removing blooms as they fade also encourages new growth and keeps the plants bushy. Zinnias thrive in hot, dry climates, but they need regular watering. Water in the morning; to prevent disease, avoid wetting the foliage.

ZINNIA ANGUSTIFOLIA

ZINNIA ELEGANS

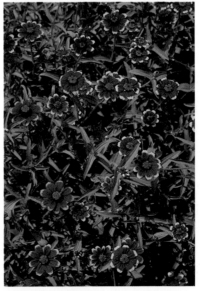

ZINNIA HAAGEANA

FURTHER READING

Ball, Jeff, and Charles O. Cresson, *The 60-Minute Flower Garden.* Emmaus, Pennsylvania: Rodale Press, 1986.

Beckett, Kenneth A., *Annuals and Biennials.* New York: Ballantine Books, 1984.

Beckett, Kenneth A., David Carr and David Stevens, *The Contained Garden.* New York: Viking Press, 1983.

Brooklyn Botanic Garden, *A Handbook on Annuals.* New York: Brooklyn Botanic Garden, 1974.

Crockett, James Underwood, *Crockett's Flower Garden.* Boston: Little Brown, 1981.

Fell, Derek, *Annuals: How to Select, Grow and Enjoy.* Tucson, Arizona: HP Books, 1983.

Ferguson, Nicola, *Right Plant, Right Place.* New York: Summit Books, 1984.

Foster, Catharine Osgood, *Organic Flower Gardening.* Emmaus, Pennsylvania: Rodale Press, 1975.

Johnstone, D. Bruce, and Elwood K. Brindle, *America's Best Garden Flowers.* Minneapolis: Burgess Publishing Company, 1978.

Loewer, Peter, *Gardens by Design.* Emmaus, Pennsylvania: Rodale Press, 1986.

MacCaskey, Michael, ed., *Complete Guide to Basic Gardening.* Tucson, Arizona: HP Books, 1986.

Pavel, Peggy Brandstrom, and Catherine Rossi, *Gardening with Color.* San Francisco: Ortho Books/Chevron Chemical Company, 1977.

Reader's Digest Editors, *Illustrated Guide to Gardening.* Pleasantville, New York: Reader's Digest Association, 1978.

Reilly, Ann, *Success with Seeds.* Greenwood, South Carolina: George W. Park Seed Company, 1978.

Sinnes, A. Cort, *All about Annuals.* San Francisco: Ortho Books/Chevron Chemical Company, 1981.

Sunset Editors, *Garden Color: Annuals and Perennials.* Menlo Park, California: Lane Publishing, 1981.

Sunset Editors, *New Western Garden Book.* Menlo Park, California: Lane Publishing, 1986.

Taylor, Norman, *Taylor's Guide to Annuals.* Boston: Houghton Mifflin, 1986.

Wilson, James W., *Flower Gardening: A Primer.* New York: Van Nostrand Reinhold, 1970.

Wyman, Donald, *Wyman's Gardening Encyclopedia.* New York: Macmillan, 1986.

PICTURE CREDITS

The sources for the illustrations in this book are listed below. Cover photograph of eustoma by Michael Dirr. Watercolor paintings by Nicholas Fasciano except pages 76, 77, 78, 79, 80, 81: Lorraine Moseley Epstein. Maps on pages 70, 71, 73, 75: digitized by Richard Furno, inked by John Drummond.

Frontispiece paintings listed by page number: 6: *Farmhouse Garden with Sunflowers,* c. 1905-1906 by Gustav Klimt, courtesy Österreichische Galerie, Vienna. Photo by Erich Lessing. 36: *Morning Glory and Frog,* Japanese painting: 18th-19th century, Edo period, Ukiyoe school, Hokuga. Sketchbook (76.41). Courtesy Freer Gallery of Art, Smithsonian Institution, Washington, D.C. 54: *Early Spring,* c. 1908 by Pierre Bonnard, courtesy The Phillips Collection, Washington, D.C.

Photographs in Chapters 1 through 3 from the following sources, listed by page number: 8: Margaret Bowditch. 10: Jerry Pavia. 12: Joanne Pavia. 14: David Scheid. 18: Audrey Gibson. 20: Steven Still. 24: Jerry Pavia. 28: Cole Burrell. 30: Saxon Holt. 32: Renée Comet. 38: Saxon Holt. 40: Horticultural Photography, Corvallis, OR. 44: Saxon Holt. 46: Thomas Eltzroth. 50: Saxon Holt. 52: Dan Clark/Grant Heilman Photography. 56: Thomas Eltzroth. 58: Jerry Pavia. 60, 64: Saxon Holt. 66: Pamela Zilly.

Photographs in the Dictionary of Annuals by Pamela Harper, except where listed by page and numbered from top to bottom. Page 84, 1: Niche Gardens, Chapel Hill, N.C. 84, 2: Robert Lyons/Color Advantage. 84, 3: Horticultural Photography, Corvallis, OR. 85, 3: Steven Still. 86, 2: Ann Reilly. 86, 3: Maggie Oster. 86, 4: Horticultural Photography, Corvallis, OR. 87, 1: Margaret Bowditch. 89, 1: Joanne Pavia. 89, 3: William D. Adams. 90, 1: Derek Fell. 90, 2: Gillian Beckett. 91, 1: Joanne Pavia. 91, 2: Ann Reilly. 92, 1: Horticultural Photography, Corvallis, OR. 92, 2: Ann Reilly. 93, 3: Saxon Holt. 94, 1: Joanne Pavia. 94, 3: Steven Still. 95, 2: Saxon Holt. 96, 1: Michael Dirr. 97, 1: Dan Suzio. 98, 2: Cole Burrell. 98, 3: Saxon Holt. 99, 1: Mike Heger. 99, 2: Saxon Holt. 99, 3: John J. Smith. 100, 2: Horticultural Photography, Corvallis, OR. 101, 2: Robert Lyons/Color Advantage. 101, 3: David M. Stone/Photo-Nats. 102, 1: Cole Burrell. 102, 3: William D. Adams. 103, 3: Michael Dirr. 104, 1: Mike Heger. 104, 2: Robert Lyons/Color Advantage. 104, 3: Steven Still. 105, 2: Patricia Christopher. 107, 1, 107, 2: Horticultural Photography, Corvallis, OR. 107, 3: Robert Lyons/Color Advantage. 108, 1: William D. Adams. 108, 2: Steven Still. 109, 3: Joanne Pavia. 111, 2: Runk/Schoenberger/Grant Heilman Photography. 113, 1: Dan Suzio. 114, 1: William D. Adams. 114, 2: David Cavagnaro. 114, 3: Robert Lyons/Color Advantage. 115, 1: William D. Adams. 115, 2, 115, 3: Steven Still. 116, 1: William D. Adams. 116, 2: Saxon Holt. 116, 3, 117, 2, Steven Still. 118, 1: Dan Suzio. 118, 2: Mark Gibson. 118, 3: Joy Spurr. 120, 2: Michael McKinley. 120, 4: Saxon Holt. 121, 1: © Walter Chandoha 1988. 121, 2: William D. Adams. 121, 3: John Colwell/Grant Heilman Photography. 122, 2: Joy Spurr. 122, 3; Niche Gardens, Chapel Hill, N.C. 123, 1: Patricia Christopher. 123, 2: Ann Reilly. 123, 3: David Scheid. 123, 4: Michael McKinley. 124, 2: Robert Lyons/Color Advantage. 124, 3: Thomas Eltzroth. 124, 4: Robert Lyons/Color Advantage. 125, 1: Cole Burrell. 125, 2: Karen Bussolini. 125, 3: Maggie Oster. 126, 1: Steven Still. 126, 2: Jerry Pavia. 127, 2: Maggie Oster. 127, 3: Joy Spurr. 129, 1: Hollen Johnson. 129, 4: Maggie Oster. 130, 2: Steven Still. 130, 3: Robert Lyons/Color Advantage. 131, 2: Michael Dirr. 132, 1: Gary Mottau. 132, 2: Ann Reilly. 133, 1: Robert Lyons/Color Advantage. 133, 2: Steven Still. 134, 2: Ann Reilly. 134, 3: Mike Heger. 135, 1: Saxon Holt. 136, 1: Maggie Oster. 136, 2: Steven Still. 136, 3: Ann Reilly. 137, 2: Jerry Pavia. 137, 3: Robert Lyons/Color Advantage.

ACKNOWLEDGMENTS

The index for this book was prepared by Lynne R. Hobbs. The editors also wish to thank: Teresa Aimone, Sluis & Groot Quality Seeds, Englewood, Colorado; Wayne Amos, National Park Service, Washington, D.C.; Sarah Brash, Alexandria, Virginia; Martha S. Cooley, Washington, D.C.; Margery A. duMond, Washington, D.C.; Barbara W. Ellis, Alexandria, Virginia; Filoli Gardens, Woodside, California; Betsy Frankel, Alexandria, Virginia; Ray Glenn, Matthews Nursery, Miami, Florida; Dr. Robert Griesbach, U.S. Department of Agriculture, Beltsville, Maryland; Kenneth E. Hancock, Annandale, Virginia; James A. McKenney, Potomac Nursery and Flower Center, Potomac, Maryland; Linda Morris, Baltimore, Maryland; William John Park, Park Seed Company, Greenwood, South Carolina; Jayne E. Rohrich, Alexandria, Virginia; Dr. Frank Santamour, U.S. National Arboretum, Washington, D.C.; Joseph Savage, Nassau County Cooperative Extension Service, Plainview, New York; David Scheid, U.S. Botanical Gardens, Washington, D.C.; Candace H. Scott, College Park, Maryland; Holly Shimizu, U.S. Botanical Gardens, Washington, D.C.; Henry Steffes Jr., Washington, D.C.; Susan Stuck, Alexandria, Virginia; Dr. Mel Tessene, Harris Moran Seed Company, West Chicago, Illinois; Dr. Scott Trees, Pan American Seed Company, Elburn, Illinois; Barbara Tufty, Washington, D.C.; Jan Umstead, Ball Seed Company, West Chicago, Illinois; Richard Weir, Nassau County Cooperative Extension Service, Plainview, New York.

INDEX

*Numerals in italics indicate an illustration
of the subject mentioned.*

REDEFINITION

Senior Editors	Anne Horan, Robert G. Mason
Design Director	Robert Barkin
Designer	Edwina Smith
Illustration	Nicholas Fasciano
Assistant Designer	Sue Pratt
Picture Editor	Deborah Thornton
Production Editor	Anthony K. Pordes
Research	Gail Prensky, Barbara B. Smith, Mary Yee
Text Editor	Sharon Cygan
Writers	Gerald Jonas, Ann Reilly, David S. Thomson
Administrative Assistant	Margaret M. Higgins
Business Manager	Catherine M. Chase
PRESIDENT	Edward Brash

Time-Life Books Inc.
is a wholly owned subsidiary of

TIME INCORPORATED

FOUNDER	Henry R. Luce 1898-1967
Editor-in-Chief	Jason McManus
Chairman and Chief Executive Officer	J. Richard Munro
President and Chief Operating Officer	N. J. Nicholas Jr.
Editorial Director	Ray Cave
Executive Vice President, Books	Kelso F. Sutton
Vice President, Books	George Artandi

TIME-LIFE BOOKS INC.

EDITOR	George Constable
Executive Editor	Ellen Phillips
Director of Design	Louis Klein
Director of Editorial Resources	Phyllis K. Wise
Editorial Board	Russell B. Adams Jr., Dale M. Brown, Roberta Conlan, Thomas H. Flaherty, Lee Hassig, Donia Ann Steele, Rosalind Stubenberg, Henry Woodhead
Director of Photography and Research	John Conrad Weiser
Assistant Director of Editorial Resources	Elise Ritter Gibson
PRESIDENT	Christopher T. Linen
Chief Operating Officer	John M. Fahey Jr.
Senior Vice Presidents	Robert M. DeSena, James L. Mercer, Paul R. Stewart
Vice Presidents	Stephen L. Bair, Ralph J. Cuomo, Neal Goff, Stephen L. Goldstein, Juanita T. James, Hallett Johnson III, Carol Kaplan, Susan J. Maruyama, Robert H. Smith, Joseph J. Ward
Director of Production Services	Robert J. Passantino

Editorial Operations

Copy Chief	Diane Ullius
Production	Celia Beattie
Library	Louise D. Forstall
Correspondents	Elisabeth Kraemer-Singh (Bonn), Maria Vincenza Aloisi (Paris), Ann Natanson (Rome)

THE CONSULTANTS

C. Colston Burrell, the general consultant for The Time-Life Gardener's Guide, is a co-consultant for *Annuals.* He is Curator of Plant Collections at the Minnesota Landscape Arboretum, part of the University of Minnesota, where he oversees plant collections and develops regional interest in the horticulture of the upper Midwest. Mr. Burrell is the author of publications about ferns and wildflowers, and a former curator of Native Plant Collections at the National Arboretum in Washington, D.C.

Wayne Ambler, a horticulturist in Richmond, Virginia, is co-consultant for *Annuals.* He is a member of the adjunct faculty at J. Sargeant Reynolds Community College and at Patrick Henry High School in Ashland, Virginia, where he teaches horticulture.

Library of Congress Cataloging-in-Publication Data
Annuals.
  p. cm.—(The Time-Life gardener's guide)
  Bibliograpy: p.
  Includes index.
  1. Annuals (Plants) 2. Flower gardening.
I. Time-Life Books. II. Series.
SB422.A57 1988   635.9'312—dc19   88-2308 CIP
ISBN 0-8094-6612-0
ISBN 0-8094-6613-9 (lib. bdg.)

Time-Life Books Inc. offers a wide range of fine recordings, including a *Rock 'n' Roll Era* series. For subscription information, call 1-800-621-7026, or write Time-Life Music, P.O. Box C-32068, Richmond, Virginia 23261-2068.